GUIDING
CREATIVE
TALENT

Look *Magazine Photo*

GUIDING CREATIVE TALENT

E. Paul Torrance

Bureau of Educational Research
University of Minnesota

PRENTICE-HALL, INC.

Englewood Cliffs, N.J.

1962

To —
my parents
my Aunts Clara, Mamie, and Lillian
and "Miss Bessie," my teacher,
who did most to keep alive a bit of my creativity
through the "fourth grade slump"

Library of Congress Catalog Card Number 62–12974

Printed in the United States of America 37152–C

PREFACE

Anyone with an interest in the problems of highly creative children will find this volume useful in guiding a wide range of creative talent at all age and educational levels. In preparing this material, I have drawn most heavily upon my own research and that of my colleagues concerning the creative thinking of children, adolescents, and adults. Although my emphasis is upon the problems of highly creative children, I believe you will find these materials useful in guiding a wide range of creative talent at all age and educational levels. I have also attempted to give these research findings and observations meaning from my experience as a teacher, counselor, and principal in a high school and as a college teacher and counselor, roles in which I have met many highly creative individuals. I have also drawn upon my research concerning behavior under emergency and extreme conditions, especially situations involving coercion.

In the first chapter, I have attempted to tell why you should be concerned about effectively guiding highly creative individuals. I have also tried to describe the nature of the unique guidance needs of highly creative individuals.

In the second chapter, I have presented material concerning the assessment of creative talent and growth. In this chapter, I have reviewed a number of definitions of creative thinking and have stated the one which has guided our research in the Bureau of Educational Research at the University of Minnesota. I have pointed out some of the deficiencies of traditional measures of intellectual talent and personality to call attention to the need for supplementing these measures with instruments involving the creative thinking abilities and characteristics of the creative personality. Then, I have reviewed the long, interesting, and not very well-known history of the development of tests of creative thinking.

In the third chapter, I have described most of the Minnesota Tests of Creative Thinking and presented some of the reasoning behind them. I

V

realize that these tests represent something of a departure from most of the approaches now in vogue. For this reason, I have tried to summarize the evidences of validity now available. In the Appendix, I have tried to present a careful description of them and their administration.

In the fourth chapter, I have discussed problems of identifying the creative personality. In doing this, I have drawn from a large number of studies of creative adults and the currently emerging studies of creative children and adolescents. These converging lines of research, I feel, offer much promise in providing information which will be useful in guiding creative talent and in helping highly creative children and adolescents maintain this talent.

In the fifth chapter, I have summarized what I have been able to find out about the development of the creative thinking abilities. Some of the phenomena are quite puzzling and differ quite markedly from the phenomena of physical development, learning, and reasoning. The evidence from many sources, however, is quite consistent. I have offered some of my own guesses concerning the explanation of some of these phenomena, because I believe they have very important implications for the guidance of creative talent.

In the sixth chapter, I have tried to identify and describe some of the most common problems of highly creative individuals. Highly creative individuals experience many problems, if they express their creative desires and develop their creative abilities. They also suffer, if they repress these desires and fail to develop their abilities. Attention has been given to both types of difficulties. Clues from research have been offered concerning the dilemma suggested by these two kinds of difficulties. The seventh chapter deals with those problems which result from repression of the creative desires and abilities.

From these considerations, I have endeavored in the eighth chapter to deduce some general and specific goals to guide counselors in working with highly creative individuals. It is believed that these goals are based on some of the peculiar needs of creative individuals and the nature of the creative process.

In the ninth chapter, an attempt has been made to formulate a concept of the peculiar nature of the kind of relationships and techniques which I believe to be essential to the achievement of these goals. I have tried to use my understanding of the creative process, incomplete though it may be, to fashion such a set of concepts.

Although the concepts which I have proposed are divergent from current counseling and educational theory, I have borrowed much from existing theories. I am particularly indebted to Clark Moustakas for his ideas concerning psychotherapy with highly creative children. I have tried to elaborate upon the basic idea by drawing upon my earlier studies of the strategies which man has always used in coercing other men and simply reversing these strategies. I had attempted this kind of reversal in an earlier monograph prepared for school counselors entitled "Struggle for Men's Minds." In attempting the present conceptualization, I found that I had not gone far enough in trying to think of the opposite of the coercive strategy when I wrote "Struggle for Men's Minds." In the re-conceptualization included in this volume, I have gone much further in describing the teaching and counseling processes as creative processes and the teacher and counselor relationships as creative ones. I hope that I have in some degree succeeded. I suspect, however, that I may have permitted much of my old orientation, training, and experience to blind me in elaborating these concepts. I also suspect that I shall for some time continue to modify them.

The tenth and final chapter deals with what I see as the qualifications of counselors, teachers, and administrators who can guide effectively creative talent. Attention has been given both to problems of in-service education and to programs of teacher and counselor education.

I hope that the reader will be indulgent of my use of the first person in a volume such as this. I know that many of you will consider this ill-mannered. Perhaps it is and perhaps I am presumptuous in intruding myself in this way between you and the words which I have written. I have long believed that the practice of writing in the third person is unnecessarily awkward, misleading, and uncommunicative. I hope that my writing in the first person has enabled me to communicate my ideas more clearly, honestly, and powerfully.

I acknowledge with gratitude the helpfulness of many people in preparing this manuscript, especially my wife, Pansy, and the members of my staff. Kaoru Yamamoto, Philip W. Jackson, Rod Myers, and Mary Jane Aschner offered a number of helpful suggestions in the preparation of the first draft, and Mrs. Darleen Ulrich and Mrs. Gwendolyn Green have patiently typed and retyped the manuscript.

E. Paul Torrance, Director
Bureau of Educational Research

ACKNOWLEDGMENTS

We gratefully acknowledge the generosity of the many individuals and publishers who have granted us permission to quote or otherwise refer to their published or unpublished works. Among those to whom we are indebted are the following: Adult Leadership, Adult Education Association; Allyn and Bacon, Inc.; American Journal of Orthopsychiatry, Inc.; American Philosophical Society; American Psychological Association; H. R. Buhl; Bureau of Publications, Teachers College, Columbia University; Clearing House; Arthur C. Croft Publications; Evans Brothers Limited of London; Mrs. Colleen Freeman; "The Gifted Child Quarterly"; J. P. Guilford and P. R. Merrifield; Harvard University Press; Banesh Hoffman; John L. Holland; Miss Joy Alice Holm; Harvey C. Lehman; Raymond W. Lowry; Donald W. MacKinnon; National Education Association; Pauline N. Pepinsky; Princeton University Press; Routledge and Kegan Paul Limited of London; Kenyon Runner; Saturday Review, Inc.; Sister Patrick Ann Brown, C.S.J.; Calvin W. Taylor; Frederick H. Voigt; Union College Character Research Project; University of Minnesota Center for Continuation Study; University of Utah Press; P. S. Weisberg and Kayla J. Springer; and William H. Whyte, Jr.

CONTENTS

IX

8

**Goals for Guiding
Creative Talent**   *142*

Specific Goals *144*.   Summary *161*.

9

**Relationships
With Creative Talent**   *162*

The Creative Relationship *165*.   Experiencing Joy in the
Individual's Creative Powers *167*.   Being a Guide, Not a
God *170*.   Genuine Empathy *172*.   Creative Acceptance
of Limitations and Assets *174*.   Search for the Truth
About the Situation *177*.   Letting One Thing Lead to
Another *179*.   A Friendly Environment *182*.   Respect
for Dignity and Worth *186*.   Summary *187*.

10

**Counselors, Teachers,
and Administrators
for Guiding Creative Talent**   *188*

Counselor Qualifications *189*.   Teacher Qualifications *193*.
Administrator Qualifications *203*.   Summary *209*.

**Appendix: Administering
the Minnesota Tests
of Creative Thinking**   *213*

Non-Verbal Tasks *214*.   Verbal Tasks Using Non-Verbal
Stimuli *222*.   Verbal Tasks Using Verbal Stimuli *238*.

Bibliography   *255*

Index   *271*

Chapter 1

CAUSES
FOR
CONCERN

Why should counselors, teachers, and administrators be concerned with the problems of creative individuals? What business is it of theirs whether or not one is highly creative? Doesn't everybody know that the highly creative person is "a little crazy" and that you can't help him anyway? If he's *really creative*, why does he need guidance anyway? He should be able to solve his own problems. He's creative, isn't he?

Unfortunately, these are attitudes which have long been held by some of our most eminent scholars and which still prevail rather widely. Most of the educators I know perk up when they discover a child with a high Intelligence Quotient or a high score on some other traditional measure of intellectual talent. They are impressed! Most of them are rather impressed if they discover in a child some outstanding talent for music, or art, or the like. Some counselors and psychologists even go to the trouble of testing such things as finger dexterity and speed in checking numbers and names. Not a counselor or psychologist among my acquaintance, however, bothers about obtaining measures of their client's creative thinking abilities. I was trained in counseling myself and did work as a high school and college counselor for several years, and for two years I served as the director of a university counseling bureau. In all this time, I never did hear anyone mention a test of creative thinking. I certainly never used one!

What puzzles me, however, is why I remained so ignorant of such instruments. I find now that many such tests have been developed only during the past seventy years. Descriptions of these tests are now fairly detailed and scoring procedures can be satisfactorily reproduced. The reason for this state of affairs is simply that we have not really considered this kind of talent important. This kind of talent has not been valued and rewarded in our educational system, so guidance workers have seen little reason to identify it and to try to contribute to its growth.

SOME LEGITIMATE CONCERNS
OF EDUCATORS

There are very legitimate reasons why educators should be concerned about assessing and guiding the growth of the creative thinking abilities. I would like to discuss a few of these.

Mental Health

Schools are legitimately concerned about the mental health of children, adolescents, college students, and adults. They would like to be able to help their students avoid mental breakdowns and achieve healthy personality growth. These are legitimate concerns of education. But what does all this have to do with creativity?

Actually, it has a great deal to do with creativity. There is little question but that the stifling of creativity cuts at the very roots of satisfaction in living and ultimately creates overwhelming tension and breakdown (Patrick, 1955). There is also little doubt that one's creativity is his most valuable resource in coping with life's daily stresses.

In one study (Hebeisen, 1960), a battery of tests of creative thinking was administered to a group of schizophrenics who appeared to be on the road to recovery. Many of them were being considered for vocational rehabilitation by the State Department of Welfare. These individuals manifested an astonishingly impoverished imagination, inflexibility, lack of originality, and inability to summon any kind of response to new problems. Their answers gave no evidence of the rich fantasy and wild imagination popularly attributed to schizophrenics. There was only an impoverished, stifled, frozen creativity. They appeared to be paralyzed in their thinking, and most of their responses were the most banal imaginable.

Although it will be difficult to prove, I suspect that schizophrenics and others who "breakdown" under stress constitute one of the most unimaginative, noncreative groups to be found. I also suspect that it was their lack of creativity rather than its presence which brought about their breakdowns. Certainly the schizophrenics tested lacked this important resource for coping with life's stresses. Creativity is a necessary resource for their struggle back to mental health.

Fully Functioning Persons

Schools are anxious that the children they educate grow into fully functioning persons. This has long been an avowed and widely approved purpose of education. We say that education in a democracy should help individuals fully develop their talents. Recently there have been pressures to limit this to intellectual talents. There has been much talk about limiting the school's concern to the full development of the intellect only.

Even with this limited definition of the goals of education, the abilities involved in creative thinking cannot be ignored. There has been increasing recognition of the fact that traditional measures of intelligence attempt to assess only a few of man's thinking abilities. In his early work Binet (1909) recognized clearly this deficiency. It has taken the sustained work of Guilford (1959a) and his associates to communicate effectively the complexity of man's mental operations.

Certainly we cannot say that one is fully functioning mentally, if the abilities involved in creative thinking remain undeveloped or are paralyzed. These are the abilities involved in becoming aware of problems, thinking up possible solutions, and testing them. If their functioning is impaired, one's capacity for coping with life's problems is indeed marginal.

Educational Achievement

Almost no one disputes the legitimacy of the school's concern about educational achievement. Teachers and guidance workers are asked to help under-achievers to make better use of their intellectual resources and to help over-achievers become better "rounded" personalities. But, how do you tell who is an under- or over-achiever? In my opinion, recent findings concerning the role of the creative thinking abilities in educational achievement call for a revision of these long-used concepts.

We are finding (Getzels and Jackson, 1958; Torrance, 1960c) that the creative thinking abilities contribute importantly to the acquisition of information and various educational skills. Of course, we have long known that it is natural for man to learn creatively, but we have always thought that it was more economical to teach by authority. Recent experiments (Moore, 1961; Ornstein, 1961) have shown that apparently many things can be learned creatively more economically than they can by authority, and that some people strongly prefer to learn creatively.

Traditional tests of intelligence are heavily loaded with tasks requiring cognition, memory, and convergent thinking. Such tests have worked rather well in predicting school achievement. When children are taught by authority these are the abilities required. Recent and ongoing studies, however, show that even traditional subject matter and educational skills can be taught in such a way that the creative thinking abilities are important for their acquisition.

Most of these findings are illustrated dramatically in a study conducted during three years in the University of Minnesota Laboratory Elementary School. We differentiated the highly creative children (as identified by our tests of creative thinking) from the highly intelligent (as identified by the Stanford-Binet, an individually administered test). The highly creative group ranked in the upper 20 per cent on creative thinking but not on intelligence. The highly intelligent group ranked in the upper 20 per cent on intelligence but not on creativity. Those who were in the upper 20 per cent on both measures were eliminated, but the overlap was small. In fact, if we were to identify children as gifted on the basis of intelligence tests, we would eliminate from consideration approximately 70 per cent of the most creative. This percentage seems to hold fairly well, no matter what measure of intelligence we use and no matter what educational level we study, from kindergarten through graduate school.

Although there is an average difference of over 25 IQ points between these two groups, there are no statistically significant differences in any of the achievement measures used either year (Gates Reading and Iowa Tests of Basic Skills). These results have been duplicated in a Minneapolis public high school, the University of Minnesota High School, and two graduate school situations. Getzels and Jackson (1959) had earlier obtained the same results in a private secondary school. These results were not confirmed in a parochial elementary school and a small-town elementary school known for their emphasis on "traditional virtues in education." Even in these two schools, however, achievement is significantly related to measures of creative thinking and the highly creative group is "guilty" of some degree of over-achievement, as assessed by usual standards.

It is of special interest that the children with high IQ's were rated by their teachers as more desirable, better known or understood, more ambitious, and more hardworking or studious. In other words, the highly creative child appears to learn as much as the highly intelligent one, at least in some schools, without appearing to work as hard. My guess is that these highly creative children are learning and thinking when they appear to be "playing around." Their tendency is to learn creatively more effectively than by authority. They may engage in manipulative and/or exploratory activities, many of which are discouraged or even forbidden. They enjoy learning and thinking, and this looks like play rather than work.

Vocational Success

Guidance workers [1] have traditionally been interested in the vocational success of their clients. Indeed, the guidance movement got much of its impetus from this concern. Of course, it has long been

---

[1] The term "guidance workers" will be used to refer to all school personnel who perform guidance functions and includes teachers, administrators, counselors, psychologists, social workers, deans of boys and/or girls.

recognized that creativity is a distinguishing characteristic of outstanding individuals in almost every field. It has been generally conceded that the possession of high intelligence, special talent, and technical skills is not enough for outstanding success. It has also been recognized that creativity is important in scientific discovery, invention, and the arts.

We are discovering now that creative thinking is important in success even in some of the most common occupations, such as selling in a department store (Wallace, 1960). In one study it was found that saleswomen ranking in the upper third in sales in their departments scored significantly higher on tests of creative thinking than those who ranked in the lower third in sales. An interesting point in this study, however, is that the tests did a better job of discriminating the high and low selling groups in what the personnel managers considered routine sales jobs requiring no imagination than in the departments rated as requiring creative thinking. Thus, creative thinking appears to be important, even in jobs which appear to be quite routine.

Social Importance

Finally, educators are legitimately concerned that their students make useful contributions to our society. Such a concern runs deep in the code of ethics of the profession. It takes little imagination to recognize that the future of our civilization—our very survival—depends upon the quality of the creative imagination of our next generation.

Democracies collapse only when they fail to use intelligent, imaginative methods for solving their problems. Greece failed to heed such a warning by Socrates and gradually collapsed. What is called for is a far cry from the model of the quiz-program champion of a few years ago. Instead of trying to cram a lot of facts into the minds of children and make them scientific encyclopedias, we must ask what kind of children they are becoming. What kind of thinking do they do? How resourceful are they? Are they becoming more responsible? Are they learning to give thoughtful explanations of the things they do and see? Do they believe their own ideas to be of value? Can they share ideas and opinions with others? Do they relate similar experiences together in order to draw conclusions? Do they do some thinking for themselves?

We also need more than well-rounded individuals. We ordinarily respect these well-rounded individuals, broad scholars, and men of many talents. Dael Wolfle (1960) has made a case for those who develop some of their talents so highly that they cannot be well-rounded. He argues that it is advantageous to a society to see the greatest achievable diversity of talent among those who constitute the society.

A recent warning by Henry Murray (1960), a well-known Harvard psychologist, sounds very much like the one Socrates gave in his day. It reads as follows in part:

> An emotional deficiency disease, a paralysis of the creative imagination, an addition to superficials—this is the diagnosis I would offer to account for the greater part of the widespread desperation of our time. Paralysis of the imagination, I suspect, would also account, in part, for the fact that the great majority of us, wedded to comfort so long as we both shall live, are turning our eyes away from the one thing we should be looking at: the possibility or probability of co-extermination. . . .—p. 10.

GUIDANCE ROLES

Many will say, "Surely, schools have a right to be concerned about mental health, full mental functioning, educational achievement, and vocational success. They ought to be concerned that coming generations contribute productively to our society. *But* how can school guidance workers contribute to the creative growth necessary for these things?"

This is a legitimate question. Parents and peers play such important roles in the encouragement or discouragement of creative expression and growth, what can school guidance workers do? There are at least six special roles which school guidance workers can play in helping highly creative children maintain their creativity and continue to grow. Each of these is a role which others can rarely fulfill. Our social expectations frequently prevent even teachers and administrators from effectively fulfilling these roles. Thus, in some cases, only counselors, school psychologists, and similar workers will be able to fulfill these roles. In many cases, however, teachers and administrators can supply these needs, if they differentiate their guidance roles from other socially expected roles.

The six roles which I have in mind are: (1) providing the highly creative individual a "refuge," (2) being his "sponsor" or "patron," (3) helping him understand his divergence, (4) letting him communicate his ideas, (5) seeing that his creative talent is recognized, and (6) helping parents and others understand him. I shall now discuss each of these roles briefly.

Provide a "Refuge"

Society in general is downright savage towards creative thinkers, especially when they are young. To some extent, the educational system must be coercive and emphasize the establishment of behavior norms. Teachers and administrators can rarely escape this coercive role. Counselors and other guidance workers are in a much better position to free themselves of it. Nevertheless, there are ways teachers and administrators can free themselves of this role long enough to provide refuge, if they are sensitive to the need.

From the studies of Getzels and Jackson (1958), we know that highly creative adolescents are estranged from their teachers and peers. Our Minnesota studies indicate that the same holds true for children in the elementary school. The reasons are easy to understand. Who can blame teachers for being irritated when a pupil presents an original answer which differs from what is expected? It does not fit in with the rest of the grading scheme. They don't know how the unusual answer should be treated. They have to stop and think themselves. Peers have the same difficulty and label the creative child's unusual questions and answers as "crazy" or "silly."

Thus, the highly creative child, adolescent, or adult needs encouragement. He needs help in becoming reconciled and, as Hughes Mearns (1941) once wrote, in being "made cheerful over the world's stubborn satisfaction in its own follies." The guidance worker must recognize, however, that the estrangement exists and that he will have to create a relationship in which the creative individual feels safe.

Be a Sponsor or Patron

Someone has observed that almost always wherever independence and creativity occur and persist, there is some other individual or agent who plays the role of "sponsor" or "patron." This role is played by someone who is not a member of the peer group, but who possesses prestige and power in the same social system. He does several things. Regardless of his own views, the sponsor encourages and supports the other in expressing and testing his ideas and in thinking through things for himself. He protects the individual from the reactions of his peers long enough for him to try out some of his ideas and modify them. He can keep the structure of the situation open enough so that originality *can* occur.

It is my contention that the school counselor or guidance worker is in a better position than anyone else in the social system to play this role, especially if such a role for him is sanctioned by the teachers and principal. Since few elementary schools have counselors or guidance workers, this role is usually assumed by principals. It is a difficult role for a principal, however. Think of the role conflicts which must be involved in the following case of a principal whose school participated in our research.

In an experiment conducted on a Monday, I had observed the exceptional creative talent of Tom, a fourth grader. Before leaving the school, I asked the teacher about Tom. She volunteered the information that he had had a struggle with most of his teachers, but that he had had a very successful experience in the third grade.

On Friday, we returned to the school to conduct the experiment in some other classes. In the meantime, the principal had observed this boy's class for an hour. During the mathematics class, Tom questioned one of the rules in the textbook. Instead of having Tom try to prove his rule and perhaps modify it or explain the textbook rule, the teacher became irate, even in the presence of the principal. She fumed, "So! You think you know more than this book!" (holding the book and tapping it with her hand).

Tom replied meekly, "No, I don't think I know more than the book, but I'm not satisfied about this rule."

To get on safer ground, the teacher then had the class solve problems in their workbook. Tom solved the problems easily and about as rapidly as he could read them. This too was upsetting to the teacher. She couldn't understand how he was getting the correct answer and demanded that he write down all of the steps he had gone through in solving each problem.

Afterwards, the teacher asked the principal to talk to Tom. The principal explained to Tom that many things came easy to him, such as solving problems, and perhaps he really didn't need to write out all of the steps. The principal also explained that there are some other things like handwriting which came easier to others than to him and that he might have to work harder than some of the others on these things.

Apparently, this principal had been able to provide enough of the "patron" role to permit him to keep alive his creativity up to this time. Soon afterwards, Tom's family moved to a nearby suburb and he was duly enrolled in a new school. On Tom's very first day in the new school, the principal of the new school called the principal of the school from which Tom had transferred. He wanted to know immediately if Tom is the kind of boy who has to be squelched rather roughly. His former "patron" explained that Tom was really a very wholesome, promising lad who needed understanding and encouragement. The new principal exclaimed rather brusquely, "Well, he's already said too much right here in my office!"

We can certainly sympathize with the new principal. He must support his teachers and maintain good discipline in the school. It is frequently difficult for a principal to play the "sponsor" or "patron" role. It is far more harmonious with the position of the school counselor. Nevertheless, it is a role which administrators and teachers may have to play. Otherwise, promising creative talent may be sacrificed.

Help Him Understand His Divergence

A high degree of sensitivity, a capacity to de disturbed, and divergent thinking are essentials of the creative personality. Frequently, creative children are puzzled by their own behavior. They desperately need help in understanding themselves, particularly their divergence. The following story written by a fourth grader about a lion that won't roar illustrates the divergent child's search for someone who will understand him:

> . . . Charlie had just one great wish. It was to be able to roar. You see when Charlie was born he quickly turned hoarse. As soon as he was nine years old, he went to ask Polly the parrot. But she said, "Go ask Blacky the crow."
>
> So off went poor Charlie to see Blacky. When he got there, he asked, "Blacky, why, oh why can't I roar?"

But Blacky only replied, "Don't you see, Charlie, I'm busy. Go see Jumper the kangaroo. She can help you."

Jumper didn't understand Charlie's problem. But she did give him some advice. Jumper said, "Go ask the wise old owl."

The wise old owl understood everything. He told Charlie, "I hate to say this, but if you really want to know, you're scared of everything."

Charlie thanked him and hurried home. To this day Charlie can't roar, but how happy he is to know why he can't.

There are crucial times in the lives of creative children when being understood is all that is needed to help them cope with the crisis and maintain their creativity.

Let Him Communicate His Ideas

The highly creative child has an unusually strong urge to explore and to create. When he thinks up ideas, or tests them, and modifies them, he has an unusually strong urge to communicate his ideas and the result of his tests. Yet both peers and teachers named some of the most creative children in our studies as ones who "do not speak out their ideas." When we see what happens when they do "speak out their ideas," there is little wonder that they are reluctant to communicate their ideas. Frequently, their ideas are so far ahead of those of their classmates and even their teachers that they have given up hope of communicating.

All school guidance workers need to learn to perform this function more effectively. They must genuinely respect the questions and ideas of children to sustain the highly creative child so that he will continue to think.

See that His Creative Talent Is Recognized

Information from many sources indicates that much creative talent goes unrecognized. In our own studies at all educational levels (Torrance, 1960c), you will recall that over 70 per cent of those in the upper 20 per cent on tests of creative thinking would be eliminated if only an intelligence or scholastic aptitude test had been used.

Of all of Elizabeth Drews' (Drews, 1961b) three gifted groups (social leaders, creative intellectuals, and studious achievers), the lowest teacher grades were achieved by the creative intellectuals. When the others were studying for examinations, they would be reading a book on philosophy or a college textbook, activities with almost no payoff in the teacher's grade book. Thus, on standardized achievement tests, the creative intellectuals surpassed the other groups as a result of their wide reading and uncredited, self-initiated learning.

Holland and Kent (1960), of the National Merit Scholarship Corporation, have questioned the effectiveness of present scholarship programs. They think that much of the $100,000,000 now available annually for college scholarships may be going to the wrong individuals, the good grade-getters who often have little creative talent. In the corporation's studies of scholarship winners, Holland (1961) found that "for samples of students of superior scholastic aptitude, creative performance is generally unrelated to scholastic achievement and scholastic aptitude." He suggests the use of nonintellectual criteria in the selection of students for scholarships and fellowships. A bold step was taken by the National Merit Scholarship Corporation in 1961 when it awarded 25 of its scholarships to individuals who had high creative promise but would not otherwise have won awards.

Getzels (1960a) has also pointed out that the tests, recommendations, and rank in class now relied upon so heavily in college admission are biased in favor of the student with "convergent" intellectual ability and social interests. He made a plea at the 1960 meeting of the American Educational Research Association that colleges recognize and find a place for superior divergent students as well as the superior convergent ones. Mednick (1961) made a similar plea at the 1961 meeting of the Association for Higher Education. He pointed out that although modern technology might soon enable colleges to admit only a relatively pure strain of "grade getters," they may in so doing breed some extremely desirable characteristics *out* of college populations.

In the second chapter, attention will be given to methods for identifying creative talent and ways by which guidance workers can fulfill their role of seeing that creative talent is recognized.

Help Parents Understand Their Creative Child

One of the most tragic plights I have witnessed among highly creative individuals stems from the failure of their parents to understand them. Frequently destructive or incapacitating hostility is the result of this failure. When teachers fail to understand highly creative children, refusal to learn, delinquency, or withdrawal may be a consequence. In some cases, the quiet and unobtrusive intervention of the counselor offers about the only possibility whereby parents and teachers may come to understand them and thus salvage much outstanding talent.

Guidance workers need to help parents and teachers recognize that everyone possesses to some degree the ability involved in being creative, that these abilities can be increased or decreased by the way children are treated, and that it is a legitimate function of the home and the school to provide the experiences and guidance which will free them to develop and function fully. Of course, these abilities are inherited, in the broad sense, that one inherits sense organs, a peripheral nervous system, and a brain. The type of pursuit of these abilities and the general tendency to persist in their search is largely a matter of the way parents and teachers treat children's creative needs.

Guidance workers can, as I see it, help parents to guide highly creative children in two major ways. The first concerns the parent's handling of the child's unusual ideas and questions, and the other involves helping such a child become less obnoxious without sacrificing his creativity.

The school should help parents recognize that criticism—making fun of the child's ideas or laughing at his conclusions—can prevent his expression of ideas. The parent's experienced eyes and ears can help the child learn to look for and to listen to important sights and sounds. The parent should stimulate the child to explore, ask questions, and try to find answers.

Many parents attempt too early to eliminate fantasy from the thinking of the child. Fantasy is regarded as something unhealthy and to be eliminated. Fantasies such as imaginative role playing, fantastic stories, unusual drawings, and the like are normal aspects of a child's thinking. Many parents are greatly relieved to learn this and out of this understanding grows a better parent-child relationship. Certainly we are interested in developing a sound type of creativity, but this type of fantasy, it seems to me, must be kept alive until the child's intellectual development is such that he can engage in sound creative thinking. I have seen many indications in our testing of first and second graders that many children with impoverished imaginations have been subjected to rather vigorous and stern efforts to eliminate fantasy too early. They are afraid to think.

Counselors and administrators can be sympathetic with teachers and parents who are irritated by the unending curiosity and manipulativeness of highly creative children. Endless questioning and experimenting can be inconvenient. Parents may not appreciate the child's passion for first-hand observation. Persistent questioning can be very annoying. A mother of a three-year old complained, "He wears me out just asking questions. He won't give up either, until he gets an answer; it's just awful when he gets started on something!"

Counselors, teachers, and administrators can help parents recognize the fact that there is value in such curiosity and manipulativeness and that there can be no substitute for it. Parents should be encouraged to help the child learn to ask good questions, how to make good guesses at the answers, and how to test the answers against reality.

Most parents find it extremely difficult to permit their children to learn on their own—even to do their school work on their own. Parents want to protect their children from the hurt of failing. Individual administration of problems involving possible solutions to frustrating situations has shown that the imagination of many children is inhibited by the tremendous emphasis which has been placed on prevention. For example, many of our third graders were so obsessed with the thought that Mother Hubbard should have prevented her predicament that they were reluctant to consider possible solutions to her problem. This may possibly be related to the criticism of some observers that American education prepares only for victory or success and not for possible frustration or even failure.

Certainly teaching of all kinds of failure is important, but overemphasis may deter children from coping imaginatively and realistically with frustration and failure, which cannot be prevented. It may rob the child of his initiative and resourcefulness. All children learn by trial and error. They must try, fail, try another method, and if necessary, try even again. Of course, they need guidance, but they also need to find success by their own efforts. Each child strives for independence from the time he learns to crawl, and independence is a necessary characteristic of the creative personality.

SUMMARY

Schools have cause for concern about the creative talent and creative growth of children which stems from their legitimate and traditional concerns about mental hygiene, fully functioning personalities, educational achievement, vocational success, and social welfare. Guidance workers are in a unique position to encourage creative talent by providing highly creative children with a refuge from vicious attacks by the world, being a sponsor or patron, helping him understand and accept his divergence, letting him communicate his ideas, seeing that his creative talent is recognized, and helping parents and teachers understand him.

Chapter 2

ASSESSING
THE CREATIVE
THINKING ABILITIES

Many writers (Barron, 1957; Hargreaves, 1927; Osborn, 1948; Simpson, 1922; Thurstone, 1952, 1953) have cited evidence concerning the relative independence of measures of intelligence and measures of creativity or imagination, especially when quality rather than fluency is considered. What, then, is the nature of these thinking abilities which are different from those assessed by tests of intelligence? What is creative thinking?

I have chosen to define creative thinking as the process of sensing gaps or disturbing, missing elements; forming ideas or hypotheses concerning them; testing these hypotheses; and communicating the results, possibly modifying and retesting the hypotheses. I have been quite willing to subsume in this definition the major features of most other definitions which have been proposed. Something new is included in all of them. Sir Frederick Bartlett (1959) employs the term of "adventurous thinking" which he characterizes as "getting away from the main track, breaking out of the mold, being open to experience, and permitting one thing to lead to another." Simpson (1922) defined creative ability as the initiative which one manifests by his power to break away from the usual sequence of thought into an altogether different pattern of thought. Concerning the problem of identification, he says that we must look for a searching, combing, synthetic type of mind. Such concepts as curiosity, imagination, discovery, innovation, and invention are prominent in discussions of the meaning of creativity.

In accepting this kind of definition of creativity, a variety of kinds of behavior are included. It is my opinion that we must continue to do this. By this, it is not meant that we should try to represent all of these abilities and/or behaviors by any single index. Neither does it mean that we are now ready to establish a set of discreet abilities or pure factors.

In order to identify and measure the abilities involved in the creative process, it is necessary to understand the nature of the creative process. Many workers have sought to describe the process, and these descriptions show remarkable agreement. Most analysts (Wallas, 1926; Patrick, 1955) identify four steps: preparation, incubation, illumination, and revision. Apparently the process flows something like the following. First, there is the sensing of a need or deficiency, random exploration, and a clarification or "pinning down" of the problem. Then ensues a period of preparation accompanied by reading, discussing, exploring, and formulating many possible solutions, and then critically analyzing these solutions for advantages and disadvantages. Out of all this comes the birth of a new idea—a flash of insight, illumination. Finally, there is experimentation to evaluate the most promising solution for eventual selection and perfection of the idea. Such an idea may find embodiment in inventions, scientific theories, improved products or methods, novels, musical composition, paintings, or new designs.

The concern of this chapter is with the assessment of the creative thinking abilities—those abilities presumed to be involved in creative thinking. The emphasis in measurement has been on the product rather than the process. Because of the nature of the creative process and of the limitations of testing situations, only rare attempts have been made to assess the process.

**DEFICIENCIES OF TRADITIONAL
MEASURES OF INTELLECTUAL
TALENT AND PERSONALITY
ADJUSTMENT**

As Catherine Cox Miles (1960) pointed out in the First Minnesota Conference on Gifted Children, Terman in his pioneer work challenged educators, sociologists, and psychologists "to produce, if they can, another concept as effective as the IQ for the delimiting of a group of talent to include the most successful students, the best achievers in the academic world, and, as he believed, in the world of human relationships and human endeavor generally" (p. 51). The prestige of intelligence tests, especially individual ones like the Stanford-Binet and the Wechsler, was so great that hardly anyone paid any attention to those rare individuals who questioned their ability to identify "intellectual giftedness" and assess mental growth. As Gallagher (1960) notes, the few complaints that were heard concentrated on the limitations of IQ tests in assessing special talents such as art, music, and dramatic ability.

Emphasis on Convergence

Now that a second look is being taken at intelligence tests, many deficiencies become apparent. One of the most obvious is their emphasis on convergent, conforming thinking. Guilford (1950), Thurstone (1952), Getzels and Jackson (1958, 1960), and others have made this clear. The full impact of this deficiency did not occur to me, until I started studying the performance of children in West Samoa on the Minnesota Tests of Creative Thinking. As estimated by the Goodenough Draw-a-Person Test, children reared in this highly conforming culture rate high IQ's. They exhibit outstanding technical skill in drawing but almost all of their drawings have a reproductive quality. Everything is drawn in the correct proportion and every person has proper eyes, ears, and noses. The children's performance on the tests of creative thinking, however, did not keep pace with the excellence of their drawings or the degree of intelligence exhibited in their drawings.

I. A. Taylor (1959) argues that "intelligence" is an invention of western culture and selects and stresses the values important in our society.

He maintains that intelligence tests "essentially concern themselves with how fast relatively unimportant problems can be solved without making errors" (p. 54). "In another culture," he continues, "intelligence might be measured more in terms of how adequately important problems can be solved, making all the errors necessary and without regard for time."

Overemphasis on Traditional Academic Values

Others have criticized intelligence tests for their exclusive concern with traditional academic value systems which have little to do with life outside this system. Smillie (1959) maintains that the limited conceptualizations of intelligence represented by the Stanford-Binet and the Wechsler tests obscure the unique and creative qualities of those who do not fit the patterns measured by the tests. The ability to memorize and to repeat arbitrary information is highly valued, and creativity, inventiveness, and originality are ignored.

Calvin W. Taylor (1959) criticizes traditional measures of intellectual talent on much the same grounds. He argues that, historically, intelligence tests were developed in such a way that they predicted academic performance of the type which was valued most highly at the time. This has tended to freeze both the nature of the tests and of academic values.

The criticisms of Smillie and Taylor find interesting, indirect support in studies being conducted in conjunction with some of the experimental science programs. When students are taught science in such a way that they learn creatively, the traditional predictors lose some of their validity. For example, Ornstein (1961) has described just such a phenomenon in connection with one of the experimental physics courses. He reports that a substantial number of students who had scored only slightly better than average on the School and College Aptitude Test (SCAT) made gradually higher scores on the physics tests administered throughout the year. Some of these "average" students scored higher than many who were at the top of the SCAT test and presumably were more gifted. Ornstein makes the guess that the students whose high SCAT scores did not correlate with their physics test scores were much better at memorizing facts and formulas (learning by authority) than at the analytical, intuitive thinking the new approach requires.

Lumping Together of Talent, Creativity, and Conformity

Another criticism of prevailing practices for identifying and guiding gifted individuals is our traditional lumping together of talent, creativity, and conformity. We have tried to make one metric, the IQ or a score on some scholastic aptitude test, represent the sum total of man's mental functioning.

Calvin W. Taylor (1960b), at the Second Minnesota Conference on Gifted Children, voiced his criticism in the following words:

> To me it is highly inconsistent to conceive of the mind as being represented by a single score or even by only the handful of scores or dimensions present in our current intelligence tests. The brain which underlies the mind is far, far too complex for us to hope that all of its intellectual activities can be represented by only a single score or by a handful of dimensions. To seriously utilize such an over-simplified picture might be considered an insult to the brain, to the human mind, and to the human being.

McNeil (1960) offered a similar criticism. He argues that if the process of creativity requires unconventional thinking, then it must be concluded that true creativity and conformity are antithetical in nature and should not be combined into any single measure. He suggests that we differentiate between the talented conformists who can be trained to become the brilliant enhancers, embroiderers, and manipulators of the ideas of others, and the equally talented nonconformists who may make imaginative breakthroughs to new knowledge.

Types of Test Responses

Group tests of intelligence and scholastic ability are being attacked on the basis of the limitations inherent in the multiple-choice type of test response. Ruth Strang (1959) has presented a case for using tests which call for creativity both in identifying gifted children and in evaluating their achievement. P. E. Vernon (1960) has pointed out the need for supplementing the objective-type tests with the creative-response-type of test.

Lou LaBrant, past president of the National Council of Teachers of English, has made the following criticism of prevailing test formats:

. . . Mechanical tests (true-false, multiple-choice with only one "right" choice) with machine-scored ratings control entrance to many of our most highly respected institutions. We may live in a machine age, but machines will not invent the imperative human relations, the necessary weighing of values, the concessions, or the daring proposals we shall need; neither will machine-scored tests discover inventors and innovators . . .—LaBrant, 1960.

E. S. Morgan of Yale University made the following criticism of multiple-choice tests in an address to Yale freshmen:

> The accumulation of information is a necessary part of scholarship, and unfortunately the part most likely to be tested on examinations, especially those wretched ones called "objective examinations" where the truth is always supposed to lie in answer space A, B, C, D, or E, but never apparently in X, Y, or Z. But the curiosity we expect of you cannot be satisfied by passing examinations or by memorizing other people's questions . . .—Morgan, 1960, p. 14.

In popular literature, devastating attacks on multiple-choice tests have been made by W. H. Whyte (1956) in *The Organization Man*, Jacques Barzun (1959) in *The House of Intellect*, and B. Hoffman (1961) in "The Tyranny of Multiple-Choice Tests." Hoffman identifies the following defects of such tests:

1. They deny the creative person a significant opportunity to demonstrate his creativity.
2. They penalize those who perceive subtle points unnoticed by less able people, including the test-makers.
3. They are apt to be superficial and intellectually dishonest, with questions made artificially difficult by means of ambiguity, because genuinely searching questions do not readily fit into the multiple-choice format.
4. They too often degenerate into subjective guessing games in which the examinee does not pick what he considers the best answer out of a bad lot but rather the one he believes the unknown examiner would consider best.
5. They neglect skill in disciplined expression.

Conformity Factored into Personality Tests

The conformity factor in personality tests has been under attack for several years. This attack has been limited almost entirely to industrial use of personality tests and has seldom been heard in education. In a conference on company climate and creativity (Deutsch and Shea, Inc., 1959), several of the panelists expressed dissatisfaction with the personality tests now in vogue. They maintained that such tests have conformity and adjustment factored into them and more often than not screen out the truly creative individuals.

Whyte's (1956) *The Organization Man* includes a rather lengthy critique of personality tests along much the same lines. For example, Whyte gives the "ideal executive" profile of Sears, Roebuck on the Allport-Vernon-Lindzey *Study of Values*. The highest point on the profile is Economic and the lowest Aesthetic, with Theoretical, Social and Political all just above the middle compared with norm groups. It is interesting to contrast this profile with those of MacKinnon's (1960) highly effective persons. In every field studied by MacKinnon, the high points on the profiles were Aesthetic and Theoretical. Whyte (1956, p. 219) also reported that not one corporation president tested had a profile that fell completely within the usual "acceptable" range.

The conformity factor in personality tests is reflected in Whyte's now classical advice for cheating on personality tests in order to get a job. He counsels test-takers to observe the following two rules:

1. When asked for word associations or comments about the world, give the most conventional, run-of-the-mill, pedestrian answer possible.
2. When in doubt about the most beneficial answer to any question repeat to yourself:
I loved my father and mother, but my father a little bit more.
I like things pretty much the way they are.
I never worry much about anything.
I don't care for books or music much.
I love my wife and children.
I don't let them get in the way of company work. (Whyte, 1956, p. 217)

MANIFESTATIONS OF CREATIVE THINKING AND THEIR MEASUREMENT

With this background of definitions of creativity and creative thinking and critiques of traditional approaches to the assessment of intellectual talents and personality, let us review some of the manifestations of creative thinking at each educational level and the approaches which have been developed for measuring the creative thinking abilities and identifying creative personalities. For convenience, I shall present this information according to four educational stages: (1) early childhood (preschool), (2) elementary school, (3) secondary school, and (4) higher education. After this summary, I shall consider problems of criteria and validity. The Minnesota Tests of Creative Thinking will be described and discussed in the next chapter.

THE EARLY CHILDHOOD YEARS

As scientifically-developed information has begun to accumulate, the nature, meaning, and importance of creativity in the early childhood years are becoming clearer. Early conceptual errors concerning the nature of the mental activity of young children has been a serious block. Many of these errors still persist and scientific information is needed to help clarify many puzzling problems.

Early Manifestations of Creative Thinking

Many scholars have denied the possibility that young children can think. In 1906, I. E. Miller in his text, *The Psychology of Thinking,* discussed this problem at length and suggested that this error which has led to the tendency to minimize the child's power to think and to overestimate the importance of receptivity can be traced to a tendency to use the terms thinking and reasoning as synonomous.

It seems clear that much of the confusion stems from the ways in which each scholar has limited his observations of the manifestations of creativity. Most of the work which has been done reflects little recognition of the fact that no single test or area of observations taps all of the resources of the individual for creative thinking and that the same test or kinds of observations are not valid or adequate at all age levels.

It is natural that many who have attempted to study creativity in the early childhood years have sought to do so through the medium of art. Conclusions from this research have varied, apparently according to the manifestations which have been admitted. Grippen (1933) recognized the following categories of "creative artistic imagination" in his studies of children from three through seven:

1. Revision of a single memory image.
2. Organization on the nature of a composite from several images, usually related.
3. Improvisation of a theme, resembling the source of sources, from a number of images.
4. Selection of various elements of aesthetic interest, to which other elements may be added, all based upon a single memorial or sensory experience.
5. Compositional expressions arising as a reaction from a single memory touching some more or less strong emotional experience.
6. Effective expressions appearing in appropriate compositional setting from a single vivid aspect of a larger experience residing in the child as a memorial experience.
7. Fusion of compositional elements or aspects into a composition of high character, from a continuing experience over a limited time interval.

Grippen's data included children's paintings and their verbalizations while painting. Sources of a child's imaginative conceptions were found to be incidents in the local and immediate environment, physical aspects of the local environment, books, magazines, pictures, and travel experiences. Limited to these observations, it is not surprising that Grippen concluded that "except in rare instances creative imagination does not function in children below the age of five years, but some children at the age of five exhibit a degree of it comparable to children seven years old." The total number of Grippen's subjects was 48, another serious limitation for a conclusion of this type.

If one observes the ways infants handle things, shake them, twist them, and manipulate them in many ways, he might find some of the beginnings of the manifestations of creative thinking. We may also see some of the beginnings of creative thinking, if we observe the infant's use of facial expressions, his efforts to interpret the facial expressions of others, and the process of differentiating his own body from the remainder of the environment. Since the infant does not have a vocabulary, he is limited in learning by authority. Thus, by necessity, much of his learning must be creative—sensing problems, making guesses, testing and modifying them, and communicating them in his limited way.

Methods of Measurement in Early Childhood

A variety of methods have been used in attempting to assess the creative products and processes of young children. McCarty (1924) used drawings. Abramson (1927) used responses to inkblots and concrete observations (subjects enumerated objects after viewing them for twenty minutes).

Andrews (1930) used a variety of methods and observations, attempting to study a variety of types of imaginative or creative activity. Three of his tests were presented tachistoscopically with the task of forming new products (transformations). The following kinds of observations were made of the imaginative play of children from two to six: imitation, experimentation, transformation of objects, transformation of animals, acts of sympathy, dramatizations, imaginary playmates, fanciful explanations, fantastic stories, new uses of stories, constructions, new games, extensions of language, appropriate quotations, leadership with plan, and aesthetic appreciation.

Andrews (1930) also described some of the unpublished work of Martha Beckman Ransohoff. As stimuli, she used the Whipple standardized inkblots 1–20 and a picture test. The pictures used in the latter were taken from current magazines and were "typical of modern advertising art." Her methods of assessing responses reflect what this writer considers to be serious misconcepts concerning the nature of creative imagination. Responses to the pictures were scored on a scale ranging from zero to two in terms of accuracy. In evaluating responses to the inkblots, she assigned the highest score to children who gave the same response to the same blot five times out of five. Both of these measures appear to be indices of convergent thinking and it is not surprising that she concluded that the imagination of young children improves with increasing maturity. Her conclusions are limited also by the fact that they are based on the study of a total of only 22 children.

As already mentioned, Grippen (1933) used constant contact methods with data consisting of paintings and verbalizations while painting.

Markey (1935) employed observational methods to evaluate performance in a variety of standardized situations and tasks, such as a housekeeping game, the fanciful naming of visual stimuli, leadership in imaginative games, and block-building. The use of this wide range of stimuli led her to conclude that no single test taps all of the imaginative resources of an individual and that the same test of imagination is not equally valid at all age levels. She points out, for example, that the lesser interest of the older children in the housekeeping game influences the trend of the age scores in that the younger children made better scores. She contends that the housekeeping materials used in one task were better suited to the younger children because of their greater interest in games involving personification and simple make-believe uses of materials. She also points out that the level of the child's understanding and comprehension influences the type of creative response. Thus, younger children give more fanciful names to objects, animals, and constructions, while older children are likely to identify the stimuli in realistic terms.

From the foregoing attempts to assess the creative thinking of younger children, there is in general a tendency for a low correlation between such measures and traditional measures of intelligence. Markey (1935) reported that the correlations between mental age and test scores were slightly higher than correlations between chronological age and test scores. It is interesting, however, that Markey sought in various ways to explain away the relatively low correlation between mental age and imaginative behavior (diversity or groups studied, etc.). Andrews (1930) recognized more clearly the difference between the two types of meaures and concluded that the correlations between IQ and imagination and mental age and imagination are so low as to indicate that "very little relationship exists between intelligence and the fantastic imagination of the young child." In interpreting his use of "fantastic imagination" it is important to note that his measure included transformations, analogies, and other kinds of performance now considered to be involved in creative thinking. Among children of two to four years of age, McDowell and Howe (1941) found that IQ was correlated positively with the degree of creative use of all the play materials (blocks, plastic clay, and paints).

THE ELEMENTARY SCHOOL YEARS

There is rather general consensus that the elementary school years are critical ones in the development of creative talent. For ages, sensitive observers have noted and deplored the rise and decline of the child's creative powers during this period. Most of them have done so in a spirit of helpless resignation or have made authoritative pronouncements concerning the solution to the problem. Sustained, imaginative research concerning these problems is lacking. Many important *beginnings* have been made, however, and an attempt will be made to summarize the status of the knowledge which has accumulated as a result.

Manifestations of Creativity in the Elementary School Years

Of the many manifestations of creativity among children during the elementary school period, greatest attention has been given to creative writing and art. More and more, adults are finding delight in the writing and art of children. More and more, teachers are beginning to value creative productions over the reproductions of adult models. Aside from the walls of school rooms, however, there are few places where such manifestations of children's creativity can be enjoyed. A bibliography of child authors by Kupferberg and Topp (1959) lists 450 titles. Most of these, however, are poorly presented, difficult to obtain, and published in few copies. Here and there exhibitions of children's art have achieved unexpected success and exchange exhibits with other countries have attracted considerable attention.

Throughout history, in spite of the "holding back operations" which seem always to be with us, there have been examples of outstanding creative achievement at a tender age (Cole, 1956, p. 27). Newton spent his childhood making water clocks and windmill models. James Hillier constructed his first microscope as a boy. Pascal wrote his famous essay at 16; the great mathematician Karl Friedrich Gauss, after performing distinguished work at 15, developed his method of least squares at the age of 18. Samuel Colt started working on his idea of the revolver at 16. At 19 George Westinghouse invented a device for replacing derailed cars.

Methods of Measurement During the Elementary School Period

As might be expected, more varied materials and tasks have been used in assessing the creative capacities of children during the elementary school period than during the preschool period. With increased ability to communicate ideas through speech and writing this becomes possible. Attention will be called to some of the more significant contributions.

Typical of many of the early efforts, was Kirkpatrick's (1900) work with four inkblots. Colvin (1902) used compositions, giving attention to such factors as invention, sense of humor, imaginative power, feeling, and perceptive power. Simpson (1922) used fifty sets of four small round dots, representing the four corners of squares, as the stimuli for drawings. Fluency, originality, and flexibility were assessed. McCarty (1924) extended the use of drawings through the third grade, and Abramson (1927), working with children of the third and higher grades, used inkblots and a task requiring the enumeration of objects after viewing them for twenty minutes. Grippen (1933) used the constant contact method, already described, through the second grade.

Harms (1939) employed a test requiring the representation of words (mostly various actions) by single lines, in grades one through twelve. Stephenson (1949) reports the use of a Poetry-Writing Test and an Art Form Test, presumably covering the same range.

Developers and users of tests of imagination and creative thinking for elementary school children have consistently found little or no relationship between scores on such measures and scores on tests of intelligence. Simpson, in 1922, declared, "By joining a creative test such as we have outlined, with a 'reproductive' test such as any general intelligence test, we shall get a more accurate statement of the worth of an individual." He argued that an intelligence test alone does not evaluate "vital creative energy."

THE HIGH SCHOOL YEARS

Of the different educational levels, the high school years have perhaps been the most neglected in creativity research. Information has accumulated concerning the preschool and elementary school years because of interest in "creative imagination." Apparently, educators have not had much interest in the "creative imagination" of high school students. Information has accumulated concerning creativity during the college years, because many outstanding creative scientists, writers, and performers of many kinds began their productivity during these years, and because it has been deemed appropriate for colleges to produce professionally trained people who will make creative contributions. No such expectations exist for high schools.

Creative growth has rarely been recognized as an objective of secondary education. Although many promising changes in objectives seem to be occurring, especially in high school mathematics, physics, biology, and chemistry, the results of a 1959–60 sample survey (Torrance, 1960j) of Minnesota social science teachers probably reflects the status of high school objectives in this regard. Each social science teacher in the survey was asked to select a course or unit and list the three most important objectives. The objectives listed were then classified according to Guilford's five mental operations with the following results:

Percentage

Cognitive (recognize, realize, become aware of, become
  acquainted or familiar with, be conscious of, etc.) 70.7

Memory (remember, acquire distinct or thorough
  knowledge of, learn thoroughly) 5.3

Convergent (behavioral norms, right attitude, right
  solution, etc.) 18.7

Divergent (independent thinking, constructive, creative,
  liberal, inquiring, etc.) 1.7

Evaluative (critical thinking, assessing, selecting,
  comparing, judging, deciding, etc.) 3.6

Manifestations of Creativity During High School Years

Although a few scientists, writers, and inventors have won eminence while still of high school age, the number has been too small for much study and in most cases they did not achieve their eminence in the high school setting. High schools have long had provisions for recognizing creative writing and speaking talent. In recent years, there have been many provisions for recognizing scientific and inventive talent. In studies of the National Merit Scholarship Corporation, a five-item Creative Science Scale and an eleven-item Creative Arts Scale based on high school experiences have proved quite valuable in predicting later creative performance (Holland, 1961). The following manifestations are recognized in the Creative Science Scale:

1. Presenting an original paper at a scientific meeting sponsored by a professional society.
2. Winning a prize or award in a scientific talent search.
3. Constructing scientific apparatus on own initiative.
4. Inventing a patentable device.
5. Having scientific paper published in a science journal.

The following kinds of manifestations are included in the Creative Arts Scale:

1. Won one or more speech contests.
2. Had poems, stories, or articles published in a *public* newspaper or magazine (*not* school paper) or in state or national high school anthology.
3. Won a prize or award in an art competition (sculpture, ceramics, painting, etc.).
4. Received the highest rating in a state music contest.
5. Received one of the highest ratings in a national music contest.
6. Composed music which has been given at least one public performance.
7. Arranged music for public performance.
8. Has minor roles in plays (not high school or church-sponsored).
9. Had leads in high school or church-sponsored plays.
10. Won literary award or prize for creative writing.
11. Had cartoon published in a public newspaper or magazine.

These are but a few of the manifestations of creativity among high school students.

Measurement of Creative Thinking at High School Level

Devices for assessing the creative thinking abilities of high school pupils have tended to be in the direction of group administered tests with verbal stimuli requiring verbal responses. Although some of the devices originally developed for use with children have been extended into or through the high school years, most of the instruments used with high school students were initially developed for use with college students or adults. Some of the major efforts will be summarized briefly.

Colvin (1902) made more use of his measures based on compositions with high school students than with younger groups. Abramson (1927) also used his inkblots and concrete observations (enumerating objects after twenty minutes of exposure) with high school students, as well as with grades three through six. Throughout grades one through twelve Harms (1939) applied his test in which subjects drew lines to represent words (mostly action words). M. D. Vernon (1948) used his Imaginative Construction Test (stories based on four colored pictures) with high school subjects, as did Stephenson (1949) with his Poetry-Writing and Arm Form Tests.

Most of the recent work with high school students has involved adaptations of Guilford's test with a few innovations. Getzels and Jackson (1958) used four adapted tasks (Word Associations, Uses for Things, Hidden Shapes, and Fables) and constructed one of their own (Make-Up Problems). In the latter task, subjects are presented with four complex paragraphs, each containing a variety of data. Subjects are then required to make up as many mathematical problems as they can which can be solved with the information given. Scores depend upon the number, appropriateness, and originality of the problems.

With seventh-grade subjects, McGuire, Hindsman, King, and Jennings (1961) used the following Guilford tests: Rhymes, Unusual Uses, Consequences, Common Situations, Seeing Problems, Mutilated Words, and Gestalt Completion. Piers, Daniels, and Quackenbush (1960) administered the following Guilford measures to seventh and eighth graders: Consequences, Plot Titles, and Unusual Uses. Guilford (1961) recently gave a progress report on current work in which he has administered his battery to ninth graders and found essentially the same factors he found with adults. These measures will be discussed in the section on higher education which follows.

HIGHER EDUCATION

Much has been written concerning the need for developing creativity in higher education, and college students have served as subjects in experiments concerning creativity phenomena. Yet there is almost no evidence of experimentation in this area in admissions practices, college teaching, or evaluation of achievement in higher education.

Manifestations of Creativity in Higher Education

College students have been known to produce almost all types of creative products—inventions, books, monographs, and original articles. Usually, however, such manifestations occur outside college requirements and activities. The well-known term paper is usually a digest of known facts or opinions of experts and is graded for correctness of form and content. The research of others is almost always evaluated in terms of correctness or methodology and is done in a critical rather than a constructive manner. Dissertations and theses, usually regarded as original contributions, tend actually to be evaluated in terms of the correctness of the methodology rather than in terms of the originality, power, and worth of the ideas developed and tested. There are, and perhaps always have been, dramatic exceptions to this generalization, which appears to represent the consensus of many observers of the higher education scene.

Measures of Creative Thinking in Higher Education

Although no reports have been located of colleges or universities in the United States which use measures of creative thinking as a functional part of their programs, a great variety of such measures have been developed for use with college students and have been in existence for many years.

In 1916, Laura Chassell at Northwestern University reported rather detailed data concerning a battery of twelve tests of originality. This battery included: Word Building, Picture Writing, Analogies, Original Analogues, Chain Puzzle, Triangle Puzzle, Royce's Ring, Completion Test, Economic Prophecies, Code Test, Invention for Sheet Music, and Novel Situations (Consequences).

In his book, *Teaching to Think* (1922), Boraas described and discussed the following eight types of tests of "imaginative thinking":

1. The interpretation of inkblots.
2. Word-building test.

3. Sentence-building test.

4. Making of similes or metaphors by combining any two of a given series of words.

5. Completion of mutilated sentences.

6. Painted cube test.

7. Imaginary journey test.

8. Production of rhymes.

Hargreaves (1927) described and presented data concerning twelve tasks which he scored for fluency and originality: Word Building and Composition, Ebbinghaus Test, Invention of Stories, Indeterminate Picture Completion, Unfinished Pictures, Ink Blots, Indeterminate Language Completion, Unfinished Stories, Writing Words, Probable Situations, and Imaginary Situations.

Meier (1939) and his associates (McCloy, 1939; McCloy and Meier, 1939) experimented with a variety of measures closely related to their interest in art education. Their tasks included: interpretative titles for pictures; critical appraisal and interpretation of completed works of art; compositions, opinions, and interpretations of paintings.

Welch (1946) has made several interesting contributions concerning the assessment of creativity as seeing new combinations. His tasks include: Block Constructions (make as many pieces of furniture or home furnishings as possible from ten blocks), Sentence Construction (from ten words), Letter Construction (from three straight lines), and Short Story Construction.

Owen and his associates (1957) have developed a series of tasks to assess creativity in machine design. These include: Power Source Apparatus Test, Design-a-Machine Test, Three-Dimensional Space Relations Test, and Figure Matrices Test. This battery is supplemented by a Personal Inventory and a Personal History Form. Harris (1960) has developed two forms of a 20-item test of creativity in engineering which has been standardized for engineering students. The content is oriented to engineering and the tasks require subjects to list possible uses of various objects and to guess "What is it?" Scores are obtained for fluency, flexibility, and originality.

Barron (1958) and his associates at the University of California have developed a battery of tasks for assessing originality among college students and adults. Among the tasks which have been described in the literature are: Mosaic Constructions, Anagram Test, Drawing-Completion (Franck), Figure Preference Test (Welsh), and Inkblot Test (uncommon responses).

Other instruments which have been used with college subjects include: Flanagan's (1958) Ingenious Solutions to Problems, one of the few attempts to assess creative thinking through multiple-choice items; Frederickson's (1959) Formulating Hypotheses Test, an attempt first to elicit creative-type responses and then to transfer them to machine-scoring answer sheets by having subjects code their own responses; and Burkhart's (1961) Divergent Questions Test which requires subjects to ask questions about a given object such as an apple or a paper clip.

The elaborate battery of tasks developed by Guilford and his associates has been used with college students both by Guilford's laboratory and other groups. Because of the lengthiness of this battery, most users have used only a portion of the Guilford tasks. A number of these were originally developed by Thurstone, the United States Air Force, and Educational Testing Service. Since his presidential address before the American Psychological Association in 1950, Guilford has continued to modify his conceptualization of the creative thinking abilities and the tasks used to assess them. In a recent monograph, Guilford and Merrifield (1960) summarized these modifications. This work has been done within the framework of Guilford's "structure of intellect." Earlier, Guilford had hypothesized that the thinking abilities involved in creativity were those he had defined as *divergent productions and transformations*. He now includes the redefinition abilities which are in the *convergent-production* category of his structure of intellect and sensitivity to problems which falls in the *evaluation* category. Thus, the following factors and tasks for assessing them may be regarded as summarizing Guilford's present theory concerning the measurement of the thinking abilities involved in creativity (Guilford and Merrifield, 1960):

FACTOR	TESTS AND DESCRIPTIONS
Sensitivity to Problems (seeing defects, needs, deficiencies; seeing the odd, the unusual; seeing what must be done)	*Apparatus Test*—Suggest two improvements for a common appliance. *Seeing Problems*—List problems that might arise in connection with common objects.

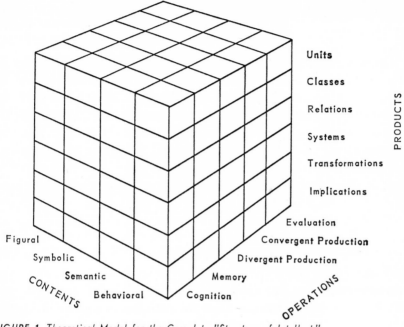

FIGURE 1. Theoretical Model for the Complete "Structure of Intellect."

FACTOR	TESTS AND DESCRIPTIONS
	Seeing Deficiencies—Point out the way in which a described plan or activity is faulty.
Figural Spontaneous Flexibility	*Cube Fluctuations*—Indicate the number of changes in perspective of ambiguous cube. (Thurstone)
	Windmill Alternations—Indicate the number of alternations from the illusion to another while observing shadow of rotating rectangular blade. (Thurstone)
	Retinal-rivalry Reversals—Indicate the number of reversals when a blue field is presented stereoscopically to one eye and a yellow field to the other eye. (Thurstone)
Figural Adaptive Flexibility	*Match Problems II*—Indicate three or four different patterns of a specified number of matches that can be removed to leave a specified number of triangles or squares.

FACTOR	TESTS AND DESCRIPTIONS
	Match Problems III—Indicate several different patterns of matches that can be removed to leave a specified number of squares.
	Planning Air Maneuvers—Select the most direct path in "skywriting" letter combinations. (USAF)
Word Fluency	*Suffixes W-1*—Write words ending with a specified suffix. (ETS)
	Prefixes W-2—Write words beginning with a specified prefix. (ETS)
	First and Last Letters W-3—Write words beginning and ending with a specified letter. (ETS)
Expressional Fluency	*Expressional Fluency*—Write four-word sentences when the first letter of each word is given.
	Simile Interpretations—Complete sentence that states an analogous idea.
	Word Arrangements—Write sentences containing four specified words.
Ideational Fluency	*Topics If-1*—Write as many ideas as possible about a given topic. (ETS)
	Theme If-2—Write as many words as possible about a given topic. (ETS)
	Thing Categories If-3—List the names of "things that are round or that could be called round."
	Ideational Fluency—Write names of things fitting into broad classes.
Semantic Spontaneous Flexibility	*Brick Uses (flexibility)*—Write a variety of uses for a brick.
	Alternate Uses—List different peculiar uses for common objects.

FACTOR	TESTS AND DESCRIPTIONS

Associational Fluency

Controlled Associations—Write as many synonyms as possible for each given word.

Simile Insertions—Write adjectival completion for a simile.

Associations IV—Produce a word that can be associated with two given words.

Associational Fluency I—Write synonyms for given words.

Originality

Plot Titles (clever)—Write clever titles for story plots.

Symbol Production—Produce symbols to represent activities and objects.

Consequences (remote)—List remote consequences of certain changes.

Semantic Elaboration

Planning Elaboration—Fill in as many details as necessary to make a briefly outlined activity work.

Figure Production—Add to given lines to produce a meaningful figure. Score is based on number of details drawn.

Figural Redefinition
(defining or perceiving in a way different from the usual, established, or intended way, use, etc.)

Concealed Figures Cf-1—Indicate which of four complex geometrical figures contains a given geometrical figure. (ETS)

Penetration of Camouflage—Locate faces hidden in pictures. (USAF)

Hidden Pictures—Find human or animal pictures hidden in a scene, as rapidly as possible. (Thurstone)

Hidden Figures—Indicate which of five figures is hidden in a given figure.

Symbolic Redefinition

Camouflaged Words—Find the name of the sport or game concealed in a sentence.

FACTOR	TESTS AND DESCRIPTIONS
	Word Transformation—Indicate new divisions between letters in a new series of words forming a phrase, to make a new series of words.
Semantic Redefinition	*Gestalt Transformation*—Indicate which of five listed objects has a part that will serve a specified purpose.
	Object Synthesis—Name an object that could be made by combining two specified objects.
	Picture Gestalt—Indicate which object in a photograph will serve a specified purpose.

Alert teachers and counselors will find useful a vast variety of evidence of creative talent. For example, one highly creative student was identified in an industrial arts course through a cheating incident. The instructor recognized the methods employed by the student in cheating as clever, unusual, and ingenious. The instructor then realized that the assignments he had been giving his student required only a reproductive kind of activity and that this was what the student was doing. To have punished the student would not have solved the student's problems for the causes which motivated him to cheat would have remained the same. Emphasizing the positive characteristics of the observed behavior (ingenuity and originality), the instructor provided challenging tasks which required creative problem-solving. The result was that the formerly unproductive and delinquent student excelled everyone else in the class, achieving at a level which merited a grade of "A."

PROBLEMS OF CRITERIA AND VALIDITY

Perhaps one of the major reasons why research related to the measurement and development of creative thinking did not catch the imagination of educators in past years lies in the failure of researchers to deal adequately with the difficult problems of criteria and validity. In most cases, the theoretical rationale of the instruments developed "made good sense," but their presumed validity wasn't convincing.

Quite interestingly, the most careful jobs of criterion development have been done in connection with personality and life experience studies rather than in efforts to validate measures of the creative thinking abilities.

Problems of criteria and validity have engaged the attention of the three University of Utah conferences on the identification of creative scientific talent (Taylor, 1956, 1958, 1959).

The 1959 Committee report on Criteria of Creativity at the Utah Conference (Taylor, 1959) presented an outline of the variables and dimensions potentially involved in criteria of creativity, summarized the work of past conferences on the criterion problem, and made suggestions for future research on the criterion problem. Their outline began with a consideration of what was to be measured. In identifying products they considered kinds of products (patents, books, monographs, copyrights, ideas, etc.) and aspects of products (novelty, number of products, comprehensiveness, generalization, new implications, surprise, valuableness, etc.). Concerning the identification of creative individuals, the Committee recommended that attention be given both to the identification of particular people in terms of their products, eminence, training and educational status, organizational responsibility, and to the identification and quantification of psychological traits. They also included the identification of the productive processes involved in divergent and convergent thinking and of work methods such as flexibility, planning, perseverance, and variety of approaches.

Attention was drawn by the Committee to problems of assigning value, including the sources of value judgments (supervisors, peers, monitors, organizational records, historical records, awards, self) and qualifications of the sources (scientific competence, opportunity for observation, skill in making judgments, etc.). Attention was also given to methodology (statistics and sampling, control variables, time dimensions), dimensions of functions, dimensions of field, and other similar considerations.

The 1955 Committee had drawn up a comprehensive system for evaluating the total lifetime creative output of the scientist and suggested means by which subjective biases in evaluation could be controlled. In 1957, favorable attention was given to the contributions of Ghiselin and Lacklen. Ghiselin had proposed that the measure of creativity of an idea is the extent to which it restructures our universe of understanding. Lacklen suggested that the creativity of a contribution (the more basic it is) may be measured in terms of the extent of the area of science which it covers. The 1957 Committee formulated hypotheses concerning the following issues:

1. The relation between level of creativity and amount of creative productivity.
2. The diversity of an individual's products and the level of his creativity.
3. The construction of a scale for evaluation of level of creativity of products following the Ghiselin and Lacklen formulations.
4. Abbreviated procedures for product evaluation.
5. The "validation" of a scale (such as in 3) against ratings of individuals who vary in their judged creativity.
6. The adequacy of official records for product evaluation.

Several interesting contributions to the criterion problem were made at the 1959 conference. Taylor reported a study in which he had obtained almost 150 measures of scientists' productivity and creativity which he reduced through factor analysis to 16. This work illustrates the overwhelming complexity of the criterion problem. Sprecher reported an approach in which he had peers and supervisors rate engineers on creativity and deliberately left them undefined. He then had them list the qualities which had determined their ratings. He thus derived definitions of creativity from the raters. Hans Selye, through Prioreschi, defined creativity as having three elements:

1. It must be true.
2. It must be generalizable.
3. It must be surprising.

Cattell presented an "across-time" approach to the problem. He first constructed personality profiles for several eminent men of the past on the basis of their biographies and then obtained personality profiles of leading men today and compared them.

Concerning future work, the 1959 Committee recommended that the products of creative behavior should be the first object of study. When such products are judged to be "creative," the behavior which produced them can be called creative. The individuals who produced them can also be considered "creative." They defined the criterion problem as consisting essentially of the identification of individuals who have positively and clearly demonstrated possession of the trait of creativity. They also recommended that the criterion measure should provide degrees or levels of possession of the trait, using the most basic and unequivocal measure available. The Committee included the following as types of creative products: new theories, hypotheses, classificatory or analytical concepts, relationships, formulas, techniques, machines, materials, chemicals, and physical or temporal patterns. They differentiated these from discoveries of things or events which pre-existed, recognizing that such discoveries might involve a creative act.

At the 1959 Utah Conference, Guilford discussed the validation process as a part of the report of the Committee on Predictors of Creativity. He recommended that longitudinal (predictive) validation studies be initiated as quickly as possible. He also commended Taylor's procedure of working first on the criterion problem and then looking for the measures which should be used to predict them. Another participant referred to this process as "post-current" or "follow-back" validity in contrast to follow-up or predictive validity. Recommendations were also made concerning the desirability of cross-validation, the use of factor or subscores rather than just combinations of them, the need for using moderator variables (co-varying factors), and validation procedures other than the regression approach (such as comparing the mean scores of the successful scientist with the means of the general population from which these scientists originally came).

Attempts at early identification of creative talent are required to satisfy the recommendations of the Guilford Committee relative to longitudinal validation studies. Taylor (1960b) at the Second Minnesota Conference on Gifted Children discussed the obstacles to this early identification. He included such considerations as the following:

1. The rarity of the highest type of creative thinking.
2. Society's failure to recognize creative products until a generation or two after the creation.
3. Society's tendency to reward recognized creative talent with promotions into positions where they are unable to continue their creativity.

4. The stress of academic programs of noncreative activities.

5. Failure of academic programs to reward creative achievement and divergent thinking.

In commenting upon Taylor's Minnesota address, I (1960b) set forth a number of arguments supporting the necessity of serious efforts to identify creative talent early in life and to study the forces which impinge its development. I pointed out the necessity for scientifically developed information concerning the nature and development of creative thinking in children in order to make possible the changes needed in education. On the basis of work already in progress, I discussed the fallacies in the concept that "creativity will win out" regardless of the obstacles. The challenge of keeping creativity alive is analogous to what medicine and other sciences have accomplished in lengthening man's life expectancy and in reducing deaths at birth.

SUMMARY

In examining a large number of definitions of creativity and creative thinking, it was observed that almost all of them involved the production of something new or original as a result of a process of sensing some kind of deficiency, formulating ideas or hypotheses concerning them, testing these hypotheses, and communicating the results. In order to assess the abilities involved in creative thinking, it is necessary to develop and apply tests which are different from those now commonly used in assessing mental functioning. Some of the more serious deficiencies of traditional instruments include: their emphasis on convergence; overemphasis on traditional academic values; tendency to lump together talent, creativity, and conformity; and types of test responses required. Conformity has also been factored into most of the personality tests being used.

The manifestations of creative thinking at the preschool, elementary, secondary, and higher education levels were described and the types of tasks which have been devised for measuring them were reviewed in this chapter. During the past seventy years a variety of tasks have been devised. The earlier measures tended to involve either responses to inkblots or analogies. The tasks which have been developed subsequently involve a great variety of types of stimuli, materials, responses and apparently a great diversity of mental abilities. Problems of criteria and validity have presented serious problems in the development of testing instruments and continue to engage the attention of conferences and leaders in the field. In this chapter, special attention was given to the recommendations of the University of Utah national conferences on the identification of creative scientific talent.

Chapter 3

THE MINNESOTA TESTS
OF CREATIVE
THINKING

In 1958 when the Bureau of Educational Research of the University of Minnesota began its studies of creative thinking, it felt that what was needed was a set of tasks which could be used from kindergarten through graduate school. Thus, it first attempted to adapt Guilford's (1951) materials with this objective in mind.

Accordingly, the Bureau developed as a start two alternate forms of the following Guilford-type tasks: Unusual Uses, Impossibilities, Consequences, Problem Situations, Improvements, and Problems. Adaptation was accomplished by substituting objects or situations more familiar to children. Thus, subjects were instructed to think of unusual uses of "tin cans" instead of bricks and to imagine all of the things that might happen, "if animals and birds could speak the language of men" instead of "what would happen, if all national and local laws were suddenly abolished."

Almost simultaneously experimentation was begun with several other kinds of tasks. The tasks developed were constructed on the basis of analyses of the reported experiences of eminent scientific discoverers, inventors, and creative writers. An attempt was made to construct tasks which would be models of the creative process, each requiring several types of thinking. This approach represents a departure from that of Guilford and his associates. Perhaps the greatest divergence is from Guilford's insistence that predictor measures should represent single factors (C. W. Taylor, 1959, p. 299). The Bureau's program has been to develop complex tasks presumed to involve the creative process and then to examine the products for evidences of various types of thinking, or, to use Guilford's term factors. A calculated attempt has also been made to develop tasks which will grip the interest of the subject and which will permit him to "regress in the service of the ego" which appears to be important in creative thinking (Schafer, 1958).

Three years of experimentation has resulted in the development and use of over twenty-five tasks varying greatly in the nature of the stimulus and the kind of thinking involved. All call for the production of divergent solutions, multiple possibilities, and some type of thinking involved theoretically in creative behavior. Detailed descriptions of the tasks, their rationale, and their administration are presented in the Appendix. Brief descriptions of selected tasks will be presented here to give the reader a general idea of the nature and scope of the tasks.

EXAMPLES OF SPECIFIC TASKS

One task, called the Ask-and-Guess Test, requires the individual first to ask questions about a picture, questions which cannot be answered by looking at the picture. (Pictures used include primarily prints from Mother Goose stories such as Tom, the Piper's Son; Ding Dong Bell; and Little Boy Blue.) Next, he is asked to make guesses or formulate hypotheses about the possible causes and then the consequences, both immediate and remote, of the behavior depicted. Responses can then be evaluated to yield scores on a number of Guilford factors such as: sensitivity to problems (number of missing pieces-of-information questions were asked), ideational fluency (number of questions and guesses), flexibility (variety of kinds of questions and hypotheses), and originality (remote consequences and causes hypothesized).

In the Product Improvement Task, common toys are used and children are asked to think of as many improvements as they can which would make the toy "more fun to play with." Subjects are then asked to think of unusual uses of these toys other than "something to play with." Responses are then scored for such factors as: fluency (number of improvements and unusual uses given), flexibility (number of approaches used in making improvements and number of categories of unusual uses), originality (number of uncommon improvements and uses), "inventivlevel" (a measure based on criteria used by the United States Patent Office in evaluating patent applications and meaning level or degree of inventiveness), and possibly redefinition.

A set of problems somewhat similar to Guilford's Common Situations has been constructed. For example, one such task requires the subject to think of all of the possible things Mother Hubbard of the Mother Goose story could have done when she found that her cupboard was bare and there were no bones for her dog.

Creative writing tasks requiring the invention of stories have also been used. Children are asked to make up stories of their choice from ten suggested topics or a similar one of their own. The topics used involve unusual characteristics of animals or people, such as:

> The Flying Monkey
> The Lion that Won't Roar
> The Man Who Cries
> The Woman Who Won't Talk

The stories are evaluated according to a variety of creativity criteria, such as originality, interest, and purpose.

The Just Suppose Test is an adaptation of the consequences type of test designed to elicit a higher degree of spontaneity and to be more effective with children. As in the Consequences Test, the subject is confronted with an improbable situation and asked to predict the possible outcomes from the introduction of a new or unknown variable. In this adaptation, the verbal statement of the improbable situation is accompanied by a black-and-white drawing or cartoon of the situation. Responses are scored for fluency, flexibility, and originality.

Several non-verbal tasks have been developed. One of these is an adaptation of Kate Franck's Drawing-Completion Test, described by Barron (1958), and labeled the Incomplete Figures Test. Another is the Circles and Squares tasks. In one form, the subject is confronted with a page of thirty-five circles and asked to sketch objects or pictures which have a circle as a major part. In the alternate form, squares instead of circles are used. A third non-verbal task, the Shape Test requires the subject to create a picture, using standardized shapes of colored paper as the base stimulus. The instructions emphasize originality (thinking of an interesting idea no one else in the class will think of) and elaboration (building onto the basic idea to make it more interesting and to tell more of a story). In both the Incomplete Figures and Shape tasks, subjects are asked to make up titles for their pictures. In addition to scoring for originality and elaboration, the products can also be scored for fluency and flexibility (circles and squares), penetration (incomplete figures), and other factors.

Recognizing that some individuals may be more creative in response to auditory stimuli than to visual ones, an audio tape created by B. F. Cunnington has been developed as a test of originality. Four unusual sound effects are presented and subjects are asked to think of word pictures suggested by the sounds. Through taped instructions, subjects are urged to "stretch their imaginations further and further" as the sounds are presented a second and third time. The tape can also be used as the stimulus for creative writing and art.

These tasks along with several others are treated in greater detail in the Appendix.

EVIDENCES OF VALIDITY

In developing and selecting the tasks which have been described above, several theoretical and practical considerations guided the Bureau. Some of these have already been mentioned in the introduction. It tried to select tasks which would make sense in terms of objectives and yet be brief enough to avoid fatigue on the part of the subjects. An attempt was made to construct tasks which would duplicate as nearly as possible the "moments of discovery." Obviously one important dimension difficult to build into tests is the time dimension, which would provide opportunity for one thing to lead to another and the incubation process to produce results.

Since a large share of the work at the University of Minnesota has been with children and with experiments to test some procedure for stimulating creative productions, validity data of the usual kind is difficult to accumulate. A variety of scattered evidence, however, is available and will be summarized here. Some experiments have already been cited in the first chapter; others will be summarized in greater detail to document some of the more relevant evidence.

Creativity and Sales Productivity

Wallace's (1960) study of sales productivity and performance on tests of creative thinking provides one kind of evidence of test validity. In Wallace's study, two aspects of sales performance were considered—sales productivity and amount of customer service.

Sixty-one saleswomen were selected on the basis of sales records (the upper and lower thirds in their respective departments) for testing. All had been employed by the co-operating department store for at least three years, the mean being approximately eleven years. All were thirty years old or older. The departmental classification was in terms of the amount of customer service involved. Departments in which the saleswomen must help the customer a great deal were distinguished from those where little customer service is required. The high service departments, such as draperies and ladies dresses, were termed "creative" while the low service departments, such as candy and notions, were designated as "noncreative."

Wallace used the following tasks in his battery: all three tasks of the Ask-and-Guess Test, Product Improvement (Toy Dog), Circles, and Unusual Uses (Tin Cans and Toy Dog). Responses were scored for fluency, flexibility, inventivlevel, and originality.

Comparisons of the means of the high and low sales groups are shown in Figure 2 and of the creative and noncreative departments in Figure 3.

The results were analyzed separately for the Ask-and-Guess Test and Test of Imagination (the other four tasks). The results for both sets of tasks, using analysis of variance, indicated that the mean of those in creative departments was significantly higher than those in noncreative departments. Also, the mean scores of subjects with high sales productivity were significantly higher on the tests than those classified as low

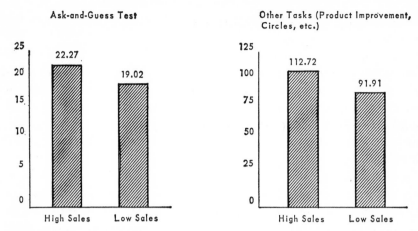

FIGURE 2. *Comparisons of Mean Total Scores of High and Low Sales Producers on Two Sets of Creative Thinking Tasks.*

sales producers. The performance of those classified as low on both variables (customer service and sales production) was considerably lower than the other groups in measured creative thinking ability. There was no significant interaction between the two variables. The total score on the Ask-and-Guess Test was more efficient in differentiating the high and low sales producers in the noncreative departments than in the creative departments.

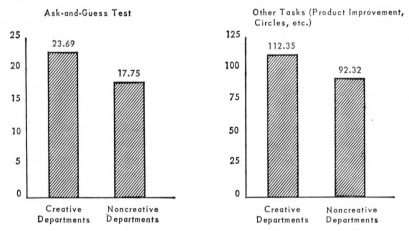

FIGURE 3. *Comparison of Mean Total Scores of Subjects in Creative and Noncreative Departments on Two Sets of Creative Thinking Tasks.*

Creative Students in Industrial Arts

In collaboration with Wesley Sommers at Stout State College, the Bureau conducted a small validity study, using creativity in industrial design as the criterion. The faculty of the college was asked to nominate individuals oustanding for their creativity and individuals notable for their lack of it. The criterion groups consisted of undergraduate students who had had opportunities to demonstrate creative thinking in their classes.

The criterion groups were administered essentially the same tasks as administered to Wallace's subjects [Ask-and-Guess Test, Product Improvement (Toy Dog), Circles, and Unusual Uses (Tin Cans and Toy Dog)]. Results were available for ten creatives and twelve noncreatives. The mean total score of the creatives was 237.4 and of the noncreatives, 179.25. The difference in mean is significant at better than the .05 level of confidence. Only one of the noncreatives achieved a score equal to the mean of the creatives.

Observations of Group Behavior

Another type of validity was obtained from experimental studies of detailed observations of creative behavior. In each class, pupils were divided heterogeneously into five-person groups on the basis of scores on a battery of the following tasks: the Ask-and-Guess Test, Product Improvement, Unusual Uses (Toy Dog and Tin Cans), Circles, Impossibilities, Consequences, Problem Situations, and Improvements. In each class, the pupils were divided into five groups according to their total scores on the battery and one from each of the five levels of ability placed in each group.

The task involved experimentation with a box of science toys. During a twenty-five minute period, each group was encouraged to experiment with the toys to discover all of the uses for the toys, both intended and unintended, and to think of as many possible scientific principles that could be demonstrated with the toys. During a second twenty-five minute period, opportunity was given for explanations and demonstrations. Careful records were made of the ideas initiated, demonstrated, and explained by each subject.

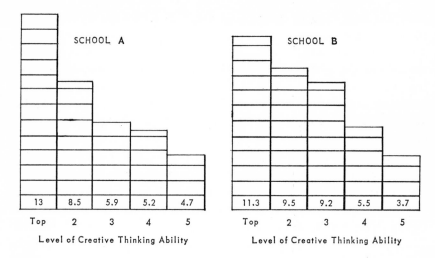

FIGURE 4. *Comparison of Mean Number of Ideas Initiated on Science Toy Task by Individuals Scoring at Each of Five Levels of a Battery of Creative Thinking Tasks.*

Although there were in many groups strong pressures to restrict the ideas of the most creative members of the group, a majority (68 per cent) managed to initiate a larger number of ideas than any other member of the group. When the number of ideas initiated and the number of ideas demonstrated and explained were tabulated according to the level of creative thinking ability and the means computed, the means showed definite linear tendencies. In other words, those who produced the most ideas on the test also tended to produce the most ideas in his group task. This linear trend is clearly observable in the two sets of means shown in Figure 4 for Schools A and B on the number of ideas initiated. When classes were divided heterogeneously according to Intelligence Quotients, no such linear trend was noted.

Sociometric Criteria

Although there are many reasons why peer groups are unable to recognize and appreciate the creativity of their most creative members, it has seemed worthwhile to use peer nominations as intermediate criteria for studying the validity of tests of creative thinking. Several types of evidence are available.

At the beginning of the term in one high school the following tasks were administered to 459 students: Product Improvement, Product Utilization (Toy Dog and Tin Cans), Circles, and the Ask-and-Guess Test. Near the end of the term, these same subjects were administered a series of sociometric or peer nominations aimed at tapping five different dimensions of creative thinking ability. The questions and the hypothesized dimensions are as follows:

1. Who in your class comes up with the most ideas? (Fluency)
2. Who has the most original or unusual ideas? (Originality)
3. If the situation changed or if a solution to a problem wouldn't work, who in your class would be the first to find a new way of meeting the problem? (Flexibility)
4. Who in your class does the most inventing and developing of new ideas, gadgets, and such? (Inventiveness)
5. Who in your class is best at thinking of all of the details involved in working out a new idea and thinking of all of the consequences? (Elaboration)

Scores were available only for Fluency, Flexibility, and Inventiveness. Raw scores were correlated with the frequency counts of nominations. Rather consistently the results for the eighth, ninth, and tenth grades were significant. The relationships in the seventh grade tend to be the lowest. This is of especial interest, since this class showed a decrement in performance below that of sixth grades in far less selective schools.

Although the coefficients of correlation are statistically significant but not very high (around .24 for the total group of 459 subjects), considering the nature of the data, the results are encouraging.

Similar sociometric data were also obtained in thirty-three elementary school classrooms studied in four different schools. Children were asked to name their best friends (pals or buddies), those who must aggressively speak out their ideas (talk the most), those who have the most good ideas, those who think of the most ways to be naughty, those who think of the most wild or silly ideas, and those who don't tell their ideas. Each child was asked to nominate three classmates in each category. Although there are slight variations from school to school, some of the general trends can be summarized by grades.

First and Second Grades. In the first two grades there was a general tendency for children chosen most frequently on the good-ideas criterion to have moderate creative thinking scores. Highly creative boys, however, were frequently chosen as having silly ideas and ideas for being naughty.

Third Grade. Highly creative girls tend to be chosen frequently on the good-ideas criterion, while highly creative boys tended to be nominated as having silly ideas and ideas for being naughty. The most highly chosen third graders on the good-ideas criterion tended to nominate one or more of the most creative but not frequently chosen children. In the third grade, pupils nominated as having ideas for being naughty or as having silly ideas tended not to be chosen on the good-ideas criterion.

Fourth Grade. Only a few of the most highly chosen fourth graders on the good-ideas criterion were in the top group (upper twenty per cent) on the measure of creative thinking. Most of the highly creative pupils, however, received a moderate number of choices on this criterion.

Fifth Grade. Highly creative fifth graders were nominated quite frequently on the good-ideas question but moderately creative subjects were named more frequently.

Sixth Grade. Most of the highly creative sixth graders were chosen rather frequently on the good-ideas criterion.

From a factor analytic study, it seemed that the children tended to perceive individuals as having good ideas if they maintain a good "batting average" of "good ideas" to "wild, silly, or incorrect" ideas. Thus, the individual with a moderate number of good ideas and no low quality ideas would be more likely to be nominated as having good ideas than one with a large number of good ideas along with a sizeable number of low quality ideas.

When the "sociometric stars" (those receiving five or more choices) on the good-ideas criterion were compared with those who received no choices on this criterion, the creative thinking scores of the stars were significantly higher.

A special study was made of the boy and the girl who obtained the highest creativity score in each class. They were then matched with another classmate of the same sex and IQ. The highly creative children were more frequently chosen than their matched classmates on the "wild ideas" and "naughty ideas" criteria. Teachers nominated them more frequently as talkative and as having "wild" ideas. The most creative boys apparently had a far greater impact on their classmates than did the most creative girls. These extremely creative boys were especially noted for the "wild" ideas.

Groups Differentiated as Highly Intelligent and as Highly Creative

Reference was made in Chapter 1 to studies in which groups of subjects identified as highly intelligent (upper 20 per cent of group on traditional tests of intelligence or scholastic aptitude but not in the upper 20 per cent on tests of creative thinking) have been compared with their highly creative peers (upper 20 per cent on measures of creative thinking but not in upper 20 per cent on traditional measures of intelligence or scholastic aptitude). Since an effort is being made here to pull together some of the scattered indications of validity, it seems appropriate to present some of the documentation. Thus, I shall present results from eight partial replications of the Getzels-Jackson (1958) study. Five of the replications have been at the elementary school level, one at the high school level, and two in graduate school situations.

Procedures

Elementary School A is a laboratory school enrolling twenty-five pupils in each grade from kindergarten through sixth grade. The following data were obtained for each subject: intelligence quotient (Stanford-Binet), educational quotients (Gates Reading and Iowa Basic Skills, including reading, language, work-study, and arithmetic skills), and scores on a battery of creative thinking tasks. In 1958, the following tasks were included in the battery of creative thinking tasks: Uses of Tin Cans, Impossibilities, Consequences, Situations, Problems, and Improvements. The 1959 battery (known as Form DX) consisted of the following: Product Improvement (Toy Dog), Unusual Uses of Toy Dog, Unusual Uses of Tin Cans, Circles, Ask-and-Guess.

Elementary School B is located in a small, Minnesota college town. A total of 354 pupils from grades one through six were tested but achievement data were available for only the fourth and fifth grades (128 pupils). The measure of intelligence used is the Otis Quick-Scoring Mental Ability Test and was administered as a part of the school's regular program. The measure of achievement is the Iowa Basic Skills battery and the creative thinking measure is Form DX already described. The only difference in Form DX as administered in School A and School B is that the picture used in the last three tasks in School B was that of "Tom, the Piper's Son" which pictures a boy running with a white and black pig and being pursued by a man with an upraised pitchfork.

Although there is a wide range of ability in School B, there are many gifted pupils in the school and emphasis on learning is strongly evident in the general atmosphere. The school principal commented that the school has a reputation for emphasizing traditional academic achievement. Almost none of the children asked questions about the examiner's directions. It was particularly striking that fourth graders did not ask how to spell words when required to write their responses. This difficulty had been quite marked in several schools tested previously, including Schools A and D.

School C is a metropolitan parochial school, enrolling 238 pupils in the fifth and sixth grades (Brown, 1960). The creativity and achievement measures are the same as those used in School A in 1959–60 and in School B. The measure of intelligence was the Kuhlmann-Anderson Intelligence Test administered as a regular part of the school's program. The creativity measure was obtained in the fall and the achievement measure near the close of the school term.

Like School B, this school has a diversity of talent distributed fairly normally but has perhaps a slightly larger number of high ability youngsters than most schools.

School D is a metropolitan public school, enrolling 110 pupils in the fifth and sixth grades. The creativity and achievement measures were the same as those used in the other schools and the measure of intelligence was the California Test of Mental Maturity. The IQ used in identifying groups was obtained by computing the mean of the verbal and non-verbal IQ's. This school has a somewhat rectangular distribution of talent, with disproportionate numbers at both the higher and lower levels of ability.

High School A is a laboratory high school. Data were obtained from

272 students from the ninth through twelfth grade. This represents about 90 per cent of the school's enrollment in these four grades. The measure of creative thinking was the same as that used in the elementary schools (Form DX). Intelligence quotients were derived from the Lorge-Thorndike Intelligence Test (Verbal Battery), administered as a regular part of the school's personnel program. Achievement data were also obtained from official records of the Iowa Tests of Educational Development. This battery consists of the following nine tests:

1. Understanding of Basic Social Concepts.
2. Background in the Natural Sciences.
3. Correctness and Appropriateness of Expression.
4. Ability to do Quantitative Thinking.
5. Ability to Interpret Reading Material in the Social Studies.
6. Ability to Interpret Reading Material in the Natural Sciences.
7. Ability to Interpret Literary Materials.
8. General Vocabulary.
9. Use of Sources of Information.

The first of the graduate-level groups studied was the 1959 University of Minnesota Summer Guidance Institute (Palm, 1959). Seventy mature teachers and counselors were enrolled in this institute and provided the data for this study. The measure of scholastic ability used was the Miller Analogies, Form G, which is used by many universities in the selection of graduate students. The measure of creativity was based upon the tasks included in Form DX already described plus additional tasks based on counseling and guidance concepts. The measure of achievement consisted of pre- and post-tests of achievement in the guidance area. All items were of the recognitive (multiple-choice) type. The duration of the Institute was five weeks.

The second of the graduate groups consisted of eighty-five students enrolled in Educational Psychology 159 (Personality Development and Mental Hygiene) at the University of Minnesota during one summer session. A total of 115 students completed the course but scores on Miller Analogies were available for only 85 of them. The measure of creative thinking was Form DX, the same used in the elementary and high school studies. A variety of measures of course achievement were used. Four types of tests were used both during and at the end of the course:

1. Recognition or multiple-choice items.
2. Memory or completion-type items.
3. Creative-application tasks, such as thinking of uses of specific information concerning personality development and mental hygiene, alternative explanations of research findings, alternative solutions of problems, etc.
4. Evaluation or decision-making tasks (decisions on mental hygiene problems supported by facts, etc.)

In addition, scores were given for critical and creative-thinking reports on research articles, self-initiated learning, and the development of a new idea concerning personality development and mental hygiene.

In all eight studies the same procedure was used in identifying the highly creative and highly intelligent groups. The highly creative groups consist of those ranking in the upper 20 per cent of the sample studied on the measure of creative thinking but not ranking in the upper 20 per cent on the measure of intelligence or scholastic aptitude. The highly intelligent groups consist of those ranking in the upper 20 per cent on the measure of intelligence or scholastic aptitude but not in the upper 20 per cent on the measure of creative thinking. Those ranking in the upper 20 per cent on both measures were eliminated. It will be noted that this procedure is simpler and more straightforward but more inclusive than the procedure used by Getzels and Jackson. It is believed, however, that the procedure is essentially the same and that the same kinds of individuals are identified in the two groups.

After the groups were identified, they were compared on the achievement measures by means of appropriate tests of significance.

Results

Ability Levels of Groups Identified.   Means on the various intelligence and scholastic ability measures of the highly intelligent and highly creative individuals in the eight learning situations are presented in Table 1. It will be noted that the differences are all statistically significant at the .001 level or better. In fact, even the layman will recognize that the differences are "big enough to make a difference." In Elementary School A, there was a difference of over 25 points the first year and about 22 points the second year. In School B, there is a difference of about 15 points on the Otis Quick-Scoring. In School C, there is a difference of about 12 points on the Kuhlmann-Anderson. In School D, there is a difference of over 27 points on the California Test of Mental Maturity. In the high school, there is a difference of about 20 points on the Lorge-Thorndike. In the Counseling Institute group, there was a difference of 23 points on the Miller Analogies and in the Educational Psychology group, 22 points.

It will be noted that most of the highly creative groups are still relatively superior on the measure of intelligence or scholastic aptitude. This is especially true in the laboratory and the metropolitan public schools. The only elementary school group below average in IQ is the highly creative group in School B, the school located in a small Minnesota town. Both of the graduate-level creative groups are relatively low on the Miller Analogies. Many graduate advisers, including the author, would usually hesitate to accept as advisees applicants scoring as low as the average member of these groups.

TABLE I

Mean on Intelligence or Scholastic Ability Measure of Highly Intelligent and Highly Creative Individuals and Per Cent Overlapping in Eight Learning Situations

Group and Date	Intelligence Measure	Number Each Group	Mean Intelligence	Creatives	Per Cent High on Both
Elementary School A, 1959	Stanford-Binet	21	152.1	126.5*	30.0
Elementary School A, 1960	Stanford-Binet	10	143.5	121.9*	33.3
Elementary School B, 1959	Otis Quick-Scoring	18	113.5	97.9*	33.3
Elementary School C, 1960	Kuhlmann-Anderson	36	118.6	106.9*	24.5
Elementary School D, 1960	California Mental Maturity	13	139.8	112.3*	40.9
High School A, 1960 (Grades 9–12)	Lorge-Thorndike	26	141.7	122.0*	51.8
Guidance Institute (University of Minn.) 1959	Miller Analogies, Raw Score (G)	10	68.5	45.3*	28.6
Educational Psychology 159 (University of Minn.) 1960	Miller Analogies, Raw Score (G)	13	72.1	49.9*	23.5

* Differences in means of Highly Intelligent and Highly Creative significant at .001 level or better.

Relationships Between IQ and Creativity.   It is of interest to note the amount of overlap between the groups identified as gifted (in upper 20 per cent of their group) by the two kinds of measures. In most of the groups studied, about 70 per cent of the most creatives would have been eliminated if a "gifted" group was being selected on the basis of the intelligence test or Miller Analogies. The two exceptions are Elementary School D, using the California Mental Maturities, and High School A, using the Lorge-Thorndike. In these two schools, there is a stronger tendency than in the others for the highly creative also to be highly intelligent. This phenomenon may be due in part to the nature of the distribution of talent in these schools or to the nature of the measures of intellectual talent used.

The virtual lack of relationship between measures of creative thinking and IQ is also shown when the two are correlated. In most cases, the relationship is little more than can be expected by chance. In fact, the relationship is no more than would be expected by chance in the two college groups and the two laboratory schools. The highest correlation was .32 between scores on the group administered Otis Quick-Scoring Test of Intelligence and the measure of creative thinking.

ACHIEVEMENT OF THE HIGHLY INTELLIGENT AND THE HIGHLY CREATIVE

Comparisons of the achievement of the highly intelligent and highly creative in Table 2 are based only on the critical or summary measure of achievement in each of the eight situations. It will be noted that in six of the eight situations the differences in means are so small that they could occur by chance. Only in Elementary Schools B and C (the small-town and parochial school) are the differences large enough to have occurred by chance less than five times out of one hundred. Thus, in only two of the eight situations is there a contraindication of the findings of Getzels and Jackson (1958). Possible reasons for this exception will be discussed later.

Differences in Various Kinds of Learning.   One might expect the mental abilities sampled by the measures of IQ or scholastic aptitude to be more useful in certain kinds of achievement than in others. Likewise, the creative thinking abilities are more important in some kinds of achievement than in others. A major difficulty, of course, is that we do not now have achievement measures appropriate for assessing different kinds of achievement of importance. We can, however, look at achievement in terms of different kinds of content and of different kinds of test performance within a content area.

TABLE 2

Means or Critical Measures of Achievement of Highly Intelligent and Highly Creative Individuals in Eight Learning Situations and Tests of Significance

Group and Date	Number Each Group	Achievement Measure	Means Intelligence	Means Creatives	F-ratio	Probability
Elementary School A, 1959	21	Iowa Basic Skills Battery	141.2	139.1	0.16	Not significant
Elementary School A, 1960	10	Iowa Basic Skills Battery	137.8	136.6	0.01	Not significant
Elementary School B, 1959	18	Iowa Basic Skills Battery	139.2	121.7	8.84	$<.01$
Elementary School C, 1960	36	Iowa Basic Skills Battery	113.4	103.8	23.61	$<.01$
Elementary School D, 1960	13	Iowa Basic Skills Battery	119.2	110.4	3.18	Not significant
High School A (Grades 9–12)	26	Iowa Tests of Educational Development	26.0	22.9	1.37	Not significant
Counseling Institute (University of Minn.), 1959	10	Pre-Post Test Gain, Achievement Test	13.4	16.4	0.23	Not significant
Educational Psychology 159 (University of Minn.), 1960	13	Total Score on Course Achievement	340.8	332.2	0.38	Not significant

In Table 3, the means on each of the four subtests of the Iowa Basic Skills Battery are shown for the two groups in each of the five learning situations studied. From this table, it will be observed that there is a fairly general tendency for the highly creative groups to be better on reading and language skills than on work-study and arithmetic skills. Some elementary teachers have observed that the Iowa reading and language tests require more interpretation than most other achievement tests. The ability to "get the right answer" through recognition, memory, or convergent thinking apparently becomes more important in the work-study skills and arithmetic skills tests.

In the Educational Psychology class there were available a variety of measures, presumed to test different kinds of achievement related to different mental operations (cognition, memory, divergent thinking, and evaluation). Different types of items were used in measuring each of these. Also available was a measure of self-initiated learning based

TABLE 3

Mean Achievement Quotients on Iowa Basic Skills Battery
of Highly Intelligent and Highly Creative Pupils in Four Elementary Schools

School and Year	Reading		Study-Work		Language		Arithmetic	
	IQ	Cr.	IQ	Cr.	IQ	Cr.	IQ	Cr.
School A, 1959	145.4	152.8	155.3	139.9	132.4	138.4	131.6	125.2
School A, 1960	145.1	143.6	140.7	137.9	133.8	136.9	131.8	127.5
School B, 1959	149.4	121.2*	149.6	128.6*	135.7	117.9*	124.6	116.3*
School C, 1960	118.8	106.8*	111.4	100.9*	112.7	104.6*	110.6	102.7*
School D, 1960	126.1	122.2	117.4	106.6*	115.9	109.2	117.8	103.3*

* Differences in means this large would occur between Highly Intelligent and Highly Creative groups by chance no more frequently than five times out of 100.

on detailed descriptions and evaluations of self-initiated experiences during the course. Table 4 presents the means of the two groups on each of these achievement measures. Although the differences are not statistically significant, the observed trends should be noted. The high Miller Analogies group tends to achieve higher scores on the recognition (true-false) and memory (completion) type items. On the creative applications, decision-making tasks, and the self-initiated learning activities the reverse is true.

TABLE 4

Mean Achievement Scores of High Miller Analogies and Highly
Creative Students in Educational Psychology 159 on Different Types of Measures

Measure	Means		F-ratio
	High Millers	High Creatives	
Recognition (multiple-choice tests)	56.46	50.92	3.760
Memory (completion items)	32.38	30.77	0.825
Creative Applications (divergent thinking, free response)	64.38	65.00	0.019
Evaluation (decision-making tasks)	52.23	54.23	0.639
Self-Initiated Learning	40.82	44.00	0.333
Total of all achievement measures in course	340.82	332.15	0.381

Note: All of the differences in means shown in this table could have occurred by chance in more than five cases out of 100.

CONCLUSIONS

Although highly creative individuals tend to learn as much as highly intelligent ones in educational situations, these studies indicate that this does not occur in all schools. We are then prompted to ask the question, "Under what conditions is the Getzels-Jackson phenomenon likely to occur and when not?" The results presented herein, together with accumulated results from other studies, provide clues but not definite answers.

One simple explanation is that individuals in some learning situations are taught in such a way that they learn creatively, and thus creative thinking abilities become important in learning. In other situations, they are taught authoritatively, and emphasis is placed on memory and conformity to behavioral norms. For example, the author and his staff, observed far more signs that children in Schools A and D learned creatively than in other schools. In School B, the principal himself observed that the community and the school placed great value upon "traditional kinds of learning." Fewer evidences of creative achievement were visible about the school than in others visited. Although the author did not visit School C and knows some evidences of creative activity in this school, one would expect that in a parochial school emphasis would be placed on learning from authorities and on the importance of "traditional kinds of learning." This explanation gains further plausibility from Coleman's study (1959) which shows that different high schools have vastly different orientations towards learning.

One might also look for an explanation in the nature of the distribution of ability. It will be noted that the average IQ of the highly creative group was lowest in School B (97.9 on the Otis) and School C (106.9 on the Kuhlmann-Anderson). Both of these schools have what might be considered a more normal distribution of ability than Schools A and D. Helpful in examining the dynamics here is Anderson's (1960) concept that we can "think of ability level in terms of thresholds and ask questions as to the amount necessary to carry on a task and then consider the factors that determine function beyond this threshold." He points out that there are cut-off points or levels above which the demonstration of ability in relation to environmental demands is determined by the presence of other factors. In other words, we might ask where this cut-off point is in terms of IQ. How high must the IQ be before a point is reached when a higher IQ makes little difference, and the creative thinking abilities become important? On the basis of my experience, as well as on the basis of studies by Roe (1960) and others, I would like to propose that this cut-off point is around an IQ of 120. It has been noted that many of the most creative children achieve IQ's in the 120's or slightly under and that these children achieve quite well, generally. Most such children would not be included in most special programs for gifted children, however. This cut-off point has generally been set at some such figure as 135, 140, 150, or even 160.

Another important clue brought to light by the present study is that we need to consider different kinds of achievement and develop measures to assess these different kinds of achievement. This is especially apparent in the data from the Educational Psychology class. Here we have in the highly creative group mostly individuals so low on the Miller Analogies that their capacity to do graduate work would be seriously questioned. Yet on creative applications of knowledge, decision-making, and self-initiated learning, they actually do as well as and tend to do better than even the most superior of their colleagues on the Miller Analogies. There is a tendency, however, for the latter to perform better on the traditional types of examinations (multiple-choice and completion) requiring primarily recognition and memory.

In summary, it may be said that the results obtained by comparing highly creative individuals (as measured by the tests of creative thinking) with highly intelligent individuals provide indirect evidences of the validity of the tests of creative thinking. Apparently highly creative individuals prefer to learn creatively rather than by authority and when given an opportunity to learn in this way achieve as well as their more intelligent but less creative peers. Further support of this contention is obtained by correcting for the effects of IQ. When this was done in School A, partial coefficients of correlation between creativity scores and performance on the achievement measures were as follows:

Gates Reading Test 0.40
Iowa Reading Skills 0.48
Iowa Study-Work 0.37
Iowa Language 0.38
Iowa Arithmetic 0.28

All of these relationships are statistically significant at the .05 level of confidence or better.

From Chapter 1, it will also be recalled that teachers rated the highly creative children in comparison with the highly intelligent ones as less desirable as pupils, as not as well-known or understood by them, as less ambitious, and as less hard working or studious.

Although more evidence is needed concerning the validity of the Minnesota Tests of Creative Thinking, the scattered bits of evidence described herein are encouraging. Performance on batteries of these tests seem to be related to sales productivity, the kind of selling to which one gravitates over an extended period of time, creativity in industrial design, initiating behavior in creative tasks, nominations by peers on criteria involving various aspects of creative thinking, and the achievement of basic educational skills. From data cited earlier, a poor performance appears to be related to mental illness. It is hoped that several studies now underway will provide more adequate evidence of the validity of the Minnesota Tests of Creative Thinking.

SUMMARY

In this chapter, I have tried to show wherein the Minnesota Tests of Creative Thinking differ from the mainstreams of testing in this area, as inventoried in the preceding chapter. The strategy has been to develop complex rather than pure-factor tasks presumed to involve creative thinking and then to examine the products for various qualities of thinking which may be inferred therefrom. An attempt has also been made to devise interesting, ego-involving tasks which will encourage "regression in the service of the ego." Specific examples include: the Ask-and-Guess Test, Product Improvement Task (involving common toys), Imaginative Stories about Divergent Animals and People, Just Suppose Test, Incomplete Figures, Circles and Squares, and Picture Construction.

I have also offered several types of evidence of validity. The tasks discriminate industrial arts students rated as highly creative from those rated as least creative, saleswomen who sell most from those who sell least, and saleswomen who work in creative departments from those who work in routine departments. With elementary school children, it was validated in terms of observed behavior in small group situations, on the basis of peer and teacher nominations, and on the basis of achievement of the traditional kinds.

Chapter 4

IDENTIFYING
THE CREATIVE
PERSONALITY

There has long been general agreement that personality factors are important in creative achievement. Even in the matter of measuring the creative thinking abilities, there have been persistent and recurrent indications that personality factors are important even in test performance. For example, Hargreaves (1927) hypothesized that the "unknown" common factor found in his measures of imagination is conative in nature. Guilford and his associates (Guilford, Christensen, Frick and Merrifield, 1957) have also been interested in determining what relationships might exist between measures of traits of temperament and motivation to measures of factors of ability within the areas of creative performance. They found a large number of significant correlations between the non-aptitude traits and the measures of ideational fluency and originality. Ideational fluency appears to be related to impulsiveness, self-confidence, ascendance, greater appreciation of originality, and inclination away from neuroticism. Those having higher originality scores tend to be more interested in aesthetic expression, in meditative or reflective thinking, and appear to be more tolerant of ambiguity, and to feel less need for discipline and orderliness.

PERSONALITY STUDIES OF HIGHLY CREATIVE ADULTS

There has been a great variety of empirical studies (Stein and Heinze, 1960) in which individuals identified as being highly creative on some criterion were contrasted with comparable individuals on personality measures derived from traditional personality tests such as the Minnesota Multiphasic Personality Inventory, Thematic Apperception Test, Rorschach, and others. I recently surveyed a large number of the studies and compiled the following list of characteristics found in one or more studies to differentiate highly creative persons from less creative ones:

1. Accepts disorder
2. Adventurous
3. Strong affection
4. Altruistic
5. Awareness of others
6. Always baffled by something
7. Attracted to disorder
8. Attracted to mysterious
9. Attempts difficult jobs
   (sometimes too difficult)
10. Bashful outwardly
11. Constructive in criticism
12. Courageous
13. Deep and conscientious conventions
14. Defies conventions of courtesy
15. Defies conventions of health
16. Desires to excel
17. Determination
18. Differentiated value-hierarchy
19. Discontented
20. Disturbs organization
21. Dominant (not in power sense)
22. Emotional
23. Emotionally sensitive
24. Energetic
25. A fault-finder
26. Doesn't fear being thought "different"

27. Feels whole parade is out of step
28. Full of curiosity
29. Appears haughty and self-satisfied at times
30. Likes solitude
31. Independence in judgment
32. Independent in thinking
33. Individualistic
34. Intuitive
35. Industrious
36. Introversive
37. Keeps unusual hours
38. Lacks business ability
39. Makes mistakes
40. Never bored
41. Nonconforming
42. Not hostile or negativistic
43. Not popular
44. Oddities of habit
45. Persistent
46. Becomes preoccupied with a problem
47. Preference for complex ideas
48. Questioning
49. Radical
50. Receptive to external stimuli
51. Receptive to ideas of others
52. Regresses occasionally
53. Rejection of suppression as a mechanism of impulse control

54. Rejection of repression
55. Reserved
56. Resolute
57. Self-assertive
58. Self-starter
59. Self-aware
60. Self-confident
61. Self-sufficient
62. Senses of destiny
63. Sense of humor
64. Sensitive to beauty
65. Shuns power
66. Sincere
67. Not interested in small details
68. Speculative
69. Spirited in disagreement
70. Strives for distant goals
71. Stubborn
72. Temperamental
73. Tenacious
74. Tender emotions
75. Timid
76. Thorough
77. Unconcerned about power
78. Somewhat uncultured, primitive
79. Unsophisticated, naive
80. Unwilling to accept anything on mere say-so
81. Visionary
82. Versatile
83. Willing to take risks
84. Somewhat withdrawn and quiescent

Most of the empirical studies seeking to determine the personality characteristics of highly creative persons have relied upon traditional personality instruments and life experience inventories. Literature records few attempts to develop personality instruments which might be used either in identifying or guiding the development of creative individuals. My associates and I are now exploring some of the potential uses of the above check list as one such instrument.

NEW AND EXISTING INSTRUMENTS FOR IDENTIFYING CREATIVE PERSONALITIES

In my opinion, present instruments for personality study are not suitable for use in guiding the creative development of either children or adults. Instruments built upon the best knowledge now available concerning the problems, development, and adjustment of creative individuals are needed. In the meantime, however, teachers and practicing counselors will probably have to accept creatively the limitations of existing instruments, observational data, and the like. As a researcher, however, I shall turn my own energies towards the search for new instruments.

Creativity research has yielded results which provide counselors with some very useful guides for maximizing the usefulness of existing instruments such as the Strong Vocational Interest Blank, the Allport-Vernon-Lindzey Study of Values, and the Minnesota Multiphasic Personality Inventory.

Some of the most useful research findings involving these instruments come from the studies of MacKinnon (1960) and his associates at the University of California Institute for Personality Assessment and Research. A finding obtained in their first study of graduate students and repeatedly confirmed in investigations of other groups is that individuals who rated high on originality reveal a characteristic pattern of scores on the Strong Vocational Interest Blank. The more original subjects, with slight variations from sample to sample, rate high on such scales as architect, psychologist, author-journalist, and specialization level; and low scores on such scales as purchasing agent, office man, banker, farmer, carpenter, veterinarian, policeman, and mortician. MacKinnon interprets these findings as indicating that creative individuals are less interested in small details and the practical and concrete aspects of life, and more concerned with meanings, implications, and symbolic equivalents of things and ideas.

As already indicated, the highest values of MacKinnon's subjects on the Allport-Vernon-Lindzey instrument are the Theoretical and Aesthetic scales. This was true of all of his highly creative groups. MacKinnon reports that his research team had not anticipated that just these two values would be high and of so nearly the same strength for all groups. The authors of the instrument had pointed out that the "aesthetic attitude is in a sense diametrically opposed to the theoretical." MacKinnon explains that if there is for most persons a conflict between theoretical and aesthetic values, a characteristic of the creative personality is the capacity to tolerate the tension of opposed strong values and to bring about integration, synthesis, and reconciliation of them.

A consistent finding from the use of the Minnesota Multiphasic Personality Inventory occurs in the realm of sexual identification and interests. All of MacKinnon's highly creative male groups show unusually high peaks on the Masculinity-Feminity Scale. For example, he found a mean standard score of 72 for his group of creative architects. These creative men were not characterized by markedly effeminate manner or appearance. MacKinnon reports that in applying an adjective check list to describe these men, his staff frequently checked both "masculine" and "feminine." They showed an openness to their feelings and emotions, a sensitive awareness of self and others, and wide-ranging interests, many of which are regarded as feminine in our culture.

In one of our Minnesota studies (Torrance, 1959c) involving the

1959 Summer Guidance Institute, an interesting supplementary result was obtained. Beginning with the male counselors having standard scores of 55 or above on the Masculinity-Feminity Scale, we identified two patterns: an independent pattern involving low social introversion, high manic and high psychopathic deviate, and a dependent pattern involving high scores on the neurotic triad and psychasthenia. On a battery of creative thinking tests devised by this author the independent-feminine group achieved a mean of 200.22 compared with a mean of 147.44 for the dependent-feminine group (significant at better than the .001 level).

Studying the same population of Summer Guidance Institute participants, Palm (1959) compared the need characteristics as measured by the Edwards Personal Preference Schedule of highly creative counselors with those scoring high on the Miller Analogies. The criterion groups consisted of the upper 20 per cent on each measure, eliminating of course those who scored high on both measures. The highly creative group were found to have significantly stronger needs than the high Miller Analogies group on deference, exhibition, succorance, abasement, and change. Thus, these highly creative counselors are characterized by what would appear to be polar opposite needs and an ability to tolerate the tensions arising from them. On one hand, they express a high need for exhibitionism and on the other they manifest needs for deference, succorance, and abasement. The need for change and exhibitionism appears to be consistent with the need to do new and different things and the sense of humor found in other studies. The high scores on abasement, succorance, and deference appear to be consistent with the openness to stimuli from external sources also found to be characteristic of highly creative individuals in other studies. The former would appear to represent independence, and the latter, sensitivity.

I attempted to study the needs of highly creative adults in another investigation through the *Stern Activity Index* (Stern, 1958). The subjects were 240 graduate students enrolled in courses in Personality Development and Mental Hygiene who were judged on the inventiv-level of original ideas developed as a part of the course requirements. The groups chosen for comparison were the top and bottom 27 per cents in rank on the original-idea project. Complete data were available for 51 of the top group and 45 of the low group. The more creative group was found to have significantly higher scores than the less creative group on the scales for achievement, affiliation, conjunctivity, ego, energy, exhibition, reflectiveness, and understanding. From the definitions of these scales given by Stern, it would seem that we have emerging for these more creative students a picture of a person who enjoys intense, sustained, and vigorous effort to surmount obstacles. Furthermore, he has a need to prove his personal worth and dramatize and display his ideas. These needs, however, are held in check by needs of self-awareness, awareness of the feelings and experiences of others, and detached intellectualization. Thus, we have the picture of an individual who is fully alive and open to awareness of his own experiences and those of others and seeks to organize them and see meaning in them.

ASSESSMENT OF CREATIVE MOTIVATIONS

In recognition of the need for a simple, easily-scored instrument for assessing creative motivations among adults, my associates and I have developed and used in several studies a device called the Personal-Social Motivation Inventory.

Personal-Social Motivation Inventory

Although we drew items from many sources and constructed some of our own, we relied most heavily upon the earlier work of the Runners (Runner Associates, 1954; Runner, 1954). Early in their work with the *Runner Studies of Attitude Patterns,* they devised a scale which they originally labeled "Creative Attitude." Later they incorporated it into their Individualist scale. Although they have accumulated a wealth of evidence of validity in industrial and educational situations, they have not yet published any of these interesting data. Kenyon Runner (1954) has, however, characterized the individualist pattern in a way that is interesting to compare with the Check List (p. 66). He lists the following as being the more common and observable attributes of the individualist:

1. Seeks change and adventure. Any system he follows will be his own system.
2. Inclined to sloppiness and disorganization. May give meticulous attention to things important to him personally.

3. Tendency not to plan activities, inclined to wait for developments, and changes plans quickly. Doesn't expect to be able to predict in detail and probably won't try.

4. Questions rules and authority.

5. Inclined to be chummy with strangers, not confining social activity to any certain groups. May talk too much or refuse to talk if he is interested in something else.

6. Thinks of people as individuals; is tolerant and open-minded and has faith in goodness of people as individuals.

7. Holds conformists in some disdain.

8. Disciplines himself to accomplishment of specific results; acts impulsively and fails to stick to any one course of action.

Following leads from the Runners and from the theoretical formulation of Tumin (1953), my associates and I assembled a 189-item inventory entitled Personal-Social Motivation Inventory. We hypothesized that individuals develop certain attitudes which facilitate creative growth and others which operate as obstacles to creativity. First, there is the creative attitude, an urge to search for the answers to puzzling questions, to explore, and to experiment. Second, there is the critical attitude, the inclination to search for defects and criticize. Third, there must be confidence in one's perceptions and willingness to believe them, if they withstand his honest tests of creativity. Taking a cue from Tumin (1953), we hypothesized five motivations inimical to creative productivity: an excessive quest for certainty, power, meaning, and social relations, and pathological rejection of social relations.

The items in this Inventory require "True" or "False" responses in terms of the subject's present attitudes and motivations. The following are examples of items in the Creative Attitude Scale:

I enjoy trying out a hunch just to see what will happen.
I like to work on problems in which the outcome is unpredictable.
I feel that it is always wiser to stick to the tried and true way of doing things.

A variety of studies are underway with adults and the items are being adapted for use with children and adolescents. Already we know that teachers ranking in the upper half on the Creative Attitude Scale have their pupils engage in a larger number of creative activities in grades three through six than their colleagues, and that their pupils show significant growth in creative writing, whereas the pupils of their colleagues do not demonstrate such growth. We also know that graduate students who develop original ideas judged to be superior have significantly higher scores on the Creative Attitude Scale than their colleagues. We have also found that graduate students having high scores on this Scale respond more favorably emotionally and in turn perform better when assigned the task of reading imaginatively rather than critically research reports and course studies.

DISCREPANCY BETWEEN "WILL DO" AND "CAN DO"

Educational and vocational counselors have always been harried by the discrepancy between what people *can do* and what they *will do*. This problem is accentuated when we attempt to predict creative behavior; the "will do" becomes even more important than in ordinary predictions.

Counselors have for a long time sought to improve the usefulness of measures of capacity by combining with them measures of motivation—interests, needs, wants. Some have sought assistance from various indicators of mental health, attempting to correct the crippling effects of maladjustment. I would like to propose still another concept for increasing ability to predict what individuals *will do* and in helping them achieve what they *can do*—the concept of risk-taking or testing the limits.

I had been verging on this concept for a couple of years as I studied the experiences of men who had survived emergencies and extreme conditions in which others would have perished and from my observations of behavior in realistically simulated emergencies and extreme conditions. It was not until Rush, Kohn, Doughty and I (1957) were in the middle of the Jet Ace Study that I began to grasp its significance.

Rush, Kohn, Doughty, and I had the privilege of studying rather intensively 31 of the 36 American jet aces and of comparing them with fighter interceptor pilots matched for rank, age, flying experience, and opportunity to shoot down MIGs (Torrance, Rush, Kohn and Doughty, 1957; Strawbridge, 1955). I think some of the findings from this study are relevant to the problems of identifying and guiding creative talent.

As we interviewed these men concerning their combat experiences and their childhood experiences, as we analyzed their responses to psychological tests and observed them in these situations, and as we listened to accounts by others of their behavior, it seemed to me that perhaps the most salient characteristic of the ace was his ability to test the limits or take calculated risks. Throughout most of his life he had characteristically tested the limits—the limits of his own abilities, the limits of his equipment or material resources, the limits of the situation. He was willing to diverge from the behavioral norms, whether rules of flying safety or classroom rules as a schoolboy, and to take calculated risks.

Using a sample of 800 fighter interceptor pilots and the number of MIG "kills" as the criterion, the various World War II and post-World War II classification test scores proved to be rather poor predictors of success. Out of 52 coefficients of correlation, only ten were statistically significant. Six of these were negative and the highest positive correlation was .18 (Rudder Control and Rotary Pursuit). A number of the life experience variables, however, proved to be quite fruitful. They differentiated between the matched aces and non-aces and correlated significantly with other measures of combat performance. One of the most significant scales was one consisting of experiences reflecting "testing-the-limits" or divergent behavior. Another highly significant one was composed of experiences indicating enjoyment of and participation in everyday activities involving risk and strategy from an early age. Still a third highly differentiating scale included experiences indicative of early independence.

Following this, Ziller and I set to work exploring the role of risk-taking tendencies as a determiner of behavior in a broader context. First, we combined the Risk and Strategy Scale with the Testing-the-Limits Scale and added other items many of which proved to correlate highly with the initial items and give the scale increased reliability (Torrance and Ziller, 1957). We then validated the scale against several external measures of risk-taking behavior. Since then, several additional validity studies have provided reasonably good evidence of validity. As our understanding of the role of risk-taking in personality development has unfolded, this variable has impressed me as being a very important one in predicting what an individual *will do* with resources and in assisting an individual in achieving something approaching his potentialities.

First, risk-taking seems essential in the development of the self-concept. One cannot know what he is capable of unless he tests his limits. I suspect that many of those who seek the assistance of a vocational counselor are people who have not tested their limits and consequently have either an erroneous self-concept or only a vague, ill-defined self-concept. It is little wonder that they have been unable to make a vocational choice or have made unwise ones. They now need the professional services of a vocational counselor to discover enough about what they *can do* in order to make a decision. It is in such cases as this that there *may be* the greatest discrepancy between what one *can do* and what one *will do*.

Risk-taking is also important in the acquisition of skills and knowledge. Curiosity does not fare very well in our society. We teach that "curiosity killed the cat" and refer to curiosity as "mere idle curiosity." It has been my observation, however, that the curious cat tests the limits very carefully and cautiously and withdraws with the greatest of speed from a dangerous situation. It has also been my observation that the curious person is never idle. The fact remains, however, that in most classrooms the child runs a calculated risk every time he asks an unusual question or advances a new idea for fear of the ridicule by his classmates and perhaps his teacher. This risk is even greater in most adult groups. Counselors and teachers in their relationships might do well to recognize this fact and to try to free such individuals to ask questions and to explore a variety of alternate possibilities, even unusual ones, in choosing a vocation or in seeking a better vocational adjustment.

It seems to me that personality development and growth can occur only though risk-taking and variation. Without it, I do not see how we can even expect a person to achieve the autonomy necessary in making a vocational choice or to achieve an accurate perception of reality. This, I suppose, is why many of those who seek the aid of a counselor want someone else to decide for them and to convince them that they can succeed in some specific vocation.

Risk-taking tendencies also appear to operate in determining the kind of vocation a person will choose. Ziller who worked with me in developing the Risk-Scale and in devising some of the objective criteria of risk-taking has explored some aspects of this problem (1957). He attempted to develop a theory of vocational choice which would include both economic and psychological variables. He argued that in the process of selecting a vocation, the vast array of alternatives is reduced enormously as a consequence of individual interests, abilities, economic limitations, and lack of information. The remaining possibilities form the individual's scale of judgment. These alternatives vary with regard to prize, price, and possibility of success, and it is these factors, along with the individual's risk-taking tendency, which determine vocational choice.

To test this idea concerning vocational choice Ziller obtained an index of utility for risk or risk-taking tendency from an objective device administered to college sophomores at the University of Delaware. He then compared the risk scores of those who had made various vocational choices. The group having the highest mean risk score were those who had chosen sales work. Then followed mechanical engineering, education, business administration, and other types of engineering. The lowest group consisted of those who were undecided concerning their vocational choice.

The results with regard to salesmen were in accord with our stereotype of the salesman. It would be interesting to determine the relation of risk-taking tendencies and success within a sales group of a particular organization. It is also interesting to speculate as to the job characteristics which lead high risk-takers to select the various vocations.

Most interesting, however, is the fact that the students who are undecided as to vocational goals at the end of their sophomore year have the lowest risk-taking score of any group. Abstracting somewhat, it may be hypothesized that indecision and risk-taking are negatively correlated and that measures of the latter may be useful in predicting the effectiveness of potential business executives who are continually faced with making decisions on the basis of inadequate and incomplete information.

McClelland (1956) explored a similar idea in his paper at the 1955 Utah conference on the identification of creative scientific talent. He attempted to make a case for the hypothesis that the successful scientist, like the successful salesman or business entrepreneur, has a higher need for achievement, in part because high achievement motivation will predispose him to take moderate calculated risks in which the success or failure of the enterprise will depend upon his own efforts.

Holland (1961) in his studies for the National Merit Scholarship Corporation developed some similar ideas and is experimenting with a revision of the Torrance-Ziller measure of risk-taking tendencies in predicting the performance of scholarship winners. Holland takes some of his leads from research findings which suggest that creative performance at the high school level occurs more frequently among students who are independent, intellectual, expressive, asocial, consciously original, and who aspire for future achievement. On the basis of the negligible relationship he found between academic aptitude and creative performance at a high aptitude level, Holland concluded that we must use nonintellectual criteria in the selection of students for scholarships and fellowships. He feels that further efforts to improve existing intellectual measures are likely to be unproductive.

PERSONALITY STUDIES OF HIGHLY CREATIVE CHILDREN

In general the study of the personalities of highly creative children has not been considered a very worthwhile or attractive pursuit. Investigators have been afraid that children identified as creative may not develop into creative adults. Given the creative adult, we may obtain some fairly reliable information about his childhood experiences, but we can never study his personality as a child. When fellow investigators criticize my interest in the study of the personalities of highly creative childen, I assure them that I know full well that many of these children will not be creative adults. In fact, I know that many of the children who stand out as highly creative in the second and third grades, especially boys, will not be highly creative as fourth graders. Some of them will never again show a high degree of creativity. Thus, I am interested in studying the personalities of children to see if I can find in them the trends, elements, or characteristics which lead to the eventual abandonment of this talent.

Two recent studies (Weisberg and Springer, 1961; Torrance, 1959) provide a wealth of leads concerning the personality of the highly creative child and his problems. The most thoroughgoing of the two is the one by Weisberg and Springer (1961) of thirty-two gifted fourth graders and their families. The criterion tests used included the Ask-and-Guess Test, Tin Can Uses, and Circles from the Minnesota battery. Their personalities were studied through psychiatric interviews, Rorschachs, and the Draw-a-Family technique. Judgments of the children and their parents by the psychiatrists on the basis of the interviews were made on six-point scales.

The ratings of the highly creative children were compared with those of the less creative ones. The highly creative children were rated significantly higher on: strength of self-image, ease of early recall, humor, availability of Oedipal anxiety, and uneven ego development. An examination of the bases for these judgments reflects what I would term a creative acceptance of oneself and a greater self-awareness. The more creative children could recall their earlier experiences more easily, even though they might have been unpleasant. In describing themselves, their reactions to school and their families, they placed themselves somewhere definite in these frames of reference, "even though that somewhere definite might not always be a pleasant place." Their Oedipal anxieties were closer to the surface, as judged by fantasy, content of early memories, and dream material. Their uneven ego development was reflected in various ways. Enthusiasm for Shakespeare and for dolls might peacefully coexist in them. Controls appropriate to adolescence or even adulthood might alternate with impulsive, almost infantile behavior during the interview.

On the Rorschach, children ranking high on the criterion measures showed a tendency toward unconventional responses, unreal percepts, and fanciful and imaginative treatment of the blots. They also gave more human movement and color responses than their less creative peers and the normal population of adults. The larger number of human movement responses was interpreted to reflect an internal locus of evaluation which allows for greater independence from environmental influences. The larger number of color responses was seen as an indication of greater readiness to respond emotionally to the environment. Thus, they are at the same time more sensitive and more independent than less creative but equally intelligent children.

The family pattern of the highly creative children developed by Weisberg and Springer is quite interesting. The family unit is not an overly close one; there is little clinging to one another. There is little stress on conformity to parental values. The marriage is not a particularly "well-adjusted" one. There is open, and not always calm expression of strong feeling. The father interacts strongly and positively with the child, and the mother also interacts strongly but is sometimes ambivalent in her maternal feelings. When the child regresses, the parents accept the behavior without great discomfort. The creative child is often an older sibling. He is not a particular favorite, however, and there is no over-evaluation of his abilities by the parents. The fathers of the more creative children have greater occupational autonomy or independence than the fathers of their less creative peers.

In one of our Minnesota Studies, I analyzed the personality data concerning the most creative boy and girl in each of twenty-three classes in grades one through six in three elementary schools. The controls were matched for sex, intelligence quotient, race, class (teacher), and age with the highly creative subjects. In addition to the data from the tests of intelligence (Stanford-Binet in one school and California Test of Mental Maturity in the others), we had available the results of the Draw-a-House-Tree-Person test, a set of peer nominations on a variety of creativity criteria, and teacher nominations on similar criteria. The two groups were compared on the peer and teacher nominations and on a number of indices derived from the drawings. Blind analyses were also made, using the guides developed by Buck (1948) and Machover (1949).

From the statistical analysis of the comparative data, three personality characteristics stand out as differentiating the highly creative children from less creative but equally intelligent children. First, the highly creative children have a reputation for having wild or silly ideas, especially the boys. Their teachers and peers agree on this point. Second, their work is characterized by the production of ideas "off the beaten track, outside the mold." This comes out as a highly differentiating characteristic both when we use the number of nonessential details in the drawings, and when we use the number of unique or unusual details. This characteristic is exemplified in the drawings by two highly creative third grade boys shown in Figures 5 and 6. This helps to explain to teachers why these highly creative children do not show up better than they do on traditional intelligence tests. Their ideas simply do not conform to the standardized dimensions, the behavioral norms, on which responses are judged. Just think how maddening it would be to try to evaluate the drawings shown in Figures 5 and 6 for IQ according to either the Buck or Goodenough criteria. Third, their work is characterized by humor, playfulness, relative lack of rigidity, and relaxation. This provides an interesting confirmation of the findings described above by Weisberg and Springer (1961) on the basis of psychiatric interviews and by Getzels and Jackson (1959) from stories stimulated

FIGURE 5. Tree and Person by Subject J, Third-Grade Boy.

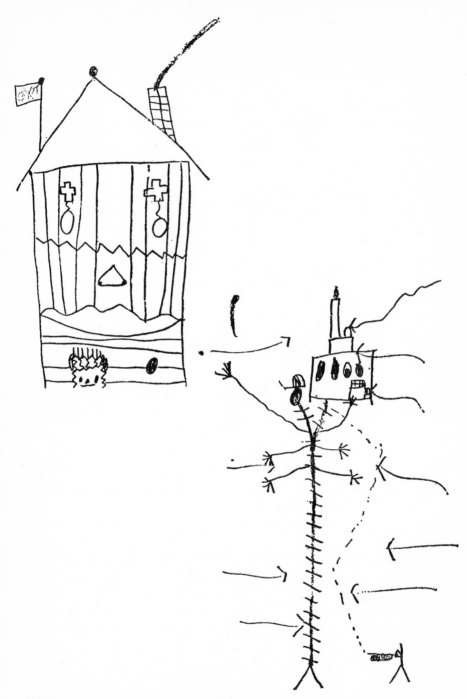

FIGURE 6. House and Person by Subject *T*, Third-Grade Boy.

by pictures similar to the Thematic Apperception Test series and rankings of qualities desired.

The three characteristics which emerge strongly would appear to be of considerable importance to teachers and counselors in their efforts to understand and guide the highly creative youngster. In spite of the fact that these children have many excellent ideas, they readily achieve a reputation for having silly, wild, or naughty ideas. It is difficult to determine what effect this derogation of their ideas has on their personality development, as well as upon the future development of their creative talents. The uniqueness of their ideas makes this a really difficult problem, because there are no standards, as in answer books and manuals. Although their humor and playfulness may win some friends for them, it does not always make them "easier to live with." In fact, it may make their behavior even more unpredictable than otherwise and this probably makes their presence in a group upsetting. Recognizing and understanding these three characteristics are important because each apparently has an important role in making an individual "creative."

PERSONALITY STUDIES OF
HIGHLY CREATIVE ADOLESCENTS

Two studies of the personalities of highly creative adolescents may be cited to supplement the two childhood studies just described. One is the study by Getzels and Jackson (1958, 1959, 1960, 1961) in which they differentiated highly creative adolescents (grades seven through twelve) from highly intelligent ones. The other is an exploratory investigation of the personalities of gifted adolescent artists (eleventh and twelfth grades) by Hammer (1961).

It will be recalled that in the Getzels-Jackson study the school achievement of the highly creative and the highly intelligent groups was equally superior to the total school population from which they were drawn. This was in spite of the fact that there was a 23 point difference in average IQ between them. The high IQ student was rated as a more desirable student than the average student but the highly creative was not. On their fantasy productions, the more creative made significantly greater use of stimulus-free themes, unexpected endings, humor, and playfulness. On the basis of these findings, Getzels and Jackson have suggested that an essential difference between the two groups is the creative adolescent's ability to produce new forms and to risk joining together elements usually seen as independent and dissimilar. They also suggested that the creative adolescent seems to enjoy the risk and uncertainty of the unknown. The high IQ adolescent prefers the anxieties and delights of "safety" to the anxieties and delights of growth. These differences are reflected in the occupational choices of the two groups. Sixty-two per cent of the creatives chose unconventional occupations, such as adventurer, inventor, writer, and the like. Only 16 per cent of the highly intelligent subjects chose such occupations; 84 per cent of them chose "conventional" occupations, such as doctor, lawyer, engineer.

Getzels and Jackson (1961) also interviewed rather intensively the parents of their two groups of subjects. The parents of the high IQ students tended to recall greater financial difficulties during their childhoods and at the present expressed greater real or imagined personal insecurity than those of the highly creatives. The parents of the high IQ adolescents also seemed to be more "vigilant" with respect to their children's behavior and their academic success. They are more critical of both their children and the school than are the parents of the highly creative adolescents. The high IQ parents focus their concern on immediately visible virtues such as cleanliness, good manners, and studiousness. The parents of the creatives focus theirs on less visible qualities such as the child's openness to experience, his values, and his interests and enthusiasm.

In the second study by Hammer (1961) of the personalities of gifted adolescent artists, an attempt was made to contrast the genuinely creative with the merely facile personality. In an intensive study of eighteen high school artists in a workshop, five were identified as "truly creative" and five as "merely facile." On the basis of elaborate psychological studies, Hammer found that the "truly creatives" differed from the "merely faciles" in that they exhibited deeper feelings, greater original responsiveness, preference for the observer role over the participant role, stronger determination and ambition, integration of feminine and masculine components, greater independence, rebelliousness, and self-awareness, stronger needs for self-expression, greater tolerance for discomfort, and a fuller range of emotional expression.

Teachers, counselors, and administrators should recognize that highly creative adolescents may exhibit vastly different personalities in school and in the rest of their world, as exemplified in the biographies of some of our most creative scientists and inventors. It is heart-breakingly apparent in the stories of many of the highly creative adolescents about whom parents and teachers write and/or tell me. For example, the mother of one rather obviously creative boy of thirteen years has described to me in beautiful contrast her son as he is at school and as he is in the rest of his world. After a steadily declining academic record, he was retained in the seventh grade "to teach him a lesson." His teachers, counselors, and principals have described the boy to his parents as extremely bright, very bored, lazy, daydreaming, and very withdrawn but not rebellious. One teacher declared to the mother, "I'll make him work, if I have to break his spirit to do it—and ridiculing and shaming him is the only way with children like him." He is not permitted to participate in science clubs because he doesn't have a "B" average. Instead, the principal insists that he play football and be "better rounded." The boy whom the parents and others outside of school sees "never daydreams; loves to learn and is always getting books from the library; works hard, many times almost collapsing from trying to work out an experiment late into the night." In the world outside of school, "he has energy enough for ten people" and has an outgoing, bubbling personality and a keen sense of humor. He talks of quitting school when he is sixteen and his parents wonder if this might possibly be his best chance to get out of the trap in which he finds himself.

SUMMARY

A great variety and number of studies have delved into the personalities of highly creative adults. In most such studies, the criterion group has been identified as being highly creative and eminent in some field and compared with some group of similar individuals not achieving such eminence. On the basis of these studies, a list of eighty-four adjectives describing the creative personality was constructed. Some studies using existing assessment devices such as the Allport-Vernon-Lindzey Study of Values, Strong Vocational Interest Blank, Minnesota Multiphasic Personality Inventory, Rorschach Ink Blots, and Thematic Apperception Test are of considerable value to counselors and other guidance workers. An attempt, however, was made to show the need for developing new instruments, and some approaches were suggested. A few personality studies of highly creative children and adolescents were described, since it is during these periods that guidance workers need to be alert in keeping alive promising creative talent.

Chapter 5

CREATIVE

DEVELOPMENT

The developmental curves for most of the abilities thought to be involved in creative thinking follow a pattern which is quite different from most other aspects of human growth. For this and other reasons it seems important that teachers, counselors, administrators, and others be familiar with the age-level characteristics of the creative thinking of children and the process by which these abilities develop. It is a well-known principle that teachers who know most about the age-level characteristics of the children whom they teach do a better job of teaching, establish better relationships with children, and enjoy their teaching more than do their less informed colleagues.

In presenting information about developmental phenomena and age-level characteristics concerning creativity, I would like to review some of the usual cautions about using such data. As with other age-level characteristics, it is never correct to make a blanket statement about the creativity of all of the children in an age group. It is possible to identify prominent characteristics which are common among children of a particular age. In using age-level characteristics, it may be misleading to look for the average behavior. It is important to look for the range of possible behaviors and to stimulate children toward their maximum possibilities. An understanding of age-level characteristics should help educators become aware of possible motivations for each child. Intelligent use of age-level characteristics requires imagination on the part of the teacher or counselor.

Many workers have made observations concerning the process by which the creative thinking abilities develop, usually without systematic documentation. Certainly there have been no studies comparable to the famous growth studies of Gesell and his associates, or of Olson and his co-workers. A few workers have, through cross-sectional studies, plotted developmental curves covering several years. For example, some have studied growth during the preschool years, while others have studied the early school years or some later period. One obstacle in studying creative growth over a wide age span has been the unavailability of tasks suited to different ages.

I shall present the data according to the different educational levels: the preschool years, the elementary school period, and the high school and college periods.

STAGES OF DEVELOPMENT
DURING THE
PRESCHOOL YEARS

The developmental stages of creativity in early childhood vary from study to study, seemingly according to the kinds of performance admitted as evidence by investigators.

Ribot (1906), one of the early investigators using the term "imagination," shows the growth and rivalry of the Imagination and Reason in most individuals in the following diagram. The line IM stands for the growth of the Imagination through the period of childhood and youth. The line R represents Reason. It begins later and grows more slowly than the other. At X the two faculties are at the same level and stand in antagonism to one another. After this, Reason fights, or seems to fight, a winning battle. According to Ribot, Imagination gives way, or at least provides nothing new, in most people, after the period of youth is over.

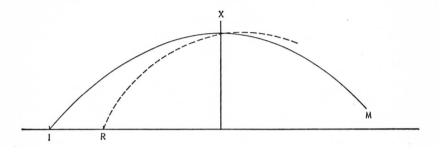

McMillan (1924) identified three stages in the development of the imagination. During the first stage, the young child has a sense of beauty which serves as a kind of shortcut to knowledge. As she says, "the city of gold with pearly gates, with crystal fountains and un-blackened skies" is real to the child at this stage. In the second stage, he comes to grips with the realities. He begins to inquire into cause and effect and to ask "why there are so many streets that are not golden, so many fountains that are turbid with filth, and so many skies that are blackened all the time." During the third stage, he begins to work out by small degrees the ideal of his first vision of the world of things as they are.

Andrews (1930) was considerably more systematic and thorough-going than other investigators in his tracing of the development of the imagination during the preschool years. He discovered that total imaginative scores are highest between four years and four years, six months, with a sudden drop at about age five when the child enters kindergarten. Ability to redefine, restructure, or recombine reached a peak between three and four years and from then on decreased; analogy reached a height during the fourth year and declined during the fifth; "don't know" responses decreased steadily with chronological age up to five years and then increased somewhat. The more creative types of imagination reached a high point from ages three years, six months to four years, six months, and their lowest ebb during the fifth year.

As already reported, Grippen (1933) concluded that creative imagi-nation rarely functions in childhood below the age of five years. Such a finding, however, seems to be inherent in the kinds of evidence recognized as relevant in this study.

Markey (1935) found that the total amount of imaginative behavior increased with age throughout the preschool period. She reports, however, that performance on the Housekeeping Game and the fanciful naming of visual stimuli decreased among the older chlidren, a finding which she discounts on the basis of interest and lack of information of the younger children.

Ruth Griffiths (1945) identified eleven stages in the creative drawings of children and relates these to the study of imagination in early childhood. These stages are:

1. A stage of undifferentiated scribble.

2. Rough geometrical shapes, usually circles and squares, with names such as doors, windows, apples, applied.

3. Making of additional objects by combinations of lines and squares and by single circles.

4. Combinations of circles and lines to make many other objects, with human figure as one of the prime interests.

5. Juxtaposition of many objects rapidly drawn and named.

6. Concentration on one object at a time, bolder work, care taken, and degree of detail present.

7. Further juxtaposition, but clear subjective association, work recognizable.

8. Partial synthesis, some items being shown in definite relationship to each other.

9. Pure picture, one picture only.

10. Multiplication of pictures, joy of representation.

11. Development of a theme by means of a series of pictures.

As a part of the Union College Character Research Project, Ligon (1957) attempted to establish age-level characteristics for the development of the imagination or vision from birth to age sixteen. From this very extensive project he also developed lists of methods for developing this and other dimensions of character. I shall summarize those which apply to creative growth.

Birth to Age Two. Ligon maintains that children begin developing their imagination during the first year. The child questions the names of things, attempts to reproduce sounds or rhythms. When he creates something, he usually names it when completed, not before. He begins to anticipate daily routines, and by the time he is two, he looks forward to special events. He is eager to experience everything through touch, taste, and sight. He is very curious, but how he expresses it depends on his unique characteristics. He learns very early that there are some things he can touch, and others that he cannot.

During this period, creative growth can be stimulated in a variety of ways. Imagination can be stimulated by simple games, large blocks, dolls, and the like. The child's desire to explore should be encouraged by making his environment safe for him to do so. This can be done by removing what he may not touch and providing barriers to prevent his doing so. It is suggested that parents play simple games with children this age and enjoy their verbal play and accept without question their names for their creations. When words gain meaning, it is suggested that parents sing songs about objects rather than ask the child to "Say dog" or "Say Daddy."

Ages Two to Four.   During the two-to-four year-old period, the child learns about the world through direct experience, and repetition of his experiences in verbal and imaginative play. He thrills over the wonders of nature. His attention span is short, and he shifts activities at random when not directed. He begins to develop a sense of autonomy and wants to do things for himself. This helps him develop confidence in his own abilities. His curiosity about his environment continues, and he explores it in his own unique way and asks questions which may be embarrassing to adults. He is learning to cope with his world as he discovers it, but fearful experiences may shake his confidence about new discoveries, the Union College study points out. Since he is testing his limits, the child at this age frequently overreaches his capacities and is apt to respond with anger to frustration.

Ligon and his associates suggest that the two-to-four year old be provided with toys which can "become" a variety of things. They point out that blocks or a ball of clay can stimulate more imagination than structured toys. They also suggest that adults share with children of this age God's wonders in budding flowers, growing seedlings, baby kittens, and pretty colored leaves in the fall. Parents should encourage two-to-four year olds to do things by themselves even when it means going on in spite of bumps. Parents need to be especially patient when the child is painfully slow or imperfect in a task. His curiosity can be

encouraged by being delighted with him over the new things he discovers or creates. Show off his "train" made of blocks. Above all, make
the discovery of new things positive and happy. Give him the freedom
to explore, but prepare him for new experiences so that he will have the
skills to react to strangeness. He needs opportunities for doing things,
although it may be necessary to remove obstacles at times and comfort
him when he is frustrated.

Ages Four to Six. Ligon and his associates say that the typical child
from four to six has a good imagination but they do not make any
observations about a lessening of imagination which others have found
at about the middle of this period. During this period, the child learns
the skills of planning for the first time. He begins to enjoy planning
anticipated play and "work." He is learning adult roles through pretended play. His curiosity leads him to search for "truth and right"
even in areas that may be embarrassing to adults. He is now able to
relate isolated events, although he may not understand the reason for
the relationship. He experiments with many roles in his imaginative
play. At this age, he starts to become aware of the feelings of others
and begins thinking how his actions will affect others.

Confidence can be developed during this period through creative
arts, new experiences, and word games. The creations of the four-to-
sixes should not be evaluated by adult standards. They may need help
in gathering things to play store, hospital, school, or the like. Their
dress-ups, store shelves, and such need only be suggestive. Parents and
teachers should permit children at this stage to contribute their ideas
in planning. Their ideas should be used at times, even though they may
not be as good as the adult's. Persistence should be rewarded, praise
bestowed when children use their imagination to care for themselves
or play alone. It is important that children's questions at this stage be
rewarded by simple but direct and honest answers. Ligon stresses that
the search for the truth should never be inhibited by shame or guilt.
Parents should share their child's discovery of new things and help
him in his search for truth by exploring the meanings of words. This
is a good age to encourage imagination in creative surprises for his family and friends. Impulsiveness can be guided by plans which include
thoughtful acts.

From my own observations and from the letters and telephone calls
which I receive from parents, the kindergarten period seems to be
especially crucial. Such a conclusion would seem to be supported by

the studies also cited which show a decline in imagination at about this time. From these sources, it is easy to guess some of the causes for this decline at about age five. The following excerpts from a report by the father of a kindergarten girl reflect much of the process revealed by the research of Andrews (1930) and others:

. . . As I watched my oldest child develop, I was impressed with her interest in the world about her. She was so different from the high school students I was accustomed to working with. She seemed so eager to learn and to explore. Then when she started talking in sentences at 14 months, I was surprised how quickly she learned nursery rhymes we had been reading to her. . . .

As she grew older, her curiosity and interest in the world around seemed to grow rapidly. She asked endless questions—everything from where babies come from to what makes the leaves turn color in the fall. I determined to answer all these questions as they came up, never putting her off with 'I don't know' or 'I'll tell you later.' I gave fairly complete explanations to her questions and showed her how we could look up answers in books to questions I didn't know. All the time I felt she was just nodding her head and accepting what I said without understanding. Soon, however, I was startled to find her asking more questions based on these first answers I had given. . . .

After her first ballet performance at age three, she decided to become a ballerina and took great pleasure in spending hours creating new dance steps to the music of Tchaikovsky and others. This interest in ballet was dulled for a period by an authoritarian teacher who insisted that she conform to the forward rolls the rest of the class was learning. However, the interest was renewed with a change in teachers and a more advanced class.

Then this year she started kindergarten. She had been anxious all summer, even though I kept reminding her that she would not be allowed to read until a year later in the first grade. . . . The first few weeks of kindergarten she was delirious with excitement. Every day she was eager for school. Show and Tell time was her favorite. She collected leaves from 22 different varieties of trees in the yard. Then she pasted them in a book, printed their names underneath and took them for Show and Tell with an explanation of what makes leaves change color. Next she took her pet turtle with her book illustrating the life cycles of fishes, reptiles and amphibians.

About November she began to complain that all the other kids were bringing their toys and dolls for Show and Tell or telling what they saw on TV. Her interest dropped further as she found that the teacher did all of the reading instead of letting the kids read. The end came when the teacher refused to let her use the Teach-a-Time clock to show the other kids how to tell time and made her paste paper instead. Her interests then began to move in the direction of what she wore that was different from the other children. She began to quote more and more what the teacher said and accepted it as law over anything else.

Interest was revived briefly when the teacher said she could bring her telescope and book on astronomy during the week they were to talk about outer space. However, the teacher didn't understand her explanation of how a reflecting type telescope works and pointed the wrong end at the sun during an observation attempt. By this time, she accepted the teacher's word to the point where she was afraid to correct the teacher and turn the telescope around. From that day on she has refused to bring another thing for Show and Tell and began talking only of when the next school vacation would begin.

STAGES OF DEVELOPMENT DURING THE ELEMENTARY YEARS

The literature concerning the stages of creative development during the elementary school years is fairly consistent, and amazingly so, considering the variety of measures that have been used and the variety of the samples studied.

Using ink spots, Kirkpatrick in 1900 reported that children in the first three grades are more imaginative than those in the fourth, fifth, and sixth grades. In his studies, there was an increase again in the seventh and eighth grades.

On the basis of compositions written by children from grades three through twelve, Colvin and Meyer (1906) found a general decline in imagination during these years. They maintained that the only type of imagination that showed substantial growth in the compositions they studied was the visual, and that this had become "symbolic and devitalized."

Simpson (1922) included grades three through eight in his studies of creative imagination. Beginning with a low point at the beginning of the third grade he found a sharp increase by the end of the year followed by a decline at the beginning of the fourth grade. This was followed by an upward trend until a peak was reached in the second half of the sixth grade, after which there was a decline in the seventh and a still further one by the beginning of the eighth.

Mearns in 1931 (reprinted in 1958) maintained that it was common knowledge that creative activity enjoys free expression during the first three grades with some remaining in the fourth and fifth grades. According to him, there is a rapid decline in the sixth and seventh grades, becoming a "vice loved in secret" by the eighth grade but eventually given up. He argued, however, that it could be revived at any age, even in adulthood.

M. D. Vernon reported in 1948 that what he called constructive imagination did not occur in the child of normal intelligence and emotional development until age eleven. He based his conclusions upon ability to "understand fully pictures and to interpret them as a whole." At the age of eleven, he found that children could "invent explanations of the scene depicted, in terms of thoughts, emotions, and activities of the characters." Apparently Vernon was tapping what I have called "ability to formulate causal hypotheses" in the Ask-and-Guess Test. The developmental curve for the ability rises slowly and gradually in the early school years and reaches a fairly good height at age eleven. Ability to ask questions about the picture and to formulate hypotheses about consequence develop much earlier and show quite different developmental characteristics.

Lally and LaBrant (1951) reported that art educators and psychologists have observed that interest in art tends to decline at each educational level through the intermediate and upper grades and on into secondary school. They admitted that this probably occurs in "schools of the old type" but expressed doubt that it occurs in schools where child art is appreciated.

Barkan (1960) makes a number of interesting observations concerning the developmental process of creativity on the basis of his intensive observational studies of a small number of elementary teachers in their teaching of art. He observed that children show greater spurts of growth at some points than at others. Degree of growth from first to second grade seems to be more dramatic than from kindergarten to first grade. He found that the insatiable curiosity of second-graders about the "why" and "how" of things changes into a more alert quest for explanations in the third and fourth grades. He found that most fourth graders tend to be perfectionistic and easily discouraged by undue adult pressure.

Wilt (1959) has written at length about the decline in creativity which occurs during what she calls the "stage of realism" and "gang age." She explains this decline on the basis of conformity to peer group standards and reports that much of the free-wheeling thinking, large swinging movements, and free action-packed art disappears. At this stage, about the fourth grade, symbols become stiff, clothes assume great importance, and male and female roles have significance. She maintains that only the unusual child can withstand the pressures to conform to behaviorial norms at this stage. She observed that in a few creativity returns after the crisis but that in most it is lost forever.

In the Minnesota studies, an attempt has been made to develop tasks suitable for studying creative development from kindergarten through graduate school. Thus far, growth curves have been fairly well developed for grades one through twelve and the graduate level. Kindergarten and the undergraduate college years will soon be included. The general pattern of the developmental curve of most of the creative thinking abilities we have assessed is as follows: There is a steady increase from first through third grade. With one exception, there is a sharp decrease between the third and fourth grades followed by some recovery during the fifth and sixth grades. Another drop occurs between the sixth and seventh grades, after which there is growth until near the end of the high school years. The developmental curve shown in Figure 7 for question-asking in the Ask-and-Guess Test is fairly typical. A major exception is the curve for the ability to formulate causal hypotheses. Apparently, children are rather slow in developing skills in causal thinking, but they continue this type of development through the fourth

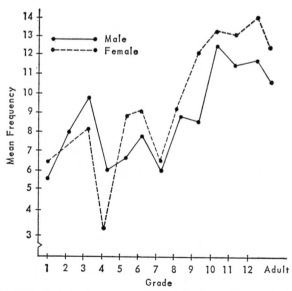

FIGURE 7. Developmental Curve for the Mean Frequency of Questions asked on Part 1, Ask, of Ask-and-Guess Test.

grade without the slump found in other types of creative thinking.

In one of our studies in which we encouraged children to write on their own, fourth graders consistently did less writing and contributed fewer poems, stories, and inventions for the school's magazine than any other grade from three through six. In an independent study, Weideman (1961) evaluated several techniques for stimulating children to create songs. Fourth graders produced fewer individual songs than any other grade from three through six. She reports, however, that fourth graders showed more interest and curiosity about the songs of other classes than did children in any of the other grades. They also demonstrated good musical judgment, choosing as best the same songs which the adult judges rated as best.

My associates and I have advanced many possible explanations concerning the sharp decreases in the fourth and seventh grades. Longitudinal studies indicate that while most children experience these decrements, some maintain their creative growth. Apparently many of those who experience this drop sacrifice their creativity rather permanently, producing a serious loss of potential talent. There are possibilities that many mental breakdowns and delinquent careers have some of their roots in the phenomena involved in these slumps in creative ability.

Research and theory in child development suggest a number of possible explanations for the phenomena observed. Particularly relevant are the theories of Harry Stack Sullivan (1953). According to him, the skills being acquired during the transition period which usually occurs between the third and fourth grades for most children include: social subordination and accommodation, ostracism, segregation into groups, disparagement, stereotyping, competition and compromise. He maintains that by this time pressures toward socialization have almost invariably resulted in a careful sorting out of that which is agreed to by authorities. Strong dependence upon consensual validation develops, and unusual ideas are laughed at, ridiculed, and condemned. The child sees those around him not so much as enemies but as sources of humiliation, anxiety, and punishment with respect to that which they communicate; and this tends to reduce the freedom and enthusiasm of communication, especially of original ideas. As the transition is made into early adolescence at about the seventh grade, still other social pressures to conformity appear. These new demands typically produce feelings of inadequacy and insecurity, as new roles are imposed. The resultant anxiety restricts awareness and produces uncertainty, making productive thinking difficult.

The various declines may also be explained in terms of reaction to new stresses encountered at each new stage of development or each transitional state in education. It will be recalled that these occur at the time of entry into kindergarten, between the primary and intermediate grades, and between elementary and high school. We know that when new stresses occur, there is a temporary decrement in performance resulting from a period of shock or temporary loss of old props or anchors. Usually, however, such periods are followed by periods of overcompensation or recovery. These decrements may possibly be little more than typical reactions to new stresses.

It may also be possible to explain these declines as expected accompaniments of physiological changes. For example, R. W. Lowry has called to my attention some visual data which may help explain the slump at about age nine. He reports that in work in developmental vision, nine-year olds have been found to have the worst possible visual organization, when compared to other years. He describes this group as very complacent. They rarely report visual symptoms (blurring, doubling, or eye watering), even though the majority depart from "ideal" or theoretical vision. Furthermore, even though the nine-year old is "falling apart visually," according to Lowry, it does not seem to be the best time for vision training or rehabilitation. Children at this age will practice endlessly with little improvement. For these reasons therapy may be delayed six months to a year. The decline at about the seventh-grade level might possibly be explained on the basis of the conflicts arising with the onset of the physiological changes of puberty.

As we complete the cross-cultural studies now underway, new light may be thrown on some of these hypotheses. The shape of the developmental curves in other cultures may be quite different from those we have found thus far in the United States. Our longitudinal studies will also make some of the phenomena clearer and more understandable.

The age-level characteristics and suggestions for prompting creative growth developed by the Union College Character Research Project (Ligon, 1957) will be summarized for the six-to-twelve-year olds as was done for the younger groups.

Ages Six to Eight. According to Ligon (1957), the creative imagination of the child between six and eight takes a turn toward realism, to the extent that he tries to reproduce details even in play. He points out that unless the child rejects pretense, he can use his imagination to personify moral principles. It has been my observation, however, that many children in the first and second grades reject all fantasy and are very impoverished in their imagination. Drawings become more representative, although the tendency is to draw what one thinks, Ligon observes, rather than what one sees. The child at this stage loves learning, if his school experiences are challenging and rewarding. His curiosity continues to develop, unless severely restricted by adults. Usually he can learn adult-imposed rules willingly, but he is apt to be too self-centered to create rules to protect someone else's rights. Some first grade teachers of my acquaintance, however, tell me that this is a mistaken notion. They find that their first graders can and do create rules to protect the rights of others and to guide their own behavior.

During this stage, Ligon and his associates recommend the encouragement of role-playing and participation in adult activities. It is a time to create through lessons, stories, or discussion, characters who personify moral principles. Children enjoy creating characters and making others guess who they are. It is important that the six-to-eight year old be given help in carrying out some of his ideas, but also that he be encouraged to go as far as he can on a project without help. Successful efforts should be displayed. It is important that adults continue to answer questions impartially and directly. Parents and teachers can help plan surprises for others.

Ages Eight to Ten. According to the Union College studies (Ligon, 1957), the child between eight and ten is increasingly able to use a variety of skills in being creative and can discover ways for using his unique abilities creatively. He likes to identify with heroes who have overcome handicaps, and he can be encouraged to use his imagination and other skills to help his friends. He can now undertake long projects which require sustained interest and effort. His ability to ask critical questions also increases and makes his quest for truth more exciting and positive. His awareness of how he differs from others may cause him to worry about things he cannot do. His feelings are frequently hurt, according to Ligon, by the imperfect judgments of what others think of him.

The Union College investigators recommend that the eight-to-ten year old be given every possible opportunity to express his originality and ingenuity. Adults should create occasions for him to use his skills and show him how his talents are useful. He needs opportunities to use what he learns, but he will need support when he fails and coaching when tasks are too diffcult. This is a time to permit him to play at vocations realistically. It is suggested that strengths be emphasized and that children be helped to realize that they cannot be good at everything.

Ages Ten to Twelve.   Children between ten and twelve delight in exploration, girls preferring to explore in books and in pretend play and boys, through firsthand experiences. It is a great age for reading. They have now become less restless and can read or think for long periods. Artistic and musical aptitudes are developing rapidly at this time. At this age, the child will try almost anything for experience but he tends to lack confidence if the results of his efforts are to be made public. His interest in detail and facility in memorizing, Ligon says, tempts adults to teach him a multitude of facts instead of challenging him to think. The child at this stage, however, is capable of deriving principles or generalizations or devising schemes to express sympathy, if challenged to do so. He seldom does so on his own initiative.

It is suggested that ten-to-twelves be given opportunities to explore, to build, to make and to read, as well as opportunities to communicate to others about his experiences. It is a time for the exploration of talents. It is also a time for helping the child learn to persist in difficult tasks and to challenge him to learn things because they are difficult. Ligon suggests making available to him biographies of those who have outstanding character traits and triumphed over difficulties. Adults need to challenge children of this age to discover the universal principles which operate in nature and among people and to cope with their fears. Children at this stage need to test out their ideas and skills. It is a time for giving experience in planning a course of action and in making decisions.

DEVELOPMENTAL PHENOMENA DURING THE HIGH SCHOOL YEARS

Although developmental phenomena during the high school years have received little attention, most of the existing evidence is fairly consistent. Most investigators have reported a decline in imaginative functioning between the sixth and seventh grades and in some studies on into the eighth. There follows a period of fairly steady growth until about the end of the high school period, at which time there is a leveling off or a slight decline.

Colvin and Meyer (1906) reported a general decline during the entire period in creative writing. Simpson (1927) found a peak which extended through the second half of the sixth grade, after which there was a decline in the seventh and a still further one in the eighth. Mearns (1931), on the basis of experiences in stimulating creative writing but apparently without any measurements, maintained that a decline which set in during the sixth grade continued throughout the high school period, unless revived by special encouragement.

In the Minnesota Studies (Yamamoto, 1960b, Torrance et al., 1960), the abilities measured show a decline between the sixth and seventh grades, after which there is a fairly steady rise until near the end of the high school period. Most of the growth curves then show either a leveling off or a slight decline.

There are some clues that the decline at the beginning of the high school period is the result of new pressures to conformity inherent in the tradition. There is a need for studies in schools having seven- and eight-grade elementary schools and for longitudinal studies to obtain clarification of the major causal factors. Throughout our search of the literature, no longitudinal studies of any type have been found.

Through the Union College Character Research Project an effort has been made to develop age-characteristics through the eighteen-year old level. These will be summarized, as for the younger ages.

Ages Twelve to Fourteen. The twelve-to-fourteen year old youth tends to be concerned with the activities of the moment, according to Ligon, and rarely plans for the future. He tends to respond to adventure more readily than to reason. Socially and emotionally it is a period of adventure. The sexes still do not mix very well. During this stage, gifted children produce remarkable performances in imaginative, artistic, musical, and mechanical fields. He is beginning to question adult regulations and wants to have a part in decisions concerning them. He feels insecure, however, because of changes in his physical and emotional make-up and a growing strangeness in interpersonal relations. He is quite fearful of rejection by his peers. He is able to stand on his own convictions, even against group pressures.

The Union College group emphasizes the need for helping the twelve-to-fourteen-year old develop specific short-range goals which require him to use what he has learned and to make a tentative vocational choice around which he can organize his present activities, even though the choice may be changed later. Exciting but difficult projects are needed. It is a time to give him experience in making decisions and carrying them out. It is cautioned that young people at this stage should not be asked to be too different from their peers but should be given skills for influencing the group and raising the level of the group. They can be given practice in sensing the needs of others and in maintaining the respect of friends by using creative solutions.

Ages Fourteen to Sixteen.   Between the ages of fourteen and sixteen much of the imaginative activity seems to be focused on a future career. Adventure is still the keyword for all phases of life for both sexes. Interests and aptitudes are developing rapidly but are still rather unstable. The youth is able to see that there are no absolute solutions to some problems but he has not yet learned how to apply creatively the principles he has learned about right and wrong. He worries about peer acceptance, and his fears cause him to avoid situations which involve exploration, testing of his abilities, and such. According to Ligon, he can, with practice, make his emotions creative.

According to the Union College researchers the fourteen-to-sixteen year period is the time for helping the individual think about his abilities and how he can use them to achieve success in his career and avocations. It is a time to help him become aware of social needs and develop ideas for meeting them through action projects. He needs help in evaluating his abilities realistically. It is also a time for learning the skills of creative problem-solving and for practicing the skill of finding "third alternatives" which are creative solutions which serve both conflicting purposes. He can be stimulated to list all of the things he can and cannot do in "hopeless" situations.

Ages Sixteen to Eighteen.   The sixteen-to-eighteen year old youth needs to give his imagination full rein, as he sorts what is and is not important, according to Ligon. In doing this he may need noncritical adults as "sounding boards." He can develop vision for his life in terms of optimistic aspirations and for the arts and social activity as means of enriched living. His interests are usually stable enough to be assessed along with his special aptitudes, making this probably the best age for vocational testing and guidance. He now has the ability to think in terms of abstractions and to translate his social ideas into specific experiences. He can also learn to channel emotional energy creatively, solve problems and participate more vigorously in groups.

During this period, adults need to make themselves available and provide provocative "food for thought" in classes. Aesthetic interests and skills should be encouraged. Adults should share with these youths as fellow learners but avoid competing with them. Various tests of interest, abilities, and attitudes toward life can be useful. Sixteen-to-eighteen year olds need problems which require creative applications of what has been learned. They also need help in finding creative ways to stand by their beliefs and to practice their social ideals. Adults themselves need to seek creative solutions when they find themselves in conflict with the sixteen-to-eighteen year old. The concept that emotional energy can be used creatively or destructively should be introduced and tested.

CREATIVE DEVELOPMENT AFTER HIGH SCHOOL

There are no developmental data for the post-high-school years comparable to those which have been presented for the other periods. A variety of experiments in many fields have demonstrated that various kinds of training and stimulation are capable of increasing the quantity and quality of the creative thinking of young people and adults. Because of the great diversity of paths taken at the beginning of this period, it probably would be extremely difficult or almost impossible to discover common developmental characteristics according to age. It might be possible to discover common developmental characteristics within relatively homogeneous career groups, especially in fields which provide opportunities for continued creative development.

Of considerable importance to persons concerned with the guidance of creative talent are the studies which have dealt with problems of age and creative productivity. Perhaps the most outstanding study of this type is Lehman's (1953) concerning the age of peak achievement in a variety of fields. He used data concerning number of contributions, expert ratings of the value of contributions, and such indicators as income and position of influence and leadership.

Among chemists, he found that the greatest contributions were made between twenty-six and thirty years of age; among mathematicians, between thirty and forty; musicians, between thirty and forty; authors, under forty-five; philosophers, between thirty-five and thirty-nine. Movie actors reached their greatest popularity between thirty and forty; executives who earned salaries of $50,000 or over usually achieved that level between sixty and sixty-four; and civic and political leaders tended to achieve eminence between fifty and fifty-five. In recent years, creativity has been exhibited at increasingly younger ages. Although numerous outstanding creative accomplishments occur at advanced ages, Lehman concluded that superior creativity generally rises rapidly to its highest point in the thirties and declines slowly thereafter.

On the basis of his studies, Lehman formulated three generalizations concerning age and creativity in most fields. He concluded that the maximum production rate for output of highest quality usually occurs at an earlier age than the maximum rate for less distinguished contributions by the same individuals. The rate of good production does not change much in the middle years and the decline is gradual for the older years. He also found that production of the highest quality tends to fall off at an earlier age and at a more rapid rate than does output of lesser merit.

Lehman (1956) has been careful to point out that it is not age itself but the factors that accompany age change that bring about a reduction in creative production. The following sixteen factors to account for this decrement suggested by Lehman should be of especial interest to counselors in guiding older creative talent (Stein and Heinze, 1960, p. 111):

1. A decline in physical vigor, energy, and resistance to fatigue occurs before the age of forty.
2. Sensory capacity and motor precision decline with age.
3. Serious illness and bodily infirmities have more negative effects on older than younger persons.
4. Creativity curves may be related to glandular changes.
5. Marital difficulties and sexual problems increase with age and may have a negative effect on creativity.
6. Indifference toward creativity may develop more frequently among older people because of the death of a loved one.

7. Older persons are more likely to be preoccupied with the practical demands of life.

8. Success, promotion, increased prestige, and responsibility may lead to less favorable conditions for concentrated work.

9. Having achieved these goals, those who desire prestige and recognition, rather than the creation of something new, strive less for achievement.

10. Easily won and early fame may lead to contentment with what has been done before accomplishing what could be the most creative work.

11. Nonrecognition and destructive criticism may lead to apathy of older workers.

12. Negative transfer, resulting in inflexibility, may be more of a handicap among older workers.

13. Older workers may become less motivated because of these factors.

14. Younger people may be better educated and have lived in more stimulating environments.

15. Psychoses, which occur more frequently in later life, may have clouded what was previously a brilliant mind.

16. Alcohol, narcotics, and such may have sapped an individual's productive power.

Most of the studies in this area appear to be in essential agreement with the findings of Lehman. Rossman's (1935) studies of inventors indicate that inventors begin their work at even younger ages than do individuals in other fields. Of 710 inventors, 61 per cent made their first inventions before the age of twenty-five. The average age at the time of the first invention was 21.3 years. The most active period of patenting was between twenty-five and twenty-nine.

These data are of special significance in guiding creative talent. They provide a strong argument for encouraging talented individuals to accelerate in our schools so that they will be in a position to be productive during the period of greatest potential productivity. It also seems plausible that imaginative counselors can use these data in helping older individuals avoid some of the inhibiting factors which accompany age and thereby increase their chances for continued creative production.

SUMMARY

In this chapter, I have called attention to the potential usefulness of information about creative development and age-level characteristics in guiding creative talent. On the basis of the information available, it seems that we may expect decrements in creative thinking ability
and in creative production at about ages five, nine, and twelve—all
transitional periods in educational careers in our society. I have tried to
summarize some of the most careful thinking which has been done
concerning age-level characteristics in creative development in a form
which will be useful in guiding creative talent. Some of the research
concerning age and peak productivity was summarized. Its implications
for accelerating gifted youngsters to positions where they can be productive during this period of their greatest potential creativity was
noted. Also ways for helping older individuals avoid some of the conditions which probably account for decreased creativity after the age of
thirty or forty were discussed.

Chapter 6

PROBLEMS

IN MAINTAINING

CREATIVITY

Inescapably, the individual who thinks of a new idea is in the very beginning a minority of one. Even when matters of demonstrable fact are involved, as in the Asch (1955) experiments, there are very few people who can tolerate being a minority of one. Since creativity involves independence of mind, nonconformity to group pressures, or breaking out of the mold, it is inevitable that highly creative individuals experience some unusual problems of adjustment. Thus, the highly creative child must either repress his creativity or learn to cope with the tensions that arise from being so frequently this minority of one. Repression of creative needs may lead to actual personality breakdown. Their expression leads to loneliness, conflicts, and other problems of adjustment. Since teachers, administrators, and counselors need to understand both types of problems, this chapter will be devoted to a discussion of the problems involved in maintaining one's creativity and the next to the problems which result from sacrificing one's creativity. The two chapters which follow will be given over to a presentation of ideas whereby highly creative individuals can be aided through sound guidance programs.

In all of the remaining chapters, considerable use will be made of the imaginative stories of children about animals and persons having some divergent characteristic. Primarily, these are used to illustrate a principle and make it more vivid. I believe, however, that these stories provide us with some deep insights into the struggles of children to maintain their creativity and their perceptions of society's treatment of divergent behavior.

Gardner Murphy (1958) has identified the basis of many of the problems of creative people. He points out that they may suffer anguish arising from specific discoveries, through social disapproval, or through the fact that the social situation causes preoccupation with a particular area and leads to poor results. He also explains that an individual may discover that he has found all there is to be discovered at his level of operation or with his opportunities for investigation. The reader will find some of these threads running throughout the problems which I have identified in the Minnesota studies and in the stories of children concerning divergent behavior.

SANCTIONS AGAINST DIVERGENCY

Many of our society's coercive influences against divergency, even against outstanding performance, are reflected in the imaginative stories concerning flying monkeys and silent lions. Many of them sound very much like cautionary tales such as "Tootle," so eloquently attacked by Riesman (1955). The following is an example of one of these cautionary tales, the story of Lippy, "A Lion that Won't Roar":

> Lippy Lion, a friend of mine, has a little problem. He won't roar! He used to roar, but now he won't. His name used to be Roarer, too. I'll tell you why.
> When Roarer was about your age, he would always roar and scare people. Now this made his mother and father worry. Everybody was always complaining. So they decided they should talk to Roarer.

They went to his bedroom . . . But when they started talking he roared and scared them downstairs. So finally they went to a magician. They talked things over until he had an idea. Then the three went home together.

The magician said his words and said, "He'll never want to roar again."

The next morning he went to scare his mother by roaring, but all that came out was a little squeak. He tried again but only a squeak came out. But he pled and pled to get his roar back, so the magician made it so he could roar. But Roarer didn't believe him. So now that he can roar he won't.

Soon they had to name him Lippy.

Teachers, parents, and peers feel threatened when highly creative children express their creativity. Some of the questioning, experimenting, and wild ideas are annoying. In many respects, however, the annoyance can be tolerated more than the threat which this creative behavior poses. Adults do not know how to evaluate these unusual ideas or respond to the many questions. Creative behavior may be interpreted as aggressive or even hostile, and certainly it soon becomes just that, if ideas and questions are rejected. Thus, one of the problems becomes that of helping the creative child maintain his aggressiveness without being hostile, as Roarer had become.

This tale brings out another problem concerning the parents' expectation of counselors and school psychologists—the expectation that they will use some kind of magic. Frequently, counselors, psychologists, and teachers are expected to play an aversive role, such as that of the magician in the story of Lippy (once Roarer). Such a role is frequently expected of the mental hygiene clinic. Guidance workers must be alert to these expectations and prepared to play more positive roles. This problem will be discussed at length in Chapters 8 and 9.

About two-thirds of the stories about flying monkeys tell similar tales of conformity or of destruction. Some cultures, however, are more indulgent of divergency than others. Stories written by gifted children in special classes are far more hopeful in outlook than those of gifted children in regular classes. In about seventy per cent of the stories of pupils in classes for high achieving children, the flying monkey is in some way able to persist in his flying. The stories written by children in a small Oklahoma town composed of Indians, whites, and a few Negroes also reflect this tolerance of divergency. In seventy-four per cent of their stories, the flying monkey succeeds. He may meet obstacles which may be overcome, but there is little question that "a monkey can fly" and should do so. Some of this spirit is reflected in the following story by an Oklahoma sixth-grade boy:

> Once there was a flying monkey named Moonbeam. This monkey had fun every day romping and flying through the trees. One day he was flying around and some men were setting traps for him. As he was walking along, "snap!" the trap sprang. Then the men took him to the alligator pits. They slowly lowered him into the pits. Moonbeam was trying to break out, but the bars on his cage were strong. Suddenly they stopped lowering him. The men started to run. Then they fell into the pits. The men fell on Moonbeam's cage and broke a bar on it. Moonbeam crawled out of the cage and flew out of the pit and went for help. When the men were pulled out of the pit, they were rushed to jail.

The imaginative stories written by French children go even further than those of the Oklahoma children in their willingness to think imaginatively about the flying monkey and the silent lion, never questioning the possibility and never bothering to explain how the monkey learned to fly nor how the lion lost his ability to roar. The stories by Greek children do not question the possibility but are devoted largely to explanations about how the conditions occurred.

The following story by a gifted Long Island boy illustrates some of the dynamics of the plight of the gifted child who lacks some quality regarded as highly important by his society. It especially communicates the depth of the anxiety of the parents under such conditions.

> Freddy was born in a cave in the Rocky Mountains. He lived there with his mother and father and his ten brothers and sisters.
>
> The first thing a lion is supposed to learn is how to roar. His ten brothers and sisters learned how to roar very well, but Freddy wouldn't roar because he was a friendly lion. First, his mother tried to teach him. She tried and tried for ten days, after which she fainted. Then his father tried to teach him for eight months, but still Freddy wouldn't roar. So finally they gave up and ordered Freddy to go and find another place to live. . . .
>
> When Freddy walked into the jungle all of the animals ran and hid in the bushes. Freddy was very sad. He tried to make friends with the monkeys but they ran up the trees. He tried to make friends with the zebras but they ran away as fast as possible. All of a sudden there was complete silence as all of the animals waited for Freddy to roar. When he didn't roar, the animals were very surprised. Slowly one by one the animals came out from behind the bushes and down from the trees and

started to form a circle around Freddy. Then one of the animals brought up enough courage to go over and touch him. When Freddy didn't do anything, the animals went over to Freddy and started to play with him. Freddy and the animals became good friends. Until this day, Freddy hasn't roared.

This story may possibly reflect the author's childlike optimism that it is possible to escape the rejection of divergency.

MAINTAINING CREATIVITY MAY ALIENATE FRIENDS

Many highly creative children find quite early that the use of their creative talents alienates them from their friends. In the stories of flying monkeys, the exercise of the talent for flying quite frequently brings about isolation, warnings by parents that the other animals won't like the monkey, and the like. In the stories of silent lions, many are afraid to roar because they will either scare away their friends or alienate others in their society. The following such story illustrates a number of the dynamics of this problem:

> One sunny day, the king of the jungle and his wife were blessed with a cub. The king was so happy that he even gave cigars to his enemy, the monkey. Many animals came to see the cub.
> The cub was growing and his parents were getting worried. He was five and he hadn't roared once. His father decided that he was old enough to go to school and then maybe he would roar. The king hired a teacher to teach his son, John, who would soon rule the jungle. John did fine in arithmetic, spelling, and other subjects. But in roaring class he refused to roar! His teacher was startled; his mother fainted; and his father was amazed.
> That night John and his father went into the study to talk. John's father asked, "Why won't you roar, son?"
> John replied, "It scares all of the animals." John then told of his adventure when he was two years old. He had roared his loudest. He saw the monkeys and the other animals he had wanted to be his friends with run away. His father understood and told him that he should learn to roar louder to scare the bad animals. John said that he would make the bad good without roaring.

This story seems to me to duplicate many of the ones which I hear from parents of highly creative children.

The implications of this problem are exemplified in a recent study by Buhl (1961) of creative engineering students. On the basis of the AC Spark Plug Test of Creative Ability, Buhl compared the upper and lower quarters of a sample of 167 freshmen engineering students. He found that the highly creative engineer has a distinct desire to have warm and close personal relationships, to share his ideas with others, to discuss problems, and to find alternative viewpoints. He also wants to be only an average student, apparently because he is afraid that excelling will alienate him from such relationships and rob him of opportunities for the kind of sharing for which he recognizes a need. Buhl sees this desire to be only average a distinct threat to the development of creative engineers. He believes that this unwillingness to show scholastic excellence is due to present-day philosophies of education in elementary and secondary schools. He points out that competition is often discouraged in grading practices and remains only in athletics. Buhl found that the highly creative student admits to being faster than most, due largely to speed competition, but believes that he must conform to the "average," except in matters connected with sports.

In my opinion, this matter of competition is one which needs reevaluation by teachers and administrators. In my own research, I have found that competition increases tremendously the production and quality of ideas produced by children. "Warm-up" procedures can compensate only in part for these effects.

CREATIVE CHILDREN MAY NOT BE WELL-ROUNDED

The highly creative child is likely to have lagged in some phase of his development. Many investigators in a variety of fields have been disappointed in finding that outstanding individuals in the field under study are not well-rounded, "all-American" boys. For example, verbal abilities frequently will be below some of their other abilities. They may even have difficulty in learning to read or write. Perhaps the most inventive and imaginative child we have tested is a boy who has had unusual difficulty in learning to read, yet his store of information and his ability to use it imaginatively in solving problems and developing ideas is fantastic.

This problem is particularly acute at the fourth-grade level. In a

number of cases, fourth graders identified by our tests as highly creative have been re-evaluated by teachers. Teachers then discover that
these children are far more knowledgeable and thoughtful than they had
imagined. I was particularly struck by a comment made by the examiner after testing orally a certain fourth grade boy. The examiner
stated: "This boy impresses me as the kind of individual who will become a top executive who can dictate to five secretaries at the same
time without becoming confused." The boy's responses gave evidence
of high inventivlevel, flexibility, and originality. This boy, however, has
a serious reading disability and ranked near the bottom of his class on
the written test of creative thinking.

Because verbal skills are highly valued in our society, tremendous
pressures are placed on children to be "well-rounded" in this area. The
relentlessness of these pressures is symbolized in many of the stories
about lions that won't roar, ducks that won't quack, and dogs that
won't bark. Some of the authors of the stories deplored the relentless
pressures exerted by adults. One referred to those who exert such pressures as "chasers and quackers." Some children resist pressures to become
well-rounded because they feel that they can win and maintain respect
in more acceptable ways than the commonly approved and expected
ways of the society. The struggle involved when this occurs is symbolized in the following story:

> In the vast wilds of the Congo jungle came the trumpeting of a bull
> elephant announcing the coming of a great contest. . . .
>
> It was the message most of the animals had been waiting for. The
> message that there was to be a new King of the Beasts. The great Bamula
> had been killed by his enemies and there had been no definite decision
> about how the new King was to be chosen.
>
> Now at last it had come. There was to be a contest testing the animals'
> strength and ability to handle all of the most difficult problems. . . . All
> of the animals, especially the lions went strutting around boasting of their
> strength and other matters concerning their beauty, intelligence, and
> swiftness of foot. At night they all sat around the water hole admiring
> and comparing their images by the light of the silver-blue moon.
>
> All of the animals were excited about the coming event, all but one.
> As you would least expect, it was a lion. He just sat on the banks of the
> Chevkrus River thinking and staring into the almost-dry ditch where
> clear waters used to run. Now and then a tear trickled down his face. . . .
>
> Why was he crying? After all, he was a lion and was as beautiful, in-
> telligent, strong and swift as any of the other animals. For one reason,

they thought he was stupid. They jeered at him and called him names and showered him with remarks such as, "You'd better watch out or you'll trip over your mane" and "Where's your cat food?"

The poor lion hadn't done anything wrong, but the reason they poked fun at him was that he was different from anyone else. He wouldn't roar. . . .

Then he decided, "I guess the only way to show them I'm not an idiot is to win that contest!"

. . . There were 300 contestants, one thousand spectators, and 57 judges. The first part of the contest was held in a gigantic arena. A chill went over the audience as into it tore a gorilla. He was the most brutal beast I have ever seen. . . . Only 249 remained to go on to the next contest. The lion was among them. The next contest was to test their intelligence. Five judges led the remaining contestants into the most savage and unknown parts of the jungle blindfolded and turned them loose. Of the 249 who entered, only 21 returned. The rest were left to die or be eaten by some unknown beast.

The lion was among the 21 and he was still just as determined to win as before. The next contest was to test their swiftness of foot. Two judges told them their route which was to cover 39 miles of rugged country. They would have to go over hot rocks, under waterfalls, and through rivers. The lion and the cheta tied for first place, but the lion beat the cheta in the last contest of beauty, for his majestic golden mane and tail and his good posture outdid the cheta, since he was too bony.

The lion has ruled all of the other beasts to this day and his subjects honor and respect him so much that he never has to raise his voice. He doesn't have to roar.

CREATIVE CHILDREN MAY DIVERGE FROM SEX NORMS

Our over emphasis or misplaced emphasis on sex roles and efforts to establish sex norms during early childhood and throughout the educational ladder makes many problems for highly creative children. We have usually thought that this emphasis takes its toll only on the creativity of women. It has been pointed out frequently that rarely do women become scientific discoverers, inventors, or composers. Over emphasis or misplaced emphasis on sex roles, however, does exact its toll on the creativity of both sexes and does create serious problems of adjustment for highly creative individuals of both sexes.

Creativity, by its very nature, requires both sensitivity and independence. In our culture, sensitivity is definitely a feminine virtue, while independence is a masculine value. Thus, we may expect the highly creative boy to appear to be more effeminate than his peers and the highly creative girl to appear more masculine than hers. Roe (1959), Barron (1957), and I (1959b) have all cited evidence in support of this phenomenon. In our longitudinal studies we are finding interesting examples of children who sacrifice their creativity in order to maintain their "masculinity" or their "femininity," as the case may be.

This cultural block to creativity comes out in many places. We first observed it in our Product Improvement Test in which children are asked to think of all the ideas they can for improving common toys so that they will be more fun to play with. In the first grade, boys excelled girls on the fire truck, but girls excelled boys on the nurse's kit. Many of the boys refused to think of anything to make the nurse's kit more fun, protesting, "I'm a boy! I don't play with things like that!" Some of the more creative boys, however, first transformed it into a doctor's kit and as such were quite free to think of improvements. By the third grade, however, boys excelled girls even on the nurse's kit, probably because girls have been conditioned by this time to accept toys as they are and not to manipulate or change them.

The inhibiting effects of sex-role conditioning also showed up in our experiments involving small groups working with science toys (Torrance, 1960b). Girls were quite reluctant to work with these science toys and frequently protested, "I'm a girl; I'm not supposed to know anything about things like that!" Boys demonstrated and explained about twice as many ideas as girls in experiments involving these materials. We know already, however, that this situation can be modified significantly (Torrance, 1960b). In 1959, we found these phenomena operating quite strongly in one school. Later I had the opportunity to report these and other results to both the teachers and parents in this school. In 1960, we conducted some experiments in this same school in which we used a different but similar set of science toys. This time, we found none of this reluctance on the part of girls; there was no difference in the expressed enjoyment of the activity of boys and girls; the mean performance of girls and boys was almost identical. In one way, however, the situation remained unchanged. The contributions of boys was more highly valued by peers than those of girls. Apparently, the school climate has helped to make it more acceptable for girls to play around with science things, but boys' ideas about science things are still supposed to be better than those of girls.

The social consequences of failure to achieve the behavioral norms associated with sex and social roles are well understood by children by the time they reach the fourth grade, if not before. Such an understanding is reflected in the following story by a young Illinois author:

> "No! No! No! I won't roar! I won't! I won't! I won't roar and scare all those little animals," said Roarless, the lion.
>
> "But that is the purpose of roaring," said his mother. "You want to roar to scare the animals. You are the king of beasts and the king of beasts roars."
>
> "No! No! No! I just won't! I won't! I won't! I don't care if I am the king of beasts and can't roar," said Roarless again.
>
> "For the millionth time, Roarless, please roar," said his mother.
>
> "And for the millionth time, I won't roar," shouted Roarless.
>
> That is Roarless and his mother arguing. Ever since he was a little cub he has not wanted to roar because he thought he would scare the other animals. When he was little his father made a roar so loud that it scared Roarless. Now, let's get back to their arguing.
>
> "All right! All right! I won't argue with you," said his mother. "I'm going out for a while. Good bye."
>
> "Good bye."
>
> Then all of a sudden Roarless said, "R-R-R-R-R-R-ROAR!"
>
> Then his mother rushed in and said, "Oh, my baby, at last you have roared. We should call you Roarful instead of Roarless."
>
> "I still think I scared the animals," sadly said Roarless—I mean Roarful.

This tale illustrates two other points of importance in guiding creative children. Counselors and teachers can expect that many highly creative children will be under severe pressure to pursue occupations which will fulfill family expectations. Many of these individuals resist these pressures for a long time, holding out for some occupation in which they can more adequately express their creativity. Unrelenting pressures such as those exerted by the mother of Roarless are extremely stressful. Even the resistant, creative youngster has his "breaking point" and cannot hold out indefinitely.

Another problem may be seen in the negative identification which apparently exists between Roarless and his father. Because of early, unpleasant relationships with the father, Roarless identifies himself as being different from his father. Thus, if roaring makes him like his father, Roarless is motivated to avoid roaring.

CREATIVE CHILDREN PREFER TO LEARN ON THEIR OWN

Many creative children prefer to learn on their own, but schools have been slow in providing such opportunities. Last year we conducted an exciting study in which we found that children would do a great deal of writing on their own, if properly motivated. In another (Fritz, 1958), it was found that gifted children in a split-shift school showed more growth in language development, science, and social studies than they did on a full-day schedule. Only in spelling was there significantly less growth among the split-shift children (seventh graders). In still another, we found that children in a split-shift school engaged in a larger number of learning activities on their own.

Since we have generally assumed that children do not learn on their own, we have seldom provided them with opportunities to do so. I have seen learning situations left "open" a sufficient number of times to have become quite excited about what would happen, if we should do so more frequently. The following story by an Oklahoma Indian girl in the sixth grade, symbolizes this situation:

> Once there were some monkeys sitting in a group. They were all alike except three monkeys. They were very different because they could fly.
> One day some men from a park zoo were looking for some monkeys because theirs had died. They came upon the three that flew. So they took them in a cage. The cage didn't have a top to it. They were in the sun one day and the monkey said to the other, "I wish we could get out of here."
> "Then, why don't we fly out of here?" said the other.
> They started to fly out. When they got about half a mile, some men came to feed them. When they couldn't find the three monkeys, they saw them flying away. One of them said, "If we would have put them in a cage with a top, we would have had a real good thing here in the zoo."

One function of the school counselor might be to help highly creative children recognize or discover the "openings" in their cages, or selves, to which they might be blinded.

CREATIVE CHILDREN LIKE TO
ATTEMPT DIFFICULT TASKS

Frequently highly creative children strongly desire to move far ahead of their classmates in some areas. They often make their teachers afraid that they are not "ready." Fortunately, however, educators of gifted children are rapidly revising many of their concepts about what can be taught at various levels of education. This terrifies many. The following recent headlines reflect such a fear:

"Caution Urged in Changing Primary into High Schools"

"Can We Rush Primary Education?"

"Don't Turn Grade Schools into High Schools, Educators Warn at Parley"

"Reading for Kindergarten, Languages Too Soon Attacked"

Some of the panic may have been eased by a recent report of the Educational Policies Commission of the National Education Association and the American Association of School Administrators (*Contemporary Issues in Elementary Education,* 1960).

Bruner's (1960) exciting book, *The Process of Education,* should give educators some very useful guidance in working out this problem. Along with revisions about readiness, Bruner develops the concept of "structure of knowledge" and offers interesting ideas about intuition and motivation. About readiness, he says, "Experience over the past decade points to the fact that our schools may be wasting precious years by postponing the teaching of many subjects on the grounds that they are too difficult. . . . The essential point often overlooked in the planning of curricula . . . [is that] the basic ideas that lie at the heart of all science and mathematics and the basic schemes that give form to life and literature are powerful." For this purpose, Bruner suggests "the spiral curriculum," one that turns back on itself at higher and higher levels of complexity.

A very frequent theme in our imaginative stories is related to this problem. The young animal or fowl asks, "When can I roar? When can I crow? When can I quack? When can I fly?" Almost always, the answer is, "When you are a little older." We are always afraid that the young one might not be ready to learn and that he would be forever scarred by even the most temporary failure. On this score, we might note the persistence of the fifth-grade Negro boy from Georgia who wrote the following story:

> Once there was a monkey that was very sad. He was sad because he didn't know how to fly. He said to himself, "Why can other animals fly but we can't fly?" Then he began to climb up a tree; he ate some bananas and coconuts. The monkey jumped out of the tree and began to fly. He fell down on the ground. Then the monkey climbed the tree again and began to try to fly. Again he fell to the ground. Again he climbed up and finally he began to fly.

A common experience in the lives of many highly outstanding individuals has been their ability to cope with failure and frustration. Certainly, almost all highly creative scientists, inventors, artists, and writers attempt tasks which are too difficult for them. Had they not attempted such tasks, it is quite unlikely that their great ideas would have been born.

CREATIVE CHILDREN MAY
UNDERTAKE DANGEROUS TASKS

In learning on their own and in testing their limits through attempting difficult tasks, creative children may also undertake dangerous tasks. This poses difficult problems for parents, teachers, playground directors, and school administrators who have responsibilities for the safety of children. I have frequently wondered if the solution to this problem doesn't lie in the technique of the parents of the jet aces of the Korean struggle. We found that the parents of these aces both exercised more control and permitted more testing-the-limits and risk-taking behavior than did the parents of the non-aces. They exercised control until skills were adequate and then permitted wide testing of the limits. Their children then could say in sincerity, "This would be dangerous for most boys or most pilots, but for me it is quite safe."

The usual type of control, however, would seem to be more in line with the theme of the following cautionary tale written by a fifth-grade boy:

There was a monkey that liked to tease people. He would pull the lion's tail and would bite the baby tiger cubs. One day he got tired of teasing the same ones. So he started thinking. "I'll tease the crocodile," he thought. The next morning he started working to fix a vine just short enough to swing down on. As soon as he was all finished, he was going to fly down by the crocodile and kick him. He was ready to try it out. He flew right into the crocodile's mouth. Now there isn't any little flying monkey to tease anyone.

This story illustrates another problem of some children in expressing their creativity. Their sense of humor is frequently not appreciated, especially if it has been tinted by hostility and resentment. It may create difficult problems of discipline for the teacher and school administrator.

CREATIVE CHILDREN ARE SEARCHING FOR A PURPOSE

It has been said that most outstanding creative achievers seem to be possessed by a purpose and to be "men of destiny." Creative children need some purpose which is worthy of the enthusiastic devotion they seem capable of giving. Some of this need is symbolized in the following story by a sixth-grade boy:

There was once a South American monkey that didn't know what he was, who he was, or why he was even alive. He decided that he didn't know even the way to figure it out, so he thought he would make up a reason.

He had seen many airplanes overhead. He had seen many ferocious animals, many nice animals, and many machines. He had always thought that it would be nice to fly, so he pretended he was an airplane.

He had also heard that buzzing sound of the engines, so he called himself "Buzz." He also decided that he was a real fast flyer so that this was the reason he was alive.

Now we all know that monkeys can't fly, but he didn't know this. Why he didn't even know that he was a monkey, so he kept trying and trying—and you know what? He flew!

Perhaps this has some implications not only concerning the need for helping children discover their potentialities but for helping them achieve their self-concepts creatively rather than by authority.

We also need to help highly creative individuals accept themselves, remembering that they may even despise an outstanding "gift," if their giftedness makes them different from others. This makes far too many gifted children willing to emasculate themselves and consciously or unconsciously hide or destroy their talents. The following story by a St. Paul girl illustrates this point effectively:

> Once in a big forest lived a monkey. This monkey was very different. He could fly. All the other monkeys in the jungle envied him. . . .
> Now one day this monkey was flying over the forest and saw a lion with a big mane. . . . He flew down and asked, "Where did you get that big mane, Mr. King?"
> "I don't know," he answered. "I guess it's just a sign of royalty."
> Then the monkey was wondering if he could have a mane like Mr. King. He flew home and asked his mother, who couldn't fly. She said, "I wouldn't like to have my son be a flying monkilion." So the monkey walked into his bedroom and sat on the bed. "Why can't I be like other monkeys?" . . .
> Then as he was turning his head, he accidentally caught sight of his mother's button box. He got up and walked over to it and took the scissors. Then he took them over to his bed and stuck them under the covers. His mother walked in, and he moved over to where he had put the scissors and said, "Yee-oowww!" as he jumped up and hit his head on the ceiling. After that, he had a big bump on his head.
> Later that night his mother asked him what he was going to do with the scissors. Of course he told the truth and said, "I was going to cut my wings off because I don't like to be odd. I want to be like other monkeys."

CREATIVE CHILDREN HAVE DIFFERENT VALUES

Counselors and teachers should recognize that the values and attitudes of the highly creative student are likely to be different from those of other students. The very fact that he is capable of a high order of divergent thinking, has unusual ideas, and is independent in his thinking in itself is likely to make his values and attitudes different from the norms of his peer group. Some of these differences have been highlighted in the Getzels and Jackson (1959) study. They found that for the high IQ group, the rank-order correlation between the qualities making for adult success was .81 (showing great similarity); for the high creativity group it was .10 (indicating little or no similarity). Among the highly intelligent, the correlation between the qualities they desired and the qualities they believed teachers favor was .67 (moderately similar); for the highly creative group, it was minus .25 (actually somewhat dissimilar). In other words, the highly creative adolescent desires personal qualities having little relationship to those he believes make for adult success and are in some way opposite those he believes his teachers favor. Thus, counselors and teachers should recognize that the desire to emulate the teacher is absent or weak among creative students. The desire to emulate peers is also weak, as I have found in some of my own studies.

Getzels and Jackson (1959) also found a certain mocking attitude on the part of the creatives toward what they call the "All-American Boy"—a theme almost totally lacking in the stories of the highly intelligent group. This highlights once more the problem of helping highly creative students learn to maintain their creativity without being obnoxious. In some way or other, this rejection of the values and rewards of the majority comes out in most studies of highly creative individuals. Perhaps this too is a function of divergency in general. This rejection of the usual values is illustrated in the following story by a New York boy of a lion that wouldn't roar:

> . . . I was on a hike in the forest with the boys in the Boy Scout pack I belong to. . . . This forest was known because some people had seen a lion. We went to prove that there wasn't one. So far there is no proof that there is one. Wait a minute! Look at this footprint! It looks like a lion's! Now that we have proof, let's go. It's funny. No roar.
> Here is a lion! A lion! Let's go!
> "I won't hurt you," he said.
> "A talking lion!"
> "Yes, I like to talk. Is there anything wrong with talking?"
> "No, but lions are supposed to roar."
> "I get a sore throat when I roar, so I gave up roaring and started talking. Old fashioned lions roar."
> "No wonder we didn't hear any roar. Will you come back to the city?"
> "Not in a cage I won't!"
> "If you don't hurt anybody, well-ll, okay."
> "But now I am hungry. I want something to eat."
> "What do you eat?"
> "Canned foods. Mostly beans. I scare hunters. They run and leave their food."

"You can have our beans. After a trip to the city, you can make a million dollars."

"All I want is to go back to a big jungle in Africa and start a tribe of talking lions and have friends. Millions of dollars later, I would buy a ticket to Africa and stay. I have no use for this money so you five boys can have it for helping me."

SOME CREATIVE CHILDREN
CAN'T STOP WORKING

Many people misinterpret the motivations of highly creative individuals who can't seem to stop working. Few creative individuals can stand the pressure of working only a forty-hour week. This is interpreted as an attempt to outdo others, rise to a position of power or favor, or such. Creative individuals, however, do not usually care for power and some of the other usual rewards. The exercise of their creative powers is itself a reward, and to them, the most important reward. One sixth-grade Oklahoma boy grasped this truth in the following story of Carlor, a flying monkey who was a fisherman:

> There was a flying monkey named Carlor. He was a fisherman. One day they went out for tuna. Carlor flew ahead to have a look. There in front of his eyes was the biggest tuna he had ever seen. Quickly he got his harpoon gun and shot it. Then he took it back to the boat.
>
> The next day they had a feast on the big tuna. Carlor ate so much his sides croaked. The next morning they headed back to land and unloaded their catch.
>
> His wife had come into a fortune of pearls, money, jewels, and other things. . . . But Carlor was very sad because he couldn't work any more now, for they were awfully rich.
>
> The next morning Carlor secretly flew back to his fishing fleet.

The creative individual is unable to stop working because he can't stop thinking. To him, there is nothing more enjoyable than work in which he can use his creative powers.

CREATIVE CHILDREN SEARCH FOR
THEIR UNIQUENESS

Counselors and teachers may become irritated with creative children who seem to create problems for themselves by trying consciously to be different—searching for their uniqueness. Barron (1958) maintains that creative individuals reject the demands of their society to surrender their individuality because "they want to own themselves totally and because they perceive a shortsightedness in the claim of society that all its members should adapt themselves to a norm for a given time and place."

Some interesting aspects of this search for one's uniqueness is reflected in the following story by a sixth-grade girl:

> There was once a monkey named Holace. Holace was very sad. He sat in his circus cage all day doing tricks when all of his monkey friends were highlights of the Cling Ling Brothers Circus.
>
> His friend, Bayberry, was an organ grinder man while his little friend Stuart was his monkey. My how everyone laughed and clapped at his friends. He rode a bicycle, but Barberry could ride one with no hands. He tried swinging on a bar by his tail but Stuart could do that. . . .
>
> One day he was swinging by his tail thinking of what he could do and he started to fall. Holace didn't want to be ashamed by falling, so he grabbed the bar that was swinging. All the people clapped for it seemed to them that he was flying through the air like a trapeze artist.
>
> When one of the Cling Ling brothers heard the noise, he rushed out. When he saw Holace flying through the air, he gasped in amazement. The next day there was a new sign that said: "The World's Only Flying Monkey." Can you guess who that is? Of course, it's Holace, the new star of the Cling Ling Brothers Circus. Now there are many who do this act, but they are all copying Holace.

As with Holace, one way in which the creative individual searches for his uniqueness is through his vocational choice. Getzels and Jackson (1960), for example, found that their highly creative subjects gave a greater number of different occupations and more "unusual" or rare occupations than their highly intelligent subjects.

THE PSYCHOLOGICAL ESTRANGEMENT OF CREATIVE CHILDREN

From the foregoing it should be obvious that a large share of the highly creative child's adjustment problems are likely to be centered in his psychological isolation and estrangement from his peers and teachers. It will be no news to counselors that peer groups exercise rather severe pressures against their most creative members. In no group thus far studied have we failed to find relatively clear evidence of the operation of these pressures, though they are far more severe in some classrooms than in others.

When we select the most creative members of each sex in each classroom and match them for sex and Intelligence Quotient with other children in the same classroom, as already described in Chapter 4, three characteristics stand out as differentiating the highly creative children from the less creative ones. First, there is a tendency for them to gain a reputation for having wild or silly ideas. Second, their work is characterized by its productivity of ideas "off the beaten track." Third, they are characterized by humor and playfulness. All of these characteristics help explain both the estrangement and the creativity.

Interesting insights are furnished by the clinical data in our longitudinal data. The handling of windows and doors in the drawings of houses suggests some hypotheses concerning the psychological accessibility of highly creative children. According to Buck (1948) the openness of the house through its windows and doors provides an index of the child's psychological inaccessibility. It was noted that some of our most creative children omitted windows and doors altogether in their drawings, drew them abnormally high on the house, or made them extremely small. Of special interest is the house shown in Figure 8, drawn by Subject J, an exceptionally creative third-grade boy. At the time the drawing was done the hypothesis concerning psychological inaccessibility was certainly valid for this subject. The teacher, principal, parents, and school social worker were all greatly concerned about this boy. At times, he would be so preoccupied with his own thoughts that he would be quite unaware of what was happening in the classroom. He was also having difficulty in learning to read and to write down his thoughts. In spite of this, however, it was quite evident that he had amassed a great deal of information, especially in science, and could use it in solving problems and in thinking of new and original ideas of a very high quality. Something of the magnitude of this boy's problem was seen when we found that twelve of his thirty-three classmates nominated him as having ideas for being naughty, and twelve as having wild or silly ideas. No one nominated him as having good ideas, in spite of his truly exceptional talent. Findings from another study by the author indicate that nominations on the "good ideas" criterion is related to percentage of good ideas produced rather than to the actual number of good ideas produced.

The results of an experimental study also helps us to understand this problem. In this study, we formed groups of five children and in each we placed one of the most creative children in the classroom, as identified by our tests. We then placed each group in a situation requiring creative thinking and involving competition among groups. The focus of observation during this hour-long activity was upon the techniques used by the groups to control the most creative member and the behavior of the most creative member in coping with these pressures. Much of the behavior observed suggests that the highly creative individual may be responsible for many of his own woes.

At the second-grade level, the most highly creative individuals were generally quite unpleasant, showing little consideration for the group, little or no goal orientation, little or no identification with the group and little or no heed to the leadership attempts of their less creative peers. In the third grade, the most creative subjects tended to work

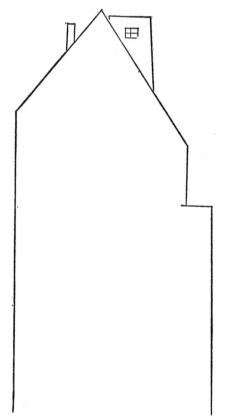

FIGURE 8. *House Drawn by Subject J, an Exceptionally Creative Third-Grade Boy.*

independently and were ignored for the most part. This tendency persisted in the fourth grade where the most creative members assumed little responsibility for leadership and were given little credit in the final ratings for the important contributions which they actually made to the group's success. The highly creatives in the fifth grade manifested more leadership attempts than in the fourth grade but brought upon themselves open criticism and attack for "being too scientific," "being too greedy," and such. These tendencies became more pronounced in the sixth-grade groups.

SUMMARY

The fundamental problem of the highly creative individual in maintaining his creativity is in learning how to cope with the discomfort which arises from divergency—of so often being a minority of one. Of the problems which arise in this process some of the more important ones include: coping with the sanctions of society against divergency, the alienation of one's friends through the expression of a talent, pressures to be a well-rounded personality, divergence from sex-role norms, desires to learn on one's own, attempts at tasks which are too difficult, searching for a purpose, having different values and being motivated by different rewards, and searching for one's uniqueness. Running throughout all of these problems, of course, are factors which lead to psychological estrangement from others—parents, teachers, and peers.

7

PROBLEMS
WHEN CREATIVITY
IS REPRESSED

Evidence from both cross-sectional and longitudinal studies of the development of the creative thinking abilities suggests that many highly creative children at almost all ages sacrifice their creativity by repressing their creative needs and abandoning creative activities. For some children, this occurs during the kindergarten period. With favorable conditions in the primary school, some of them recover, but apparently some do not. The next really serious period of abandonment occurs near the end of the third grade or at about the beginning of the fourth. Again, some recover while others apparently sacrifice their creativity permanently. The third period of decline occurs at about the time the individual enters junior high school, and another occurs near the end of the high school period.

In this chapter, I shall present some ideas concerning the problems which arise for those who choose to sacrifice their creativity by denying their creative needs at these various periods of educational development. In attempting to do this, I shall begin with some of the milder problems arising from this repression and proceed to some of the more severe consequences, if the stifling of creative needs is severe and/or prolonged.

FAULTY OR UNCERTAIN SELF-CONCEPT

The creative child who abandons his creativity sometimes becomes a very conforming, too obedient child. As a consequence, he is likely to grow up with a lack of confidence in his own thinking, be uncertain of his self-concept and be overly dependent upon others in making decisions. An effort was made in the fourth chapter to show the importance of being free to test one's limits through experimentation and exploratory activities. Without this, a child cannot know his capabilities and potentialities.

Leo, the lion in the following story, is an example of failure to develop potentialities as a result of refusing to explore one's limits:

> Leo, the lion, walked softly in the forest. He was a very beautiful lion with a thick mane and a very, very soft roar. In fact, I wouldn't call it a roar. It was just a soft meow. As he was walking one day, he met Mrs. Deer.
> "Why," asked Mrs. Deer, "don't you roar?"
> Leo grinned sheepishly, "The fact is I never tried except once and I scared myself half out of my wits."
> "Why don't you try now?" asked Mrs. Deer. "I'm sure we can quiet your roar."
> "No," disagreed Leo. "Someday later."

Children may also fail to develop realistic self-concepts because they have not been provided situations in which it is safe to practice without evaluation. They realized that their productions do not measure up to those of adults and therefore fear rejection or failure. The following story of the lion that wouldn't roar because he was ashamed of his small roar illustrates this difficulty:

> Once there was a lion that wouldn't roar because he was ashamed of it. It was only a little roar like a mouse's.

One day he went out in the village and tried to roar big and loud but the same little squeak came out. He went home not happy because everyone had laughed at his little roar.

So he roared only at home where no one would hear him. One day he was at home trying and trying hard to roar until his throat got sore. . . . He tried again one day and he got the same little squeak, but he never stopped and about when he was ready to give up he stopped and he could roar big and loud.

Many of the stories differ from the one above in that they reflect the belief that persistent practice and the gradual development of deficient skills is not necessary. If there is a genuine need, the skill will be available. The following story of John, another lion that won't roar, illustrates this rather widespread belief:

Once there was a lion named John. He had two friends, Steven and Chester. Chester always roared so loud that other animals were afraid of him. Steven roared very loud, too. But John would not roar because he didn't want to scare any animals. . . .

On the second day of school, the children lions had a roaring bee. The teacher wanted to find out who could roar the loudest, but John would not roar at all.

In a few weeks they had a test. One of the questions was, "If you are in danger should you roar?" Everyone put "yes" for an answer except John. John put "no."

One day John took a walk in the jungle. Soon he met a hungry elephant. The elephant did not have very good eyesight (in fact, that very day he broke his glasses) and he thought John was some food. The elephant started after him and John did not know what to do. He started thinking and then he remembered something on the test. It was: "If you are in danger, should you roar?" He knew the answer was "yes." He tried to roar and he roared so loud he broke the elephant's ear drums. . . .

The really tragic kind of disability occurs in the case of the potentially creative individual who never finds anything which challenges him, anything worthy of his best efforts. The trouble is that he fails to learn basic skills and later bogs down because he does not have the fundamental skills for doing the creative work which he desires to do.

Over self-evaluation can be as damaging as under-evaluation and this type of unrealistic self-concept is usually fostered by the kind of adaptation symbolized by the behavior of the lions in the two preceding stories.

Some potentially creative children develop very unrealistic self-concepts because of incorrect diagnoses. I have known some truly creative children, as identified both by their observed behavior and by individually administered tests of creative thinking, who have been labeled as "slow learners" or "stupid." Since no one expects them to learn and they are not given challenging tasks, they make little progress until something happens to change the diagnosis, usually some accidental happening such as a substitute teacher, tests administered by an outsider, or the like. Such was the case of the lion named Harold in the following story by a sixth-grade girl:

> Harold was a lion, a very timid lion. He wouldn't eat meat like the other lions would or growl when people came near. On top of that, he wouldn't roar. All he would do was make a sort of whimper. Lion tamers didn't like him because he was already tame.
>
> One day, when the usual feeder of the animals was sick, a resourceful young man took his place. He thought he would give the lions a new kind of meat. He wasn't told that Harold wouldn't eat meat, so he gave it to Harold anyway.
>
> Now Harold had never had this food before. He wondered what it was. He thought he would try some. He did and he loved the stuff. Then he got it every day and soon he got to feeling so good he started roaring louder than the other lions.

LEARNING DISABILITIES

Children who repress their creativity may develop serious learning disabilities. They learn to repress their natural tendency to learn creatively by questioning, guessing, exploring, and experimenting. As a result, they learn to prefer learning by authority. From her clinical experience Leah Levinger has given an excellent example of such an intellectually gifted boy:

> Rod, a new student, is a sophomore in my high school. He came of his own initiative to my office, worried because he is doing less brilliantly now than in the lower grades, and wanting to know if his powers were slipping or whether it was the fault of the way this school taught. His teachers' reports merit quoting . . . not only to illustrate this example, but to give us brief samples of the way creative teachers articulate and conceptualize about the learning process. . . .

The Spanish teacher reports: "Rod had Spanish before and made straight A's. Here at the beginning he made straight D's. He relied too heavily on his previous record and did not really study, though he put in the required time. He tended to feel his poor work was due to our methods. He was accustomed to learning piecemeal for small tasks. He had no idea how to relate different aspects of grammar study into an expressive whole." The English teacher concurred, although she noted he had done considerably more reading than the class requirement. "His interests seem to lie primarily in factual areas, and I doubt that he is either interested in or challenged by work on style or finer points of analysis. He is still quite immature and easily confused when he is asked to do something that requires thought and judgment; what he wants is a step by step outline of each assignment or procedure. I don't think he is exclusively a grade-getter, but he is certainly more interested in grades than he is in some of our work, which probably seems unnecessary or impractical to him." The same pattern occurs in Rod's favorite subject, mathematics. This teacher commented that his approach was probably more appropriate for elementary school demands of mastering computation than for the critical thinking he required in mastering modern mathematics.

When I gave Rod a battery of psychological tests I saw a truly brilliant mind, grimly focused on how well he was doing, devoid of curiosity or delight in solving problems. As Rod and I have had counseling contacts we have discussed what is making him examination fodder, unable to use his gifts. I told him about Wertheimer's *Productive Thinking* and he was startled by the concept of "sensible errors." He is so imbued with the need for the right answers that I do not know whether, at the age of 15, he can recapture a love for questions, or develop tolerance for the unknown. . . .—1959, pp. 294–95

When prevented from learning creatively, some children will lose interest in learning and refuse to learn by authority. Elizabeth Drews (1960) has given us an excellent example of such a boy:

Tim, a fourth-grader, gave every evidence of developing into a scientist. His interests ranged from electricity through crustaceans and birds to geological specimens. Most of these interests were displayed in one way or another on, in and around his desk. He had dry cells, rocks, an abalone shell from California, and a robin's egg from the year before.

His previous teacher had encouraged his far-ranging interests and his willingness to share with his classmates. This year he had a new kind of teacher, a young man just out of military service, who was accustomed to neatness and discipline and took a jaundiced view of Tim's projects.

One day the teacher ordered the boy to take the clutter home and keep it there. Tim did, but his heart was broken. From that time on, he refused to learn. When he took his standardized achievement tests, he ranked below grade level! His only educational venture in the classroom for the rest of the year was to learn the Morse code and teach it to his classmates.

We also find such learning disabilities described in the stories by children about animals and people with special disabilities. Here is one about a lion that wouldn't roar. He is afraid to try to roar, because he is afraid that his roar might not sound like a lion:

> There was once a lion that wouldn't roar. His mother and father tried everything. They set all kinds of animals in front of him except an elephant. But the little lion still would not roar. Then finally the little lion's mother and father called a lion doctor. The doctor told the mother and father lion that the little lion was afraid to roar because he thought that it might not sound like a lion.
> So one day the little lion was walking through the jungle and saw a great big elephant. He was so scared that he ran off *roaring*. . . .

It is frequently difficult, even for an understanding teacher or counselor, to help some children overcome their awe of masterpieces, to recognize that even a roar is achieved only by trying, improving, modifying, and perfecting.

Feelings of inadequacy in one area also cause a highly creative child to develop learning difficulties in other areas where there are no fundamental defects. These sometimes show up in speech problems, as in the following story of Kenny, another silent lion:

> Kenny the lion was going to roaring school for the first time. On the way to roaring school, he met another lion named Steven.
> Steven said, "Listen how I roar!" and he roared so loud he scared Kenny.
> Then Steven said, "Let's see how you roar."
> Kenny roared and Steven said, "That was a sissy roar."
> At school when it was Kenny's turn to roar he got scared. He roared and everybody laughed. The teacher said, "You don't roar good, Kenny."
> Kenny went to school until report cards came out. He had failed in roaring and his father said, "You should listen to your teacher."
> The next morning when his mother came up to his room, he pointed to his mouth. His mother said, "What's the matter, Kenny?"
> He wrote on a piece of paper that he couldn't roar or talk. . . . The doctor said, "I don't know what's wrong with him."
> His mother took him home and told his father that Kenny couldn't roar or talk. . . .

. . . Kenny went to the Magic Man and bought some roaring serum. He went into the jungle with it and roared. That roar was a sissy roar. An elephant nearby heard it. He came and saw Kenny. Now Kenny took the serum. All of a sudden the elephant charged and he roared. It was such a scary roar, it scared the elephant away. He went home and told his mother and father the story and he could really roar and talk all of the time.

BEHAVIOR PROBLEMS

The teacher or school counselor is likely to meet many highly creative children who are behavior problems. In the early grades, highly creative children receive many more nominations for "think [ing] of the most ideas for being naughty" than average or highly intelligent children. After gaining this kind of reputation it is difficult for the teacher or classmates to see the good ideas as anything but silly or naughty.

Our flying monkey and silent lion stories include examples of both the aggressive and withdrawn types of behavior. Most frequent is the monkey who "tears things up" when an effort is made to restrain him from flying or when sanctions are exercised against him. The silent lion is also a potential threat, as we see in the following story by an Oklahoma sixth-grader:

Once in the dark continent of Africa, there was a group of silent lions that couldn't roar!

One day there was a safari going through the land of the silent lions. It was quiet! Too quiet! But the safari kept going.

All at once the lions jumped out of the bushes and killed every man! About a year later another safari was attacked by the same lions. Then about a year later another safari was wiped out.

It happened again and again and again!

Then about 20 years later a group of scientists from America came over to Africa to investigate the happenings. They found out where the lions were and killed every one of them.

And this was the end of the silent lions.

Catherine Patrick (1955) has offered some interesting hypotheses concerning the creative thinking of the psychopathic personality. She explains that such individuals have experienced severe conflicts. Faced with difficult problems and being distressed and unhappy, the psychopathic deviate finally has a hunch. According to Patrick, "this 'wonderful idea' gives him such pleasure after his severe unhappiness that the psychopathic individual clings to it and is loath to undergo the discouragement inherent in the final stage of revision and verification." Because he shrinks from testing his solution, he spends hours elaborating upon it instead of verifying and revising it. Or he rushes out and applies his erroneous solution and gets into difficulty.

It seems, then, that the creative child with behavior problems is likely to have two major deficiencies in his thinking. First, he jumps to a premature closure or actually thinks of too few possibilities. Second, he fails to test and revise his hunches or hypotheses, and consequently, he fails to learn from experience.

There are many possible reasons why highly creative children who sacrifice their creativity become behavior problems and develop the deficiencies in their thinking described in the preceding paragraphs. I suspect that one of the primary reasons is the failure of the school to give them challenging tasks. Thus, much misbehavior may be seen as a reaction to the unchallenging, boring, reproductive tasks given them in school. In other words, they are on a "sit down strike" for better "food," as we see in the following story:

> It was 7:45 and I was sitting in my chair. (I work for the Ace Detective Agency.) I got a call from the Jungleland Zoo. Mr. Green, owner of the zoo, said that their best lion would not roar. He said that the lion might have been doped by someone from a competitive zoo. He wanted me to find out what really was the matter. I accepted the job.
> It is 10:05 the next morning. I asked the trainer to show me the cage where the lion was. I asked him to give me some of the meat that they had been serving the lion. When he was doing this, I saw some white powder around the lion's mouth. To get this powder for examination, I tied some cotton onto a long stick and I rubbed the cotton against the lion's mouth. I got the powder and the meat and then I went to my laboratory.
> It is 12:06. The white powder which I found on the lion's mouth was only dried up milk, but the meat was spoiled. The reason the lion won't roar is that he was going on a sit-down strike for better food.

A number of our most creative children even in the primary grades present behavior problems. Personality trends of a psychopathic-deviate-like nature appear quite strongly in the personality sketches of some of our most creative children and quite possibly may destroy their present promise. These personality sketches are "blind" analyses of the House-Tree-Person records and later checked against interviews with teachers, sociometric data, and classroom observations. Such tendencies are emphasized in the following sketch of a second-grade girl:

> This subject is likely to place little value on education and intellectual values. She is blunt and direct in her approach to people. She is ready to make contact with people but is likely to manifest considerable hostility in her social relations. She is conscious of authority figures as a source of power both in the home and outside of it and feels a crippling lack of autonomy. Although she feels no need to mask her feelings, she is characterized by a generalized feeling of insecurity and is likely to obtain little satisfaction from her environment. Although she has a heightened sensitivity in many respects, her aggressive-reactive tendencies are not well suppressed and is likely to exhibit a marked lack of control of her actions. She is much at the mercy of her body drives which all too frequently overwhelm her. Although this child is not likely to be easily coerced by social pressures, she will probably be in continual trouble in her relationships with teachers and peers. Unless she encounters some unusually positive influences, she is not likely to develop a sound, productive type of creativity.

As in regard to the discussion of all of the other consequences of the repression of creativity, the reader may raise an important question here. Does the abandonment of creativity lead to the disability (behavior problem, neurosis, schizoid withdrawal, etc.), or does the disability in effect destroy or seriously cripple the creativity of the individual? To me, the evidence is not clear. My contention, however, is that the expression of creative desires brings upon the individual certain sanctions which produce tensions. At this point the child needs healthy guidance in coping with his problems. With the proper guidance, he can learn to cope with these problems and still maintain his creativity. Without such guidance, he finds it necessary to distort or abandon his creativity in one or more of the ways discussed in this chapter. This obviously applies also to what I shall say about both neuroses and psychoses.

NEUROTIC CONFLICTS

Another consequence of the repression of creative needs is neurotic conflict. Many people, however, have maintained that one must be neurotic in order to be creative. Many neurotic artists, writers, musicians, and scientists have refused psychotherapy for fear that they would lose their creative spark. Kubie (1958), Roe (1959), and others cite evidence that this belief is erroneous. Kubie argues that the neurosis is "the most banal and undistinguished component of human nature." He contends that it is only when an individual is not hamstrung by conscious fear and guilt that the preconscious processes operate. "The contribution of preconscious processes to creativity," Kubie (1958, p. 37) explains, "depends upon their freedom in gathering, assembling, comparing, and reshuffling of ideas." He concludes that creative activities can be used as one ingredient in the therapeutic process, but that creative activity alone can never be a cure.

Hutchinson (1949, pp. 66–67) also points out that when creative desires are stifled, "the hidden enterprise bobs up in hydraheaded forms producing sometimes melancholy, anxiety, fatigue, inflation of ego. She warns that when the creative desire is active, intense, aroused, but for the time restricted in expression, the chief psychological symptom is tension.

Children in their stories recognize intuitively that the repression of creative needs results in disabling neurotic symptoms, as reflected in the following story by a St. Paul girl:

> Once there was a rooster. He was quite a one too. You see he was quite a curious rooster. One day he saw a farmer chewing tobacco and he wondered about it. Another day the farmer left some out. The rooster found a piece and ate it. Then he started to hiccup. From that day on when the sun comes up, he would not cock-a-doodle-doo. He would go "hiccup." He is not curious any more.

Even in personality studies of highly creative children, I find neurotic-like trends which already seem to be interfering with their creative growth. To illustrate some of these trends, I shall present a few of the personality sketches constructed from the House-Tree-Person protocols. The following sketch of a first-grade girl is an example of how the exceptionally strong desire to be well thought of (which is so characteristic of hysteria in adults) may interfere with creative growth:

> This subject places much importance on education and intellectual values. Capacity to deal rationally with and coordinate impulses has not yet been achieved, however. She is characterized by a remarkable aware-

ness of her environment—intent, quiet observation, visual curiosity, reaching out with hands to explore the environment. She is reasonably accessible psychologically and has some maturity striving. Socially, she appears to have a firm footing and is motivated for social approval. She is characterized by an unusually high degree of uniqueness for a girl. There is likely to be a serious struggle between her motivation for social approval and her uniqueness and assertiveness. If the social pressures are great it is likely that she will sacrifice her creativity.

Depressive tendencies are also likely to hamper healthy creative growth. Such tendencies seem to be interfering already in the development of the highly creative second-grade boy whose personality data are summarized below:

> This second-grade boy seems to be experiencing a great deal of inner tension and is likely to be depressed rather than expansive. He places much emphasis on intellectual control of bodily impulses and places importance on education and intellectual values. Although self-oriented, he is characterized by wide-eyed curiosity, manipulativeness, and virility strivings. He feels quite uncomfortable in his environment and feels a great need to structure his environment and to test reality. He is fairly accessible psychologically but in a cautious, reserved way. If he can have positive guidance in coping with his inner tensions, generalized anxiety, and tendencies to become depressed, he may be able to achieve the creative productivity of which he gives promise.

Even some of our most creative children give indications through our personality studies and observations of their behavior that they have neurotic-like fears of exploring their environment and of expressing their ideas. Such trends are seen as possible deterrents to creative growth in the following personality sketch of a highly creative third-grade girl:

> This third-grade girl is quite restrained. She is neither verbally nor socially aggressive. In fact, she is likely to be quite "tight-lipped," but may be described as open-eyed and curious, but quiet. She places much importance on intellectual values and would like to reach out to explore her environment but the inhibiting forces either within herself or her environment are quite strong. She feels inferior and is likely to be dependent, infantile, and inadequate in social contacts. She is quite feminine, wants to be attractive, and sees herself as a part of a fairly well-organized network of interpersonal relations. She is likely to need support in daring to reach out and explore her environment and maintain her wide-eyed curiosity.

PSYCHOSES

If creative needs are strong and if their repression or suppression is severe or prolonged, tension is likely to be overwhelming and psychosis a possible result. The process by which this occurs is apparently varied. A common feature, however, is a paralysis in thinking or a lack of verification or revision in imaginative thinking.

There are a number of other ways in which we must be careful to differentiate between psychotic and creative behavior. As a consequence of the way a creative person is treated by society, he develops some traits which resemble those of psychotics. For example, a highly creative individual because of the very superiority of his thinking and production may be threatening to others. In actuality he may experience a great deal of persecution. His reaction to this reality may be very much like the behavior of the paranoid personality in some respects. Or in order to accomplish significant creative work, an individual may have to behave in ways which are judged as withdrawn or schizophrenic. As Barlow (1952, pp. 140–41) has pointed out, scientists who withdraw from society and absorb themselves in research, often make epoch-making discoveries because they are able to concentrate on their problems without social distractions. The shy, sensitive poet may transform society's ridicule and dislike for him into rhythms of great beauty. Musical composers frequently assume certain schizoid-like traits. Their source of inspiration may be found in fantasy and daydreaming which they use in their adaptation to these stresses. Such behaviors, however, are vastly different in other ways from truly psychotic behavior.

Strong schizoid-like trends are described by a gifted sixth-grade girl in California in the following story of a silent lion. Note the withdrawal, blocking, and lack of affect. It is interesting that a sixth-grade girl can describe so deftly this type of adjustment to sanctions against divergency.

> In Africa there was a large lion cub named Sam. Now Sam had brothers and sisters, of course, but they were different from Sam. Whenever Sam tried to roar like his friends, he would only hiss in a very kittenish manner. Soon everyone mocked and scolded him so he crept away ashamed.
>
> Sam grew very rapidly as lions do, but he had a great love for the

small animals of the region who became his dearest friends. When Sam was about two years old, he expressed a great yearning to roam. After bidding his friends farewell, Sam left for adventure. Needless to say, Sam remembered his friends and after months of travel, he started for home. When he was near home, he heard a great roaring in a large thicket which held a large clan of lions. He hurried to the thicket and saw a great array of hunters and nets with a mad scramble of roaring lions. All the lion cubs were running to their screaming mothers. He walked calmly into the thicket, unnoticed because of his quietness amid the noisy crowd.

After the hunters left, there was one lone lion left. As he saw fellow lions being hauled away, Sam let out one long mournful roar and plodded slowly home.

Although I have a hunch that the repression of creativity is prominently involved in much childhood schizophrenia, I have tested only two children who have been so diagnosed. Both were undergoing treatment as outpatients at the time of testing and were quite productive during the first part of the test but became preoccupied before its completion and were unable to produce ideas. One was retested after several months of treatment and produced an outstanding record without the blocking and preoccupation which occurred during the first test. Although none of our most highly creative children could be diagnosed as psychotic, insofar as I know, some of them are already showing trends which, if continued, would lead to psychotic-like adjustments and soon will interfere with healthy creative growth. The following sketches of a first-grade boy and a third-grade boy are examples:

First-Grade Boy

This subject is not very accessible psychologically; teachers and others will probably have to work very hard to get to know him or to establish any kind of real relationship with him. He is not very communicative, fears scolding, is afraid to reveal his feelings, and is evasive about frictional aspects of interpersonal relations. He seriously lacks confidence in social contacts. He has strong visual curiosity but is otherwise rather closed to his environment. He is likely to lack physical aggressiveness and to do little to win social approval. He feels dependent and inadequate but tries to conceal his emotions and lacks the capacity to deal rationally with his impulses. His personality is characterized by a high degree of uniqueness. At the present stage of his development, there is little or no indication that he will sacrifice his creativity for social approval. In fact his estrangement from peers and teachers may interfere with the development of a found type of creativity and teachers and counselors may have difficulty in establishing a helping relationship with him.

Third-Grade Boy

This boy is highly inaccessible psychologically and denies all direct access to others. Although his uniqueness is of a high order, his contact with reality is quite poor and his ego strength is weak. At the present time he seems preoccupied by physical adequacy strivings. He is likely to be intermittently aggressive and withdrawn. Both peers and teachers will have difficulty in understanding and appreciating his inventiveness and creative ideas and he is likely to be in continual difficulty in school on this account. If he can achieve a reasonably adequate personal adjustment and learn to cope with his personal problems, he is likely to achieve a high level of creativity. This, however, is likely to pose serious problems, because of his withdrawal.

SUCCESSFUL STRATEGIES FOR COPING WITH CONFLICTS BETWEEN EXPRESSION AND REPRESSION

Lest the conflict between expression and repression of creative needs be made to seem like an unsolvable dilemma, something should be said about successful strategies for coping with such conflicts. Many promising leads have come from Pauline Pepinsky's (1959, 1960) research on what she has termed "productive nonconformity." Her studies have included intensive investigations of productive independence in three different natural situations: a university campus, a research institute, and an architecturally planned neighborhood.

Mrs. Pepinsky, as a result of these studies, has identified the following seven strategies of productive independence (1960, p. 85):

1. The individual translates his own ideas into the language of relevant others so that they can see his contribution as instrumental to (or as in minimal conflict with) their own ends.
2. He states his criticism in a positive and constructive way.
3. He makes it evident that basically he stands for something that commands the respect of others in the group.

4. He minimizes personal threat to others by granting them dignity; he will listen.

5. He builds up a "credit rating" and "buys" more freedom over a period of time by initial service in terms of existing demands and requirements.

6. He focuses upon the job to be done, not on "personalities," and not on acquiring status as an end in itself.

7. He takes into account matters of timing; he is able to delay response as well as act upon them.

Of her productively independent student, Pepinsky has the following to say (1959, p. 39):

> That they were able to persist and often to prevail may be explained in large part, not only by their unusual personal qualities, but by (1) their skill in social strategy, (2) the support of prestigeful patron-sponsors, (3) their previously acquired status as organizational leaders, and, to some extent, by (4) the very nature of the tasks they undertook, and (5) the significance of them of the issues at stake.

Essentially these same strategies are employed in the stories of children about animals and persons with divergent characteristics who maintain their unusualness and are at the same time productive. The flying monkey wins the affection of the other animals of the jungle by flying them out of the blazing jungle on his tail, by getting the best bananas for them, and similar acts. The dog that won't bark foils the robber or rescues the child from some great danger. These themes are rather frequent in the stories from all cultures. For example, the following is a translation of a story written by a sixth-grade Turkish boy:

> Once upon a time, there was a father and his son. One day the father and son caught a lion. After this, the father treated the animal cruelly. The lion wasn't doing anything against them but was only staring. One day after he was beaten, he couldn't roar any more. Many years passed. One day a wolf entered into the father's sheep herd. The father and the son grabbed their rifles. But it was no use. The wolves weren't defeated and were getting more. At that moment . . . the lion jumped among the wolves and killed many wolves. The father and the son were very glad. Then the father and the son grabbed their rifles again. They killed about 200 wolves in all. They sold these 200 wolf skins in the market and became rich. They built a home and lived happily with the lion that won't roar.

A strategy not mentioned by Pepinsky but observed in small group experiments and in the stories of divergent animals and persons is the use of joking and clowning. Frequently, this is a technique to win the favor of peers, to appear to be "one of the boys." At times, it appears to be a "safe" way of poking fun at those who ridicule them, as is seen in the following story by an eleven-year old French boy:

> The jungle was very silent. A monkey met a lion and called to him, "You, who rule the mysterious jungle, why aren't you roaring?"
> "If you knew what I have—"
> "Oh, good, is that why you aren't roaring?"
> "I have a sore throat."
> "So that's why you don't roar."
> The lion had talked enough so he walked away and went to the village.
> "Good morning!" Mr. Milch said. "Can I do anything for you?"
> "Perhaps you can give me something for my throat."
> "Why, or course, right now!"
> "Thank you very much, and how much do I have to pay?"
> "Nothing! It gives me pain not to hear you roar."
> "Is this what makes me roar, for I will not swallow the syrup."
> "At whom will you roar?"
> "Instead of boring me and talking, look at those two managers in front of the door who are talking about me. They will be surprised if I won't roar. I want to play a trick on them and afterwards I'll tell them the truth."

Many of the clues provided by Pepinsky's research will be followed up in Chapter 8 concerning the goals of teachers, counselors, and administrators in guiding creative talent. In both Chapters 8 and 9 I shall present some ideas which I believe will be useful in guiding highly creative individuals and helping them develop successful strategies for coping with the dilemma of expression versus repression of their creative needs and abilities.

SUMMARY

In the preceding two chapters an attempt has been made to identify and describe some of the common problems of highly creative individuals. The theory was advanced that basically the creative person's problems stem from the fact that inescapably the originator of a new idea is in the beginning a minority of one. If he goes ahead and expresses and develops his creative capacities, he encounters social sanctions against divergency. He is likely to be "one-sided" in development, to want to learn on his own, to attempt difficult tasks, to search for purpose, or to try to achieve uniqueness. Highly creative children are likely to feel isolated and psychologically estranged from their parents, teachers, and classmates.

Problems also spring from attempts to repress creative needs and to restrain one's self from thinking creatively. One obvious consequence is an unrealistic or uncertain self-concept. Serious learning disabilities and behavior problems may also result from prolonged, enforced repression of creative needs. Even delinquency, neurotic conflicts, psychoses, and other types of personality disorganization may result.

Many successful, effective individuals have developed strategies for coping with the conflicts which arise from the fight between expression and repression. These include such things as translating one's ideas into the idiom of the group, stating criticisms in positive and constructive ways, making it evident that one is trying to accomplish something important, minimizing personal threat to others, building up a "credit rating," focusing upon the job to be done, timing actions appropriately, and camouflaging one's talents so that they are not noticeable.

Chapter 8

GOALS
FOR GUIDING
CREATIVE TALENT

Highly creative individuals usually have very strong creative needs. They are attracted to the mysterious, to the unknown, and to the unexplained. They have a strong need to question, to explain, to test ideas, and to communicate the results of their testing. Creative individuals, however, need outside encouragement to keep up their efforts. Society in general does not supply this encouragement, but teachers and counselors are in a position to supply much of this support.

It should be recognized, however, that the goal of guidance is not to promote just individuality and creativity but to encourage healthy kinds of individuality, creativity, and conformity. As shown by Pepinsky's findings cited in the preceding chapter, creativity and conformity are not antithetical to each other. Many creative individuals, however, need guidance in achieving the balance between creativity and conformity so that they enhance one another. This is a guidance task for teachers and counselors at all levels of education, because the creative personality does not emerge suddenly and dramatically. It must be nurtured through many crises from kindergarten through graduate school.

Kris (1951), Maslow (1954), Rogers (1954), Stein (1956), Barron (1958), Kubie (1958), MacKinnon (1960), and others have discussed the essentials of the creative personality from various viewpoints. Before suggesting some specific goals in counseling and guiding creative individuals, I would like to review briefly some of the personality requirements which have been outlined. Kris (1951), Kubie (1958), and others have stressed the role of the preconscious in creativity and the personality characteristics and environmental conditions which permit the preconscious mental processes to function. Kris and others have described the role of ego-regression in preconscious thinking. Earlier workers had identified ego-regression in sleep, in the process of falling asleep, fantasy, intoxication, and in psychotic conditions. Kris identified this phenomenon in various types of productive processes. In these productive processes, the individual demonstrates the ability to regress, to assume a naïvete or a childlikeness, without "losing control" or becoming overwhelmed by tension. Its operation has been described by our most eminent inventors, scientific discoverers, and other creators. They strain consciously to develop a solution and finally it comes when they are shaving, in the bathtub, or sitting in church.

McPherson (1960), Maslow (1954), and others refer to this as *primary creativeness* and say that it comes from those who can play, imagine, laugh, loaf, be spontaneous, and accept their softness and femininity. Since the specific goals of guiding creative individuals should support the conditions which will make possible preconscious thinking, ego-regression, or primary creativeness, guidance workers should be aware of these conditions.

By synthesizing the findings of various investigators, we might list the following as necessary conditions for the healthy functioning of the preconscious mental processes which produce creativity:

1. The absence of serious threat to the self, the willingness to risk.
2. Self-awareness—in touch with one's feelings.
3. Self-differentiation—sees self as being different from others.

4. Both openness to the ideas of others and confidence in one's own perceptions of reality or one's own ideas.

5. Mutuality in interpersonal relations—balance between excessive quest for social relations and pathological rejection of them.

Another general goal in guiding the highly creative individual of course is to help him counteract some of the many pressures which push him towards the mean. Evidences of the existence of these pressures and of the power of their influence are widespread. Wolfle (1960) cites as examples the use of uniform lesson assignments, methods of selecting students for the next higher educational level or for scholarships, advertising procedures, trade union policies, wage scales, and such.

Pressures from parents are especially difficult to deal with and the research evidence on this count is rather strong. Getzels and Jackson (1960b) found that the parents of both the highly intelligent and highly creative children are not interested in nurturing giftedness in their children. Parents prefer that their children be "well adjusted." Lyle Spencer (1958) quotes the mother of three gifted children as saying, "I'm not interested in geniuses, all I want to do is to raise my kids to be normal, well-adjusted adults" (p. 42).

From my observations of many elementary and secondary teachers, it is clear that many of them endeavor to reduce the variability among the students whom they teach. Some of them admit frankly that they work towards such goals. DeHaan and Havighurst (1957) quote one teacher as saying, "When I am finished with my class in June, the slow children are a little faster and the fast have slowed down a bit."

SPECIFIC GOALS

Rewarding Diverse Contributions

Research has repeatedly shown that people will develop along whatever lines they find rewarding. Whenever only two or three types of talent are rewarded or receive a major share of the rewards, the conditions for creativity cannot be met. Teachers and counselors must acknowledge spontaneously and respectfully the questions, ideas, and other requests or contributions of creative individuals rather than respond with shock, withdrawal, or arbitrary rejection.

The social conditions necessary for rewarding diverse, even unique, talent are symbolized in the following story by a fifth-grade boy:

> Once there lived a lion named Leo. Leo could not roar for he was born that way. Leo's mother and father were very unhappy. So one day they decided to send him away. It just happened that Leo was listening. The next morning Leo's parents came to see him but Leo was not there. He had gone away to make his fortune.
>
> At first Leo was afraid. Then he met a monkey. The monkey had run away too. They met a rooster that could not crow. They all got different jobs. Now, the rooster is a proud weather vane. The monkey is working in the Twinkle commercial on TV. The lion, Leo, is the lion at the beginning of the movies and doesn't roar at all.

Vocational counselors have, of course, long accepted the goal of helping individuals find the niche where their unique talents will be rewarded. Schools, through their emphasis on developing well-rounded personalities and because of their remoteness from vocational placement, may neglect this goal. It is natural for the counselor to want to help a pupil consider as many opportunities as possible and discourage a vocational goal in which there are few employment opportunities. This poses a difficult problem in guiding creative adolescents, since many of their vocational choices are likely to fall in the category of rare or unusual occupations.

Many pieces of evidence spell out the failure of educational institutions to find ways of rewarding divergent kinds of achievement. One of the more recent of these is a study by Elizabeth Drews (1961b) of three types of gifted high school students: the studious, the social leaders, and the creative intellectuals. The poorest teacher-grades were made by the creative intellectuals. In competitive examinations sampling a wide range of information, however, they performed better than either of the other two groups. Drews found an interesting "tip-off" when she obtained information about their activities prior to important examinations. The studious group reviewed and prepared for the examinations, as usual. The social leaders, who read very little, studied what they knew would yield a good "pay-off." The creative intellectuals, however, would more likely be reading some book in philosophy or some other book which would be of no help in achieving a high grade on the forthcoming examination.

National talent searches which make use of examinations sampling a great diversity of knowledge and skills have probably served a useful purpose in rewarding self-initiated learning of the type reflected in the activities of Drews' creative intellectuals. The recent action of the National Merit Scholarship Foundation in awarding scholarships to individuals who are not so well-rounded and to individuals with creative promise appears to be a forward move. Pleas such as those of Getzels (1960) and Mednick (1961) concerning the development of admissions criteria which do not eliminate the bright nonconformist, the underchallenged, and individuals with highly specialized ability seem to point in a promising direction.

Recognizing Value of One's Own Talents

Many creative individuals desperately need help in recognizing the value of their own talents. Otherwise, they will continue to despise what could be their most valuable assets. Itchy, the flying monkey in the following story by a sixth-grade girl, recognized the value of his flying talent only after painful experience:

> Itchy was a monkey who lived in a deep, dark jungle in Africa. He came from a very fine family, but Itchy was ashamed of himself because he didn't have a long tail like his father or curly hair like his mother. He didn't even look good at all because he had a short, wide tail and smooth hair. But what made him look real bad were two wide wings just below his shoulders.
>
> One day while Itchy was lying in the grass, looking up at the sky, he saw a flock of birds. . . . Then he started thinking (for he was a very smart monkey), "If the birds can fly, why can't I?" So he climbed to the tallest tree in the jungle and jumped. Right away the wings below his shoulders started working and Itchy was flying.
>
> "Why," said Itchy, "I shouldn't be ashamed of myself because how many monkeys can fly?"
>
> And off he flew to show his family that he was as good as they were.

This guidance goal is not an easily achieved one. It is indeed difficult to believe that a talent is of value when almost everyone ridicules its display. This is true even though the individual may receive very rich intrinsic rewards from the exercise of the talent. Such a situation is portrayed in the following story of Hoppy, a flying monkey who enjoyed flying but quit because it brought him ridicule.

Once there was a monkey. His name was—well, I don't think he'll want me to tell you because he is ashamed of it, but I'll tell you. But I better be good—his name was Hoppy.

One day Hoppy wanted to fly so he went to the Wizard. He said he wanted to fly. Well the Wizard didn't think much about it but he said he would help.

So home went Hoppy gaily flying. He liked it very much until one day all the people in the neighborhood started to laugh. He got real mad and he ran into a pole. He didn't want to be laughed at, so he decided to quit.

But he couldn't quit. . . . Finally, he called on the Wizard to help again. . . . He said that Hoppy should never want to fly again. Hoppy promised that he would never do it again and he never did.

It might seem to some that teachers and counselors could accomplish this goal easily by administering tests to discover giftedness and then simply telling the individual the results. In some cases this may be helpful, but inevitably the locus of evaluation will be the individual, not the teacher, counselor, or psychologist. There are numerous other techniques whereby counselors and teachers can help the creative individual recognize the value of his talents.

Avoiding Exploitation

Since highly creative individuals frequently do not recognize the value of their talents, especially when these talents are ridiculed, they are especially susceptible to exploitation of various types. This may result in the ill-use of the talent, loss or debilitation of the talent, or unrewarded talents. Children recognize this possibility in their stories of divergent talent. The psychological needs of exploited individuals are usually such, however, that they need guidance in recognizing that they are being exploited. In the case of children, teachers and counselors may have to intervene actively to prevent undue exploitation.

The following story of Charlie, a flying monkey, symbolizes the problem of exploited talent:

"Well! What is it?"

"Boss," said BeBo, "Charlie has escaped!"

"Didn't I tell you to put him in a cage!"

"Yes, but—"

"Yipes!" said the boss, "what was that?"

"That's what I tried to tell you, boss, Charlie can fly."

"Wait! I just got a great idea," said the boss. "We'll star him as the world's only flying monkey on our trapeze act." That evening millions came to the circus. There was only one thing wrong. Charlie wouldn't fly. Then BeBo got an idea. He threw bananas up and Charlie flew up and caught them. Then the boss threw up peanuts. Charlie caught them. Then the boss knew Charlie wanted peanuts before he'd fly.

The boss called his friend on the phone, "Guess what—my star act works for peanuts!"

Accepting Limitations

Inevitably there will be limitations both within the environment and the individual. Parents, schools, and communities will be unable to provide all of the resources which creative children need to develop and test their ideas. The children will lack some of the abilities and skills they need to fulfill their dreams. Both kinds of limitations must be accepted, not cynically or with resignation, but creatively. In an early study of the psychology of inventors, Rossman (1931) found that this characteristic differentiates inventors from non-inventors. Non-inventors only curse the defects of their environment and of themselves. Inventors, however, take a more constructive approach, saying, "This is the way to do it." I like this story in which a fifth-grade boy in Massachusetts shows how the lion can accept creatively his inability to roar:

Once there was a lion named Roary. He was the king of the beasts. But he didn't roar. Mostly every creature laughed at him and didn't listen to him. Everyone thought they should vote for another animal. They were trying to decide. Then the monkey said, "Can't I be the king? I'm very strong."

The animals said, "You'll have to prove it!" So the monkey did, but the animals weren't satisfied.

Then one day King Roary came out and said, "Even if I can't roar, I can hunt. And I'm very fierce."

But the animals said that they didn't think so because a lion that doesn't roar, doesn't sound very fierce. Then the lion said that he would prove it. So the lion went into the deepest part of the jungle. There he sat. It was very dark. Then a monkey came and teased Roary. Roary got angry and tried to scare the monkey away, but the monkey wouldn't go. He said, "I'm not scared of a lion who won't roar."

. . . Then one day the animals were frightened by the hunters. They told Roary, "Please save us!"

But Roary said, "I can't save you because I can't roar."

The animals said, "It's no time to be joking."

The hunters saw Roary. They started laughing because he couldn't roar. But Roary had a record player and the record was called "How to Learn to Roar." So he played it. Then he opened his mouth and the roars came from the record player. And it seemed as if he was roaring. Roary scared the wits out of the hunters. They ran like lightning. The animals were saved, thanks to Roary. So they asked, "Roary, did you really roar?"

Roary said, "That's my secret." So now they wanted Roary for king even if he can't roar.

In the case of the school counselor and the creative individual, the "record player" may be a hearing aid, a pair of eye glasses, a prosthetic device, a wheel chair, or a similar aid. Or, help may be needed in accepting creatively such limitations as tallness or shortness, a long nose, stuttering, or other differences.

Developing Minimum Skills

Quite obviously the psychological conditions described in the introduction cannot be maintained, if the individual does not possess the minimum skills necessary for survival and for entry into situations where creativity can be expressed. Many possible causes might be cited for the failure of highly creative individuals to develop some of the fundamental skills essential to any kind of achievement. Perhaps one of the most frequent, however, is the popular fallacy that gifted children do not need guidance and good instruction. The following story by a Long Island boy illustrates some interesting dynamics involved in this problem:

In the jungles of the Congo there was a family of lions and they were the most ferocious in all the Congo. One day a baby was born into the family. It was an exceptional kind of lion. It had a tremendous roar. His mother was terrified by it, so they threw him out and he wandered all over the Congo.

He was getting thinner and thinner because he didn't know how to hunt. After one week, he came upon a baby leopard. The baby leopard saw how hungry he was, so he called his mother and the mother of the leopard got some food for the lion and adopted him. When the father came home he saw something that would have made him faint. There in front of him, his son was playing with a lion. Just then the leopardess came over and told him about the lion their son found that was very hungry. At first, the father thought it would be dangerous but then he heard the magnificent roar. Then the father leopard wanted to keep him because the louder the roar the better the hunter. So that day they went out to hunt. And was the father angry when he saw that the lion couldn't hunt. So the father then started teaching the lion. . . .

Buhl (1961) in his study of creative engineering students found that members of this group were encouraged as children to make decisions regarding clothes, friends, and activities. They were also given guidance and encouragement and plans and goals to work toward achieving. I also found these characteristics to a far greater degree in the backgrounds of the jet aces than in those of their less successful colleagues of the same rank and similar training and experience.

Utilizing Opportunities

Frequently questions are asked concerning the role of chance in scientific discovery (Taton, 1957). Certainly many great discoveries have resulted from the exploitation of a chance occurrence or unexpected incident. Because of their problems of adjustment, creative individuals may be blinded and fail to see such opportunities. It should be the teacher and counselor's goal to help free such individuals from this blindness.

The following imaginative story by a sixth-grade boy illustrates the child's intuitive understanding of the importance of being alert to the opportunities of the moment:

> Elmer Monkey was sitting on some springs by his jungle home. He was talking to a lion that wouldn't roar. He came to Elmer because Elmer was a doctor.
> One night when the lion was sleeping a mean little monkey had tied the lion's lips together. Just as Elmer was feeling the strings which tied the lion's lips together, he had a fantastic hiccup which sent Elmer flying and the strings breaking on the lion's lips. The lion quickly ran away because he could roar again.
> Elmer soon got so he could tell when these fantastic hiccups would occur and when they did occur, he could fly for hours by using and flapping his hands.

Developing Values and Purpose

Studies of outstanding individuals in various fields almost always reveal that such persons seem to be impelled by feelings of mission or purpose. They believe that what they are doing is tremendously worthwhile, and they are thereby aroused to all-out effort. When learning and thinking are made to be "tremendously important and worthwhile," schools will become exciting places. Even gifted children may achieve more than we thought possible. Such is the experience of the monkey, Nickerbocker, in the following story by a sixth-grader:

> Once there was a monkey whose name was Nickerbocker. . . . His master was Mr. Anthony Malucci. They worked together with his organ grinder. While Anthony cranked, Nickerbocker did his antics to make people laugh and give more money.
>
> When Tony and his monkey got home, he kissed his wife and the 24 children.
>
> Then he said, "Our children are crying from hunger and we are gaining more children all the time. Mama! I know you are kindhearted but do you have to take in every stray and runaway bambino that wanders around here? It was bad enough when we had 10 children but 24 is way too much!"
>
> Tony started laughing then, because he was always happy, no matter what happened. Right then and there Nickerbocker decided he must go out and work. So he did. . . .
>
> At one o'clock in the morning he fell asleep at Tony's doorstep. As Tony picked him up, Nickerbocker started flying around. Tony gasped with surprise for he knew now the family's stomachs would not cry from hunger because of the money this gifted monkey would bring them.
>
> And we know that he was given this gift because of his faith and loyalty, by some great magic that we can't understand.

Since the values of creative individuals are different from those of their teachers, it may be that the school counselor is the only person in some schools who can assist them in finding and holding to their purpose.

Holding to Purposes

If pressures continue unabated over too long a period, even the strongest personality is likely to "break." In the case of the highly creative individual, this "break" may include the sacrificing of his creativity or his purpose. One of the problems of the teacher and the counselor is to help creative individuals to accept the necessity for tolerating discomfort for long-range goals and purposes. This is an especially difficult feat to accomplish in guiding highly creative children from the lower socio-economic classes where immediacy and inability to delay gratification are strong. The following story by a fourth-grade girl about a German-speaking lion provides an interesting example of "delayed payoff":

> One day Lilly Tiger, queen of the jungle, had a baby. The lion cub refused to roar. He felt that the other lions, tigers, and cubs were silly because they roared. He would only talk German. Lilly felt her son was acting like a show-off.
>
> Lilly named her son Long Tail. He grew up very fast. All the lion cubs disliked him.
>
> A few months later a big, big ape named Noddlehead came through the woods. Everyone was frightened. They ran to their homes. The big ape went toward Long Tail's home. Long Tail screamed in German and just before the ape made his way to his home, German troops were marching around and came to the rescue.
>
> One day the ape came back. Everybody screamed again. Long Tail jumped up and down on the ape. The ape got scared and ran away. The next day they elected Long Tail as father or king of the jungle and so to this day, this tribe of lions all speak in German and do not roar.

In studies of talent, commitment to a purpose or a creative career seems to be tremendously important in success. In guiding creative talent, teachers and counselors may have to help such individuals develop a commitment to some purpose or career which they regard as important. The following story by a Long Island girl illustrates the importance of commitment:

> He was a plain little monkey. Well, at least I think so. One day this little monkey went job hunting. The only thing that he thought he could handle was in a circus. He thought the ad in the paper said, "Help Wanted: Playing Monkey," but it sure didn't say that. It said, "Help Wanted: Flying Monkey." But the monkey didn't care. He said he could fly but he really couldn't. He took a tryout. He flew. The next day the show opened. He was supposed to fly out and over the crowd. He only flew out as far as the end of the stage and tried very hard to fly way over the heads of the crowds. Do you know what he did after two more tries? He flew! He flew higher than any monkey had ever flown before. He knew he could do it and sang out, "I'm flying," and he flew all the rest of his life.

In general, it isn't necessary for teachers and counselors to push talented children, although some may need help in finding ways of self-discipline. Commitment to a purpose or goal frequently helps them achieve this discipline and stick to a line of development until they have achieved something worthwhile.

Avoiding Equation of Divergency with Mental Illness or Delinquency

Many highly creative children need help in recognizing that divergency should not be equated with mental illness or delinquency. Since our culture does generally equate them, the counselor may have to explain away their misconceptions and attitudes. The widespread existence of this misconception is reflected in the stories of children. Flying monkeys in our stories are frequently thought to be crazy or devils or under the spell of witches. Lions that won't roar and cats that won't scratch are thought to be mentally ill. One of the stories which follows should make us more aware of the ways by which parents intensify this problem. The one following painfully shows how both parents and professionals fail in understanding divergency:

> Once there was a little monkey who was always doing what his mother told him not to do. One day when he was playing outdoors with his sister he said to her, "I can do something that you will never be able to do. I can fly."
> The little sister said that he could not fly, so he said, "I will prove it to you." He went to the end of the branch and began to fly. First he gave a leap and off he went. His little sister was so surprised that she ran as fast as she could go to tell the mother monkey. At first, mother monkey did not believe that a monkey could fly. She told the little monkey to go and play and not to bother her.
> The sister finally convinced her mother to come and look. At first she sat and looked for a while. Then she told the little flying monkey to come back here, but he said that he would not come back.
> So that night when father monkey came home she told him all about it. And he went and got the little monkey and said for him not to fly anymore or the other animals will think he was crazy and out of his head.

Although this parental concern is especially common in the stories collected in urban areas, a very different parental reaction is a recurring theme in the stories written by Negro children in Georgia. Instead of being ashamed of having a flying monkey in the family and influencing him to sacrifice his talent, the parents of the flying monkey created by the Negro children are proud and encourage the talent.

The following story of the cat that doesn't scratch illustrates another aspect of our treatment of divergency:

Once there was a cat that could not scratch. A lady came and the cat followed her so she took the cat home with her. The cat meowed and meowed, so the lady gave him some milk and he spilt the milk all over himself. So the lady put the cat in the bath tub and gave him a bath, but the cat did not scratch her. The lady did not understand so she took the cat to the cat hospital. The veterinarian did not understand so she let the cat go and that is the end of the cat that would not scratch and the lady and the doctor that did not understand that cat.

In our studies of highly creative children, we find many evidences that they feel that their parents and teachers do not understand them. Their teachers themselves admit that they do not know these children as well as they know highly intelligent (IQ) pupils (Torrance, 1959a). For some creative individuals only a school counselor may be able to provide this understanding.

Reducing Overemphasis on Sex Roles

The inhibiting effects of overemphasis or misplaced emphasis on sex roles was discussed in Chapter 6. It is mentioned again since this overemphasis interferes so strongly with the achievement of the general goals outlined at the beginning of the chapter. The primary creativeness described by Maslow, McPherson, and others requires that the individual be able to accept his softness and femininity as well as his intellectual autonomy. For "regression in the service of the ego," one must have a sense of being in touch with his feelings and being free to have subjective experiences which imply how it was to have been a child and to have felt feminine, receptive, and helpless. He must also have the intellectual independence to be able to maintain his "anchors in reality," as he regresses.

Becoming Less Obnoxious

Both our experimental and longitudinal studies (Torrance, 1960b) and studies of outstanding creative persons reveal that highly creative individuals do in fact possess characteristics generally considered somewhat obnoxious. They do, in fact, create problems for their parents, siblings, peers, teachers, and supervisors. Many of our elementary school authors recognize this problem, but most, like the sixth-grader who wrote the following story, feel that considerable sacrifice of creativity is necessary:

My brother was born a day before I was. But there was something wrong with him. He had wings! Can you imagine that? A monkey with wings!

He could fly where other monkeys couldn't get to, so they teased him. Well, he got tired of being teased and I got tired of being his brother (because, of course, I was teased too). We decided to fly to some other place. So I climbed up on his back and away we went.

The other monkeys were sorry then because my brother has always gotten the best bananas for them. Everyone was sad, even my brother and I. We couldn't find anywhere to go and he was getting tired. Finally, we turned around and started walking back.

When we got back, everyone was happy again! But sometimes, for spite, the "flying monkey" wouldn't get the best bananas for them and then the teasing would start again.

Finally, he learned how to keep his "wings" out of sight. After that he hardly ever used them and was never teased again.

We also need to help children recognize that outstanding talents may threaten others and make them uncomfortable and afraid. Our young authors recognize this and offer some interesting philosophies, as we see in the following story:

Once upon a time, there was a lion who lived in a great big woods. He was the only one in this forest. Why? Because he had such a terrible roar. But one day he tried to roar at a little bird that was sitting on a branch. All he let out was a little squeak.

The bird was so frightened that he flew out to tell his friends what happened. When he got there all his friends weren't there. Two hours later he came upon another bird. The little bird asked the big bird if he knew where all his friends were. The big bird told the little bird they were hiding in some trees right underneath me.

As I went down to see what was happening I saw all my friends sitting in a corner shaking like leaves. The little bird asked them what was the matter. They told the little bird that the lion's squeak was even worse than his great big roar. . . . The little bird told all the rest that they were just babies. They all got so mad that they went and told the lion to get out or they would hurt him bad.

The moral of this story is: If you have something that other people are scared of, don't scare them with it and if you lose this thing they will not be mad at you for doing it.

The performance of important services and courageous deeds on behalf of the larger social group is seen by our juvenile authors as one way of reducing the social pressures on divergent individuals. The following is typical of the large number of stories with this theme:

The only thing wrong with Roger was that he was the only flying monkey in existence. He could fly around in the forest to get his food while all the other monkeys would just swing from limb to limb. So they wouldn't have anything to do with him.

One day a lion came to where the monkeys all lived. There was one thing wrong. He could climb trees exceptionally well. All the monkeys ran as fast as they could but the lion ran faster. Now the flying monkey saw the lion chasing the other monkeys. He swooped down on the lion. He had protection. He could fly and the lion couldn't.

After that, no matter how different he might be, the other monkeys always played with Roger just like he was one of them. . . .

In the terms employed by Pepinsky (1959) Roger had built up a "credit rating" with his peers through his service to them, and they had accepted his divergency.

In conserving creative talent, the problem resolves itself into one of helping the child maintain those characteristics which are essential to his creativity and at the same time help him acquire skills for avoiding or reducing to a tolerable level the social sanctions against him. Stein (1958) on the basis of his study of research chemists, has offered a set of helpful principles whereby creative research chemists can become less obnoxious without sacrificing their creativity. I have tried to translate this advice to make it apply to gifted elementary pupils as follows:

Help the gifted child maintain his assertiveness without being hostile and aggressive. He must be aware of his superiors, peers and subordinates as persons. He may work alone but he must not be isolated, withdrawn or uncommunicative. In the classroom he must be congenial but not sociable; outside the classroom he must be sociable but not intimate. He must "know his place" without being timid, submissive, or acquiescent and must speak "his mind" without being domineering. As he tries to gain a point, he can be subtle but not cunning or manipulative. In all relationships, he must be sincere, honest, purposeful, and diplomatic. In the intellectual area, he must learn to be broad without spreading himself too thin, deep without being "bookish" or "too scientific," and "sharp" without being overcritical.

This model probably asks too much of the gifted child, but at least it provides a model which may be useful in guiding him in becoming less obnoxious without sacrificing his creativity.

Reducing Isolation

Considerable attention has been given in professional literature to the problems stemming from the isolation of gifted children. Isolation has been a favorite technique for handling individuals having almost any kind of divergent characteristic. As already reported, research has shown that highly creative children are especially estranged from teachers and peers. This must be especially difficult for the highly creative individual because of his unusually intense need to communicate.

Teachers and counselors must help the creative child learn to tolerate his separateness or they must help him in his search for someone with whom he can communicate. In some cases, the counselor may become the person to whom the creative child communicates. In others, it may be a teacher or principal.

In the imaginative stories by urban, middle-class children, the following reaction is fairly common.

> . . . His mother was so surprised to see him flying. She said that she didn't want any flying monkey in her family so she sent him away to some other part of the jungle.

One of the most successful techniques in the stories of our young authors is the discovery by one divergent individual of someone else with a similar divergency. This happens to both the flying monkeys and the silent lions. The following lion story illustrates this principle:

> . . . This lion was a very different kind of lion. This lion didn't roar. It wasn't because he couldn't roar. It was because he didn't have the heart to scare away animals. This lion was supposed to be the king of beasts; he was but he didn't act like it.
> One day the lion met up with a dog that didn't bark for the same reason. The dog was supposed to be scared of the lion but he wasn't. Instead he was very friendly with him. They had great fun together.

Several current streams of research (Drews, 1961; Torrance and Arsan, 1961) suggest that various kinds of homogeneous groups may provide means by which the isolation of highly creative children may be reduced and communication increased.

Coping with Anxieties and Fears

Neither gifted children (Torrance, 1959c) nor creative scientists (Roe, 1959) are free of handicapping anxieties and fears. Many creative children desperately need help in coping with their anxieties and irrational fears. Otherwise they may fail to be fully functioning mentally; they will be afraid to break away from the safest, most frequently traveled paths.

An unusually frequent theme in the stories of animals and persons with divergent characteristics is the fear that one's own talent will bring injury or destruction. The following pathetic story by a gifted Illinois girl represents her extreme fear of her talent:

> . . . I will tell you about a lion named Elmer who was afraid of anything. Elmer had no friends at all. In the day he layed around all the time. At night he hunted for food. He saw his shadow, he started crying. All the animals came running. The tiger, Mr. Peabody, said, "Why are you crying?"
>
> Elmer just sat there. Then an elephant, Mrs. Atlas, said, "Why are you crying?"
>
> Elmer said nothing. Then the lizard, mouse, horse, cat, cow, and hen tried but could not get him to answer. Then a little boy said, "Why are you crying?"
>
> Elmer looked up and said, "I saw my shadow and I'm scared of it."
>
> "I don't see it," said the boy. The lion looked down. It was not there. He started to roar, then started to cry. The boy said, "Why are you crying?"
>
> "I'm afraid of my roar," Elmer said. All the animals and the boy laughed.

Less severely handicapped is Mickey, a dog that wouldn't bark, in the following story by a Twin Cities author:

> I once visited a farm. The four children who lived on the farm had a big, black mongrel dog who never barked. I wondered why, so I devoted my vacation to finding out. . . . I soon found out it wasn't because he was lazy. Mickey certainly wasn't lazy. Sally, one of the children, and I tried to tempt him with meat he couldn't get at, but it didn't work. So she gave him the meat. He never barked at cars. Once a robber entered the house. Mickey didn't bark; he just bit the robber. That's how we know what happened.
>
> Then one day we were all sitting around the piano singing when Mickey picked up his head and howled. The minute he did, there was a sur-

prised look on his face and he ran under the table and put his paws on his head as though afraid of something. "So that's it!" I exclaimed. "Mickey is afraid of his own bark. He probably didn't want to scare others either." Mickey was the bravest dog otherwise there is.

In one story, a lion would not roar because he was afraid that his roar might not sound like a lion's. Another would not roar because he was afraid that a banana might fall down his throat when he opened his mouth to roar. On and on, the animals created by gifted children are shackled by some of the same kind of fears which shackle these children. Quite interestingly, almost all of these handicapped animals are able to rise to the occasion and transcend their fears when some necessity arises.

Learning to Cope with Hardships and Failure

All of the studies of eminent individuals with which I am familiar emphasize the role of coping with hardship and failure. This comes out clearly in the recent study by the Goertzels (1960) and in an earlier study by Anne Roe (1952). On the basis of these and other studies, some workers advocate that we deliberately and calculatedly subject gifted children to hardships. It is my own opinion that gifted children should learn how to cope with hardship and failure, but they should not be forced to do so deliberately. Gifted children are resistant to and are embittered by hardships which seem to them unfair, wasteful of their energies, and unnecessary. If they are encouraged and permitted to explore, experiment, test ideas, initiate projects on their own, and assume responsibility, they will encounter enough hardships and failures in the natural course of events. This is especially true if freedom to try out ideas without penalty is permitted against a background of high standards.

The role of trying and failing and trying and failing again and again which has already been emphasized is illustrated in the following story by a gifted sixth-grade girl:

> In a deep, dark region of Africa, there is a family of monkeys. They have a baby named Sloop. He is a queer monkey because no matter how you bribe him, he will not climb trees.
> It all started when he was born. . . . He fell out of a tree and was so scared that he never tried to climb again. . . . Since he wouldn't climb

trees, he had to find some way of getting around. Finally, he thought of flying.

The art of flying is not easy to master. He fell 61 times before he got the hang of it. He stood on one foot and flapped his arms. Sloop didn't believe it when he found that he could zoom up into the air and circle the jungle. No one else did either. From that very day he was famous. . . .

The importance of skills in coping with hardships is reflected in Anne Roe's (1952) finding concerning the disproportionate number of her eminent subjects whose fathers had died during the subject's childhood. It is also reflected in one of Peter Freuchen's (1954) stories of his first year with the Thule, Greenland, Eskimos. On one occasion Freuchen was deploring the plight of certain orphan children in the tribe who had to fight for survival. The chiefs of the tribe scolded Freuchen, telling him not to feel sorry for these orphan children because they would be the future leaders of the tribe. They pointed out to him that each of the present leaders had been an orphan. They also explained that they realized that they should permit their own children to experience more difficulties and hardships but that they had grown soft and would not permit their children to expose themselves to cold, danger, or similar hardships. In most societies it takes some kind of accident or adverse circumstance to force adults to permit their children to attempt to master the skills of coping with difficulties. Even some of the imaginative stories of children give recognition of this need:

> Once there was a timid baby lion. His father was the king of the lions and he wanted his son to be king when he grew up. But he was so timid that he was afraid to roar at a mouse.
>
> Well, one day two lion hunters went to Africa to catch a lion. They were particular because they only wanted the king of the lions. Well, one day they caught the baby lion's father. They were going to shoot him. The baby lion saw this and was afraid to roar and help his dad. Well, he made up his mind he was going to help his dad. He did the loudest roar ever made. They could even hear the roar in the United States. They were so scared they jumped so high they landed on the moon. That's how the baby lion learned to roar and become king.

Apparently necessities such as this bring out "all-out efforts" which far exceed what seems possible. I doubt, however, that contrived hardships would challenge such heroic efforts. Even highly motivated, intense creative children balk at using such expensive energies, if they see no justification for it.

SUMMARY

In this chapter I have tried to identify the general goals in guiding creative talent and some of the specific goals necessary to achieve the general goals. General goals include the encouragement of a healthy kind of individuality and the development of conditions which will permit primary creativeness as described by Maslow and others, and regression in the service of the ego as described by Shafer and others. It is also necessary to counteract pressures towards regression to the average. In order to achieve these general conditions, the following specific goals seem essential: rewarding diverse contributions; helping creative persons recognize the value of their own talents, avoid exploitation, accept limitations creatively, develop minimum skills, make use of opportunities, develop values and purposes, hold to purposes; avoiding the equation of divergent with mental illness or delinquency; reducing overemphasis or misplaced emphasis on sex roles; helping them learn how to be less obnoxious without sacrificing their creativity; reducing isolation; and helping them to learn how to cope with anxieties, fears, hardships, and failures.

Chapter 9

RELATIONSHIPS
WITH
CREATIVE TALENT

There has long been rather general agreement that interpersonal relationships are important both in classroom teaching and in counseling and psychotherapy. Ideas concerning the nature of the good teacher-pupil or counselor-counselee relationship and how these relationships can be created are quite divergent, however. Research in both of these areas continues to demonstrate the importance of good relationships in guiding growth, whether we are concerned about growth in personality or growth in the ability to apply principles in mathematics. Some convergence concerning the nature of this relationship is also beginning to develop.

Fiedler's (1950ab) study of the therapeutic relationship provided some extremely important information about good interpersonal relationships in general. Using a Q-technique design with statements concerning relationships in counseling and psychotherapy, Fiedler (1950a) found that therapists of different schools (psychoanalytic, Adlerian, non-directive) did not differ in describing their concept of an ideal therapeutic relationship. Further, he (1950b) found that the ability to describe the ideal relationship is a function of expertness rather than theoretical allegiance. He also found that nontherapists can describe the ideal therapeutic relationship in the same manner and about as well as therapists. He concluded from this that the therapeutic relationship may be only a variation of good interpersonal relationships in general. Using analyses of recorded interviews, Fiedler (1950b) found that expert psychotherapists of any of the three different schools created a relationship more closely approximating the ideal relationship than the relationship created by nonexperts. The relationship created by the experts resembled more closely the relationship created by other experts than that of the nonexperts within the same school.

The most important aspect of good interpersonal relationships revealed by Fiedler's study is related to the therapist's ability to understand, to communicate with, and to maintain rapport with the client. The ability to maintain an "appropriate emotional distance" also emerged as important. For our purposes, it might be useful to list the eight statements judged in this study to be most characteristic of the ideal relationship:

1. The therapist is able to participate completely in the patient's communication.
2. The therapist's comments are always right in line with what the patient is trying to convey.
3. The therapist is well able to understand the patient's feeling.
4. The therapist really tries to understand the patient's feelings.
5. The therapist always follows the patient's line of thought.
6. The therapist's tone of voice conveys the complete ability to share the patient's feelings.
7. The therapist sees the patient as a co-worker on a common problem.
8. The therapist treats the patient as an equal.

At the other end of the scale, we find the following statements rated as least characteristic of an ideal relationship:

1. The therapist shows no comprehension of the feelings the patient is trying to communicate.
2. The therapist cannot maintain rapport with the patient.
3. The therapist's own needs completely interfere with his understanding of the patient.
4. The therapist feels disgusted by the patient.
5. The therapist is hostile toward the patient.
6. The therapist is punitive.
7. The therapist is very unpleasant to the patient.
8. The therapist acts in a very superior manner toward the patient.

In the classroom situation, we can probably substitute in almost all of these statements the word "teacher" for "therapist" and "pupil" for "patient." In the counseling situation, we can use the terms "counselor" and "counselee." In the home situation, we can substitute "parent" and "child."

An illuminating study in a very different setting is McCardle's (1959) investigation of teacher characteristics and pupil achievement in first-year algebra. McCardle administered to twenty-nine first-year algebra teachers the Minnesota Teacher Attitude Inventory, an instrument which was validated on the ability of teachers to establish good relationships with pupils. By carefully correcting for measured intelligence and initial achievement, he studied the relationship between the MTAI scores of teachers and the achievement of their pupils in algebra achievement, which required primarily the ability to manipulate symbols, and he found that the relationships were statistically significant for arithmetic understanding and functional competence in mathematics, involving skill in using what had been learned. One may infer from these findings that the pupils of teachers unskilled in creating good relationships may become as skilled in manipulating algebraic symbols as those teachers more skilled in creating good relationships but these pupils are not likely to become as skilled in using what they have learned from their thinking.

From the goals for guiding creative talent which were identified in Chapter 8, it follows that the relationships and strategies needed to guide creative talent should be such as would support the creative process and avoid driving it "off course." As I have mulled over this requirement, observed teachers and counselors in operation, and studied the various possible teaching and counseling strategies, it has seemed to me that this relationship should itself resemble the creative process.

I shall attempt now to describe what I consider the nature of creative relationships and strategies.

THE CREATIVE RELATIONSHIP

The characteristics which emerged as most characteristic of the ideal therapeutic relationship in Fiedler's study include many of the features which I consider important in the creative relationship. To achieve the relationship described by Fiedler, one must enter imaginatively into the thinking and feeling experiences of another. Only by doing this can one participate completely in another's communication, keep his comments in line with what the other is trying to say, understand his feelings, follow his line of thought, and share his feelings. There is a co-experiencing, as they struggle as co-workers on a common problem.

If we analyze the nature of the ideal relationship as described by Fiedler's subjects, it meets most of my requirements for a creative relationship. Of the relationships which have been described in the literature, one offered by Moustakas (1959) comes closest to the one I have in mind. The creative relationship requires a willingness on the part of the guidance worker to embark over untraveled pathways. As in creative thinking, he must be willing to permit one thing to lead to another, be ready to get off the beaten track or break out of the mold —rather than look upon the individual in traditional ways and thus fail to relate to him as a real person. This is in contrast to the comfort and safety of the previously tested process and well-traveled road.

This kind of relationship is in sharp contrast to most teacher-pupil and counselor-counselee relationships which have been described. Most current conceptualizations are reactive ones in which the teacher or counselor responds to the stimulations of a particular individual, and in turn the individual responds to the stimulations of the teacher or counselor. In fact, this stimulus-response conceptualization of teaching and counseling seems to be definitely in the ascendancy. Most of the thinking concerning teaching machines is oriented to such a conceptualization. Apparently, most educational leaders see counseling relationships in the stimulus-response framework. Conant (1959), for example, has urged repeatedly that gifted students *be persuaded* to enroll in mathematics and science courses and attend college. Many of the speeches and discussions at the 1961 meeting of the American Personnel and Guidance Association reflected a similar point of view. Feder (1961) in his presidential address at these same meetings, however, warned of the serious dangers of "Conantism." Feder particularly decried the implication that counselors and teachers have the "right" answers for every student in our schools, and therefore they must make a concerted drive to establish this pattern as "right" for all of America's superior youth.

On the other hand, Wrenn (1961) in his preliminary report on the future of guidance in American schools, reported that one of the possible future developments in guidance may stem from Skinner's concept of "operant conditioning." He pointed to studies which show that "specific responses can be insured if appropriately timed rewards are given for the desired behavior." "A counselor can anticipate specific responses from a student or can reinforce desired reactions," Wrenn explains (1961, p. 10), "if verbal and nonverbal cues are appropriately rewarded." Thus, "operant conditioning" promises to be the "ultimate" of the stimulus-response counseling relationship.

In all of the stimulus-response conceptualizations, emphasis is on the correctness of the stimulus and/or response. The creative counseling relationship is not a stimulus-response one. It involves a "living" relationship, a co-experiencing.

As Moustakas (1959) explains, errors or mistakes in the creative relationship are irrelevant. It is a matter of *being*, rather than one of acting and being acted upon. Educators have frequently been puzzled by the outstanding success of some rare teacher or counselor who seems to violate almost every rule of good teaching or counseling. Their errors don't matter. The pupil's creative problem-solving processes continue unimpeded because the relationship is an open, non-threatening, creative one.

How does the creative relationship come about? What can the counselor or teacher do to bring about such a relationship? Apparently, it happens in much the same way that creative thought takes place. No matter how much one strains to think of a new idea nor how fervently he may want to think of one, he may fail altogether. Then it seems to "just happen." It occurs through the preconscious processes. It is what happens when the inventor or scientific discoverer thinks of his big idea in church, the bath tub, or bed. Like creative thinking, it requires an openness to experience, a willingness to participate in the relationship once it happens.

To elaborate further upon the conceptualization I have in mind, I would like to examine and reverse the coercive strategies man has always used to control other men and contrast them with the creative relationships. I have chosen these coercive strategies because they sharpen the issues; represent primitive, overlearned behaviors; and are frequently used by teachers and counselors to influence pupil behavior. These strategies were originally identified in my study of coercive methods in a wide variety of situations in history from the extortion of witchcraft confessions and brainwashing by the Chinese Communists in the Korean struggle and in everyday living from "high pressure selling" to the control of infant behaviors. In the reversal of these strategies I shall attempt to delineate my conceptualization of the creative guidance process.

EXPERIENCING JOY IN THE
INDIVIDUAL'S CREATIVE POWERS

In order to establish creative relationships, many teachers and counselors will have to change from the "strategy of powerlessness" to one of experiencing genuine joy or pride in the creative powers of pupils or counselees. One of the favorite strategies of the teacher, administrator, or counselor who wants to control students is to make them feel powerless. This is the basic strategy of coercive influence.

The purpose behind the strategy of powerlessness is to convince the subject of the uselessness of resistance to influence, to make capitulation to the will of the influencer less damaging to self-pride than the consequences of his resistance. The ultimate objective is to reduce the subject to simple, animal-level concerns for physiological and safety needs, all high in man's hierarchy of needs.

The means of implementing this strategy are legion. The basic element is to strip the individual of his defenses and props. Figuratively speaking, this is achieved in ways analagous to one of the oldest, cleverest, and most powerful tricks employed by enemies to make a prisoner feel powerless—strip him of his clothes. Counselors and teachers do not strip children of their clothes. They do strip them of their defenses in order to control their behavior or to influence them to adopt certain behaviors and postures. This may be done by probing and insistence that a counselee give reasons for everything he does or says. It may be done by an overconcern with his daydreaming, his feelings of hostility, or his lack of interest in dating. He may temporarily need these defenses against something more threatening. Communication is made a one-way process.

A second technique for inducing feelings of powerlessness is to deprive a subject of his physical needs such as sleep, rest, water, food, sanitation, and heat. Men have perhaps always sought to control other men in this way. Here again, perhaps no school counselor or teacher has ever gone to this extreme in controlling pupil behavior. Counselors and teachers do, however, resort to milder variations of this technique that may condition individuals for later more extreme techniques. These take the form of threats of deprivation as a consequence of not adopting certain behaviors.

A third procedure for making others feel powerless is to create as much uncertainty as possible. In the hands of the enemy, this is achieved by such measures as irregular schedules, inconsistent discipline, withheld information about plans on decisions, no relaxation, and true feelings kept hidden.

Perhaps unconsciously, teachers and counselors employ techniques to maintain their power to the detriment of the ego development of the pupil and his subsequent ability to cope with life's demands. Such techniques make the individual dependent upon the teacher or counselor in making decisions, in knowing how to behave, and similar problems. An added technique employed by many guidance workers is to withhold various types of information, including the results of psychological tests of aptitude, achievement, or personality. In doing so, they communicate the idea that they possess more information about the individual than he does, and this gives them the power over him. They keep him at a "safe" distance and make it difficult for him to know where he stands.

I think the evidence is rather clear that all of these methods of implementing this strategy can be shown to decrease creativity. Rogers (1954) and others have cautioned against any condition which threatens the worth of the individual, and certainly the techniques which I have described are calculated to do just this. It seems to me that herein lies the fallacy in the arguments of those who say that we must calculatedly subject children to discomfort in order to make them think creatively. I wish some of the proponents could have participated with me in a recent experiment. I wanted to describe the nature and evaluate the degree of creative growth taking place during a two-week science and art summer camp by means of a battery of pre- and post-tests. The campers had given many evidences of creative growth. They had many exciting and stimulating experiences, making many self-discoveries. Their curiosity had full range. Their morale was high; they gave every indication of wanting to do well on the post-test. The post-test, however, fell on the hottest day the area had experienced in over five years. In spite of the fact that the examiner did everything possible to make the room comfortable and to make the children feel physically and psychologically comfortable, their struggle to think showed quite clearly in their performance. The combined effects of practice, stimulating experiences, behavioral evidences of creative growth, and learning creatively failed to produce expected gains. In fact, there were statistically significant losses on almost all of the test tasks. Too much of their energies were spent in drinking water, fanning, and otherwise trying to cope physiologically with the high temperature. Even those who sat still, trying to concentrate, were unable to summon the extra energy required to produce ideas. If this is an example of what occurs when a natural force, such as weather, reduces one to animal concerns, one can only speculate concerning the impact of such conditions created psychologically by man.

In sharp contrast to the strategy of powerlessness and its varied techniques of implementation is the proposed replacement strategy of experiencing genuine pride or joy in the creative powers of the individual. Self-esteem is a human need which ranks high in man's hierarchy. Sometimes, I think it ranks high also in the hierarchy of needs of many animals. Self-esteem is most likely to flourish when others feel pride in one's creativity.

In employing this strategy the teacher or counselor respects the individual's need for certain defenses and recognizes that they may be necessary to protect him from overwhelming anxiety until he has developed the skills for coping with the anxiety or the forces which induce it. He respects the counselee's need for privacy, perhaps his manner of dress or manner of speech, or some other prop temporarily adopted to help him control his inner tensions and cope with the demands of his environment. Appointments are respected, information is freely given, feelings are expressed, and the atmosphere is relaxed, at least most of the time.

One of the primary characteristics of the creative relationship, as I conceive it, is the acceptance of thinking as a legitimate activity. In school, we usually feel that we must keep children busy doing something, leaving them little or no time for thinking. By five or six, the child is almost never alone. We are disturbed, if he talks to himself, invents songs, or engages in unsupervised daydreams. In the creative relationship, it is not necessary for the teacher or counselor to keep children—or adults either—busy talking. They can tolerate periods of silence because they recognize that the individual may be busy thinking.

BEING A GUIDE, NOT A GOD

Teachers and counselors are especially susceptible, because of their attributed roles, to the temptations of the strategy of omnipotence and omniscience. In fact, there are times when they have difficulty in escaping this role, because students and counselees insist upon making them omnipotent and omniscient.

Through this strategy the subject is made to see the one in power over him as invulnerable and as knowing everything about him. Again, the purpose is to convince the subject that it is futile for him to resist and that nothing is to be lost by complying. An enemy may achieve this by obtaining a small bit of information about the subject's private life in some way. From this, he makes clever inferences from known information to exaggerate the amount of information possessed. The enemy magnifies the power he has over the subject and promises improved conditions as a reward for following his will.

It is easy for guidance workers to use test scores and information from teachers and other students in much the same way as the enemy uses his bit of information gleaned from the captive's hometown newspaper or fellow prisoners. Students frequently believe that the teacher or counselor knows things about them that they themselves do not know. This may be brought about quite unconsciously by the teacher or counselor, either as a function of his personality needs or because it is a strategy he learned early to enable him to control others.

This strategy could have been labeled "the strategy of bluff." Certainly, the maintenance of an aura of omnipotence and omniscience requires bluff. Deans and administrators may easily be tempted to assume postures of omnipotence, whereas teachers and counselors are susceptible to assuming postures of omniscience. While such postures may be immediately gratifying, the ultimate effect is likely to be disappointing in terms of the educator's own satisfaction and certainly in terms of the creative growth of the student. It might be well, however, for the teacher or counselor to understand the psychological function of bluff. Fundamentally, the function of bluff is to redress the balance between one's own adequacy and the other person's superiority. This cannot be done in actuality but only by psychological devices, which are independent of tangible resources. Counselors and teachers are particularly likely to employ this strategy when they feel threatened by creative pupils who ask unusual questions or propose unorthodox solutions. They use this strategy "to keep such pupils in their place" and to prevent their becoming "too big-headed."

More compatible with the objectives of counseling creative individuals than the strategy of omnipotence and omniscience is what I have termed the strategy of *being* a helpful guide. In posing this as a replacement strategy, there is no inference that the counselor should abdicate the power role which he may possess as an expert in human relations, careers, or whatever the field of expertness. The counselor must permit himself and his resources to be used by the creative individual in his inquiry, his testing of hypotheses. Similarly, the teacher need not relinquish the power he possesses by virtue of his subject matter knowledge or professional competence.

Another label for this strategy might have been that of "mutual exploration" or "mutual investigation." This would have denied the inescapable influence of the teacher or counselor. I believe this to be unwise. One of man's most fundamental needs is for anchors in reality —some kind of structure, someone or something to help remove the fear of the unknown. A guide serves such a role. The counselor can help the creative student structure his world by helping him explore his assets and liabilities, through testing or whatever means are appropriate, the requirements of various alternative courses of actions, and the possible consequences of his ideas. It is not easy, however, to resist trying to play God through the use of tests and other tools available to teachers and counselors.

The acute need of the highly creative person for someone to help him find anchors in reality is reflected in the following description by Carl Rogers (1954) of the feelings accompanying a creative production: "I am alone. No one has ever done just this before. I have ventured into territory where no one has been. Perhaps I am foolish, or wrong, or lost, or abnormal." What such a person needs, however, is a guide, not an omnipotent or omniscient dictator.

You will note that throughout I have used the term "*being* a guide." I have no where used "guide" as a transitive verb in a stimulus-response sense. Such a role would destroy the creativeness of the relationship. One can still be a guide and permit the individual to initiate, to propose, even to test. I would permit this guide to express opinions, make judgments, give information. The individual can then get his anchors from these, and the locus of the evaluations he makes will be himself rather than the teacher or the counselor.

GENUINE EMPATHY

One important basis of power to influence, according to French and Raven (1958), is referent power, based on ability to engender in others the desire to identify with the person exerting the influence. It is even a common strategy of control of the enemy. The goal is to make the adversary see himself as being one with the enemy in some way. He tries to convince the adversary that they have mutual desires, that he understands what the victim is going through, and that the victim should aid him. The purpose is to make the individual abandon his goals and forget that he is dealing with an enemy. To implement this strategy, the enemy is pleasant, agreeable, accepting, and sympathetic. He tries to gain sympathy and to find some common emotional basis for identification; for instance, they both may have been reared on a farm.

Leaders, teachers, and politicians have long understood and exploited this strategy in influencing the behavior of others. Social science research has repeatedly shown that people are influenced most by those whom they perceive as being like them. Some teachers and counselors apparently have a tremendous talent for inducing identification and thereby provoking in others the desire to give up all their secrets to please them. In so doing, the student or counselee may prematurely surrender psychological defenses important to his well-being. Others who possess this talent, by reflecting their own deceitful inner world, can more easily provoke hidden lies and fantasies in others.

Although highly creative individuals may feel this identification, their independence is frequently so great as to enable them to resist the influence. This is illustrated by an account of one investigator who was evaluating the effects of group psychotherapy with a group of "underachievers." Some weeks after the conclusion of the experiment, one of the subjects met the investigator and apologized for "letting him down by not making all A's." He explained, "I wanted to help you by making all A's but I was just so busy learning so many things, I didn't have time to make good grades." In inducing identification, counselors need to be aware of their own motivations. Their motivations may be to manipulate the counselee, or it may be a concern for this growth. If the identification interferes with the creative individual's independence of thought, it could be damaging, regardless of the teacher or counselor's motivation.

The strategy of *genuine empathy* is necessary to replace the strategy of *identification*. Basically the influence psychology is reversed. In using the strategy of identification, the counselor tries to make his client see that they are really alike and that the client should help the counselor by going to college, making good grades, deciding to be a scientist, or whatever the behavior the guidance worker is trying to influence. No one wins in such a game. The teacher or counselor is likely to feel guilty for "tricking" the student into this decision. The student may despise himself for being seduced in this way. As a result he may abandon immediately the approved behavior or be more resistant than ever, later on. In using "genuine empathy" the teacher or counselor will try to view things from the internal frame of reference of the student. He will try to imagine how the student feels about things. This, then, gives him the basis for helping the individual meet the requirements of the situation, whatever it is, as something that he is doing for himself rather than something he is doing to accommodate the teacher or counselor. This is usually a stronger and more lasting motivation.

**CREATIVE ACCEPTANCE OF
LIMITATIONS AND ASSETS**

Exploiting or "taking advantage" of another's weaknesses or vulnerabilities is another basic strategy of control. The purpose, as with other coercive influence strategies, is to increase control over others.

The coercive agent may implement this strategy by creating a friendly, informal, relaxed atmosphere. He then pounces on bits of information revealing the subject's weaknesses and uses this as a wedge for forcing compliance. He uses common, human, cultural, and personal vulnerabilities. The enemy has discovered that almost all people behave in certain ways because they are human and finds these to be reasonably reliable guides to coercion. For example, needs for sleep, rest, food, and water are universal and their deprivation or threatened deprivation usually produces certain predictable reactions. Members of a particular culture also have certain peculiar vulnerabilities which provide a degree of guidance in shaping coercive pressures. British and American POWs of World War II exploited repeatedly the Germans' blind obedience to their officers. Our own enemies have exploited our tendency to make concessions to comfort. Finally, the enemy looks for personal idiosyncrasies which can be exploited. They have found the following types particularly easy to exploit:

> *The servile*—the person who bows, scrapes, and "kow-tows" to anyone in authority, acting in a very self-demeaning manner.

> *The talkative*—the person who talks so much that inevitably he betrays himself and others, giving information which can be used against himself and others.

> *The frightened*—the person who is afraid of everyone and can be bluffed easily into doing almost anything.

> *The arrogant*—the person who bluffs and bullies, giving others the feeling that he is "riding for a fall" and makes you want to "take him down a few notches."

> *The selfish*—the person who thinks first of his own interests which makes it easy to pit him against someone else and obtain compliance.

The naive—the person who has been overprotected or has not been exposed to the "ways of the world" and doesn't seem to know what "it's all about," which makes it easy to influence his behavior.

Judging from the personality studies of outstanding creative persons summarized in Chapter 4, the teacher or counselor may expect to find some of these types more frequently among highly creative individuals than among less creative ones. In his busy schedule and in his desire to influence these youngsters, the teacher or counselor will find it tempting to exploit such weaknesses to shortcut the decision-making process and to obtain what he sees as the "right" decision. The trouble is that it may not be the "right decision" and even if it is, it may not be one that the individual actually accepts. It may amount to "behavior without conviction." The immediate and apparent influence may be satisfactory, but it is not likely to be lasting. Eventually, it is likely to produce resentment and hostility and is not likely to facilitate creative growth.

Originally, I was tempted to label this replacement strategy as "giving the sucker an even break." I rejected it immediately for two reasons. First, it implies a lack of genuine respect for the servile, the frightened, the arrogant, the naive, and similar types. Healthy influence and effective communication require respect. Second, "giving someone an even break" represents only a small part of what I consider an adequate replacement strategy. Thus, it has been labeled "the strategy of developing creative acceptance of limitations and assets or exploring the positive forces in personality."

It is usually possible to identify in all personalities forces for healthy growth. This is especially true of highly creative individuals. Through exploration, such individuals are usually able to identify such characteristics in themselves. Whether the problem is one of vocational choice, delinquent behavior, or scholastic failure, the teacher or counselor will accomplish far more by exploring positive forces in personality than by exploiting weaknesses. This does not mean that the guidance worker should not seek to understand the dynamics of a personality vulnerability. For example, an understanding of the process by which a given individual became "servile" may reveal the achievement of some very valuable characteristic. In becoming servile, he may have achieved a deep sensitivity to the feelings and needs of others. In remaining naive, he may have retained his openness to his environment. Thus, in achieving his vulnerabilities, one may have increased his creative capacity. These characteristics might be positive forces in career success in some occupations, in achieving a better relationship with others, or even in achieving scholastic success. Or, positive forces quite unrelated to the vulnerability may be identified and reinforced.

The following actual case described by a high school teacher shows how this strategy can be used to help highly creative individuals who have been labeled as "hopeless cases" (Holm, 1957):

> Bob was nervous, withdrawn and sad. He was failing every subject except gym and art and could not read well enough to keep up his work. He was not high school material according to his teachers but instead of being able to make the most of the courses that would help him prepare for his future, he was becoming more antisocial and unhappy and less able to participate in anything that involved being with other people. He felt inadequate and began to withdraw, even in basketball games. He had been a fine athlete but, losing self-respect in situations that demanded reading and talking, he soon lost his confidence altogether. He painted football games with no players on the field and made many sketches of boys huddled in blankets on the bench, watching the game. Other drawings he did showed himself alone on the bench, alone in the locker room after the game with a group of players talking together in the distance, alone at the sidelines in his basketball uniform but leaning against a post watching the game. . . .
>
> Fortunately, Bob was in my English class so in addition to having reading drills after school, he illustrated the stories we read to show he had understood the material. The poetry which was read aloud in class he envisioned richly and his clarity of visual images was a revelation. It showed that he understood the thoughts and transformed them into vivid pictures. He could not write a quiz on the meaning or details of a poem or story, nor could he talk about them, but his drawings showed understanding. In Robert Frost's poem "Mending Fences," Bob drew the neighbor ". . . like a stone savage armed" with a determined expression, while he pictured Frost with his head to one side in sad contemplation of the unfriendly act of mending the fence. Even the details of the kinds of trees each man had were pictured. Frost's trees were apple and his neighbor's were pine, which made an important point to emphasize the meaninglessness of the wall. All this Bob understood and visualized but could not express in words. The pent-up ideas and feelings and the strain of failing for lack of ability to use words were wearing Bob down, making him withdraw and changing his entire personality. His grade school teachers said he was "sweet but dumb," but at this point he was too sad to be sweet.

Finally, after his illustrations were exhibited first in the English class and then in the art class, he realized he was doing something important. Other students admired his work, expressed envy for his talent and bolstered his morale. He drew and drew, from lonely scenes of himself at a window and himself alone on the basketball court, to himself fighting with "ghastly men," to himself in many under-sea battles with fish. Drawing these conflicts was a cathartic to a pent-up boy and after almost a year of illustrating his way through English class and drawing and painting away his conflicts by externalizing them, he was able to increase his skills in reading and participate again in sports. He got back into "the crowd" and became "himself" again, a quiet, good-natured boy with more than his share of artistic ability.

An important aspect of Miss Holm's relationship with Bob was her willingness to embark with him on an untrodden path. What teacher would know how to grade a boy's English paper consisting of illustrations of poems, stories, and other literary works? By "going along with" Bob in this unorthodox fashion, a "hopeless case" learned to read and perhaps escape a life of serious withdrawal.

SEARCH FOR THE TRUTH ABOUT THE SITUATION

The strategy of the "big lie" is another favorite of those who use aversive pressures to control others. This strategy may range from simple distortions of fact to the outright creation of a situation to achieve the purpose of the coercive agent. Psychologically, the purposes of this strategy are to destroy the victim's accustomed props, take away his anchors in reality, and make him more dependent upon the coercing authority. This may be accomplished by arousing feelings of doubt concerning perceptions and motivations, making the important unimportant and vice versa, enforcing trivial demands, manipulating perceived consensus of group norms, and the like. The coercive agent may try to create the impression that the victim's friends have all turned against him, that he is alone and might as well take advantage of the situation afforded him by the benevolence of the enemy to "feather his own nest." In the purest form of this strategy, the coercive agent emphasizes the fact that the victim is now in a world completely different from the one to which he has been accustomed, and the ideas of justice are different (but better), and that his old defenses and props are no longer valid. Certainly such strategies are inimical to creative growth.

Counselors rarely, if ever, employ this strategy in its purest form. Principals and student personnel workers charged with disciplinary responsibilities sometimes use it in attempting to obtain conforming behavior among students, particularly new students with reputations as trouble-makers. Many of the auxiliary techniques, however, are items in the practiced repertoire of teachers and counselors. These, mentioned already, include: making the unimportant important, enforcing trivial and absurd demands, overemphasizing small differences between the present situation and a previous one. Guidance workers should recognize that the ready compliance with regulations or with group norms obtained by such means is likely to be only temporary and disruptive of creative growth. Most students are likely to consider this type of pressure as not legitimate—not right and just, and it is likely to have a "boomerang" effect of lasting consequences. For one thing, this strategy once applied may make it impossible for the particular teacher or counselor to be useful to the student in the future. It also makes it difficult for others to serve a productive function for the individual for years to come.

A special variety of the "big lie" is the manipulation of group consensus. Since attitudes and actions are influenced by one's perception of the consensus of his group, coercive agents are ever alert to manipulate perceptions of group consensus. Too frequently individuals accept manipulated consensus rather than rely on their own perceptions. Knowing that students are powerfully motivated by what they regard as group consensus (what everybody else thinks or does) but that perceived consensus is frequently erroneous, teachers and counselors can frequently assist students in arriving at a more realistic appraisal of the group's attitudes or actions. Students are frequently relieved that consensus is not what they supposed it to be, when consensus is contrary to the perceptions or values of the student, the teacher or counselor can assist him in resolving the conflict.

If guidance workers are not honest in their attempts to formulate perceptions of group consensus, they may expect counteraction techniques. Students will be noncommittal and untrusting and develop strategies for keeping teachers and counselors confused concerning their stand. Only the enthusiastic *search for the truth* is appropriate in guiding highly creative individuals.

The well-intentioned teacher or counselor probably uses the strategy of the "big lie" only to make a student wake up and realize the seriousness of his situation. He wants to motivate the student to take the adaptive or compensatory action necessary to solve his problem or face successfully the danger which confronts him. My studies of men in emergencies and extreme conditions have made me fully aware of the stubbornness of man's resistance to accepting the seriousness of his situation in the face of grave danger. This is evident even in the accounts of men who have lived to tell their stories of survival in emergencies and extreme situations. Aircraft accident statistics show that a large proportion of fatalities occur from bailouts which have been delayed too long. Air-sea rescue studies show that pilots resist accepting the possibility that they cannot "make it" and fail to send proper distress signals or make adequate preparations for ditchings. Students of disasters find that it is exceedingly difficult to influence people in flood disaster areas to recognize the seriousness of the situation and evacuate or take other adaptive action.

In the face of these difficulties, resort to the "big lie" or the magnification of the danger is understandable. The student who has reasonably good contact with reality, however, is more likely to be influenced by a "search for the truth." Counselors can aid creative individuals in thinking out imaginatively the consequences of their actions and decisions. Apparently a part of the reason for resistance to accepting the seriousness of the danger and to taking adaptive action is caused by inadequate structure or anchor in reality. The teacher or counselor can aid the student in his search for structure. To take adaptive action, one needs to know how he stands and what to do. An earnest search for the truth is healthy—in fact, the dangers become less frightening since they are understood and methods for coping with them can be devised. In other words, they allow the creative individual to use his own creativity to solve his problems.

LETTING ONE THING LEAD TO ANOTHER

The strategy of singleness of purpose is used by coercive agents with those who try to be evasive, vague, and indefinite. For example, an enemy interrogator or interviewer will keep steadfastly to his goal and will not be seduced into accepting vague abstractions or generalities which may have no meaning. He guards against the victim's interrogating him and distracting him from his purpose. He shows the victim that he is "onto his tricks" and that it is futile to resist his influence.

One method of applying this strategy is to pin the victim down and make him give specific, concrete, precise information. If an individual maintains that he does not know, the coercive agent will require him to give an estimate or opinion. The agent will then permit the victim to change the topic temporarily but will return doggedly to the sensitive point at the opportune moment. The strategy is uniquely suited for ferreting out those little intimate things an individual tries to hide or keep private. It is easy to spot the things a person is sensitive about.

Teachers and counselors will ask, "Well, what is wrong with this technique in guidance? Isn't it a teacher or counselor's job to stick to the goal and compel the student to work on his problem rather than evade it?" He certainly has to be sensitive to the resistance of the student, but the techniques used to help a person transform his resistance into positive, creative action may be quite different. Certainly the purpose is different. A teacher or counselor may "chase a student down the abstraction ladder" to assist him in his growth processes and to explore feelings which interfere with his creativity and his adjustment but not to demonstrate to him that the teacher or counselor is onto his tricks. The purpose might be to help him become aware of the tricks he is playing on himself.

The strategy is apparently a potent one in influencing or controlling the behavior of others. It is widely used in interviewing in criminology and law. The guidance worker should of course recognize its potency but must guard against using it in such a way as to violate the personal integrity of the student. This involves both subtle differences in technique as well as differences in motivation from those of the interrogator or indoctrinator.

There are several reasons why the strategy of singleness of purpose is neither the best guidance technique nor the most effective one in implementing the creative process. Perhaps the most serious is the failure to permit one thing to lead to another. In addition to the fact that this failure throws off course the creative process, it involves a subtle kind of lack of respect for the other, the arousal of resistance to communication, failure to understand the other, and failure to recognize blockages in communication. The teacher or counselor who pursues doggedly his singleness of purpose is likely to fail to understand the student's problem. He certainly cannot be sensitive to the needs of the student. In desperation, the student may seem to acquiesce but may not follow the advice at all because he "knows" that the teacher or counselor does not understand his problem.

It is frequently emotionally difficult for teachers to permit "one thing to lead to another." Observe how one fourth- and fifth-grade teacher managed what is an anxiety-producing kind of situation to most teachers to establish or reinforce a creative relationship with her class:

> One boy brought a cocoon to school. After two weeks, the moth hatched. We put the moth into a large glass container. The children read about moths in books. Through their reading, they learned it was a male cercopia moth. Every morning they would observe the moth carefully. In their reading, they had learned moths lay eggs. So morning after morning, no eggs. I made no comment. I listened.
>
> Finally a boy said, "I know; it's a male and males don't lay eggs." Another boy said, "Males do lay eggs."
>
> There was some silly giggling among the fifth grade boys (above average ability group) as much as to say, "Don't you know?"
>
> Then I said, "I think I know what you mean. I think you mean that a female can't lay an egg alone." "That's right," said a boy, and there was some more silly laughter and uncomfortable behavior. I said, "I haven't heard it said that a male lays an egg. A male passes a seed to a female and then after some time, the female produces its own kind."
>
> We talked about some of the animals that lay eggs and the hatching of eggs.
>
> The topic became realistic to the boys and, I hope, added respect to their knowledge which they had thought silly and which made them uncomfortable. Since then they have shown me nature books they are reading on plants and animals and discussed them without embarrassment.

Contrast the above handling of the situation to the method described below by a fourth-grade teacher in a similar situation:

> We had a rabbit in our classroom and the discussion centered about it. All of the class was very much interested in the discussion. A boy asked, "Why do we need two rabbits to have little rabbits?" Everyone joined in and wanted to know.

My immediate thought was, "I can't teach sex in school!" My action was to laugh and casually change the subject.

There was keen interest in the question and I observed that a couple drew a little color. I told the class that there are many questions that are asked that are good but hard to answer without going into research.

Everyone sort of shrugged it off with a "teacher-doesn't-know-anything" attitude.

In this case we find that it is the teacher who is evasive. She failed to recognize that questions such as the one asked by these fourth graders *can* be answered truthfully in concepts that they can understand.

A FRIENDLY ENVIRONMENT

The strategy of the totally unfriendly environment as used by a coercive agent requires that no one show friendliness or sympathy. For example, an enemy interrogator or indoctrinator contrives to make the victim feel that his "buddies" are not standing behind him or have actually "ratted" on him. He tries to exercise tight control of his own desire to be liked and to be on guard against flattery and similar guiles. He tries to avoid giving any evidence whatsoever of human feelings, particularly of sympathy. He contrives even to have others apply the cold, silent treatment.

Teachers and counselors are likely almost never to employ this technique in its purest form. Many, however, because of their own psychological needs may communicate the feeling that they are the student's only friend and by so doing reinforce the perception of his environment as hostile. Because of different needs, others may avoid giving any evidence of affect or human feeling. They are afraid that they will become too involved in the problems of their students or counselees. Consequently, they present themselves as cold, objective and unfeeling. In a sense, such devices constitute a pattern not too different psychologically from the strategy of the unfriendly environment and are about as damaging in their effects. This problem is especially acute in working with sensitive, highly creative individuals.

Two subsidiary techniques favored by coercive agents in executing the strategy of the unfriendly environment are: destroying cliques and encouraging members to give criticisms of or reports on other members, commonly referred to as "ratting." Similarly, there is a tendency among educators to regard cliques as "bad" and to try to destroy them. Research evidence, however, indicates that cliques do develop in almost all kinds of groups and *may* be quite healthy. In many of the imaginative stories of children, the solution for many of the flying monkeys is to find another flying monkey or for a cat that won't scratch to find another cat that won't scratch.

Cliques may be needed by groups and by the individuals who compose them as defenses. Their destruction may rob the group of healthy modes of adapting to the demands of the situation. Unhealthy conditions may be encouraged in school groups by using one clique as a model for others. This would appear to be particularly dangerous in dealing with highly creative individuals, whether they are members of the model group or not.

Educators are ambivalent concerning "tattling" or "informing" on members of school groups. On one hand, the practice may help them maintain power over the group, yet it may create extremely unhealthy group conditions. Teachers and counselors, particularly in discipline cases, face this problem in the use of information one student gives in confidence about another. In general, using the teacher or counselor as a "spy" for the administration is likely to place in great jeopardy their future effectiveness. One ex-POW, training young recruits a few years ago, was interviewed by a reporter studying military training. He asserted that many of the men he was training were traitors and collaborators already. Even though he discouraged the practice, men still informed him about the schemes and "secret" behavior of their "buddies." Such behavior was *probably* learned and reinforced in school.

Coercive agents also seek to control behavior in groups through techniques which unintentionally create hostile relationships. This is especially easy to do where creative individuals are involved. Giving special privileges to particular members, having students perform special tasks for the teacher or counselor, and recognizing the cooperative behavior of individuals are a few practices which may produce such consequences. Counselors and teachers may disagree with this idea and maintain that such practices are useful in bestowing self-esteem and status for meritorious work. If such purposes are in fact achieved, these practices may be desirable. These practices, however, may actually create suspicion and distrust and gain for the recipient the label of "teacher's pet." What is intended to be rewarding is in fact punishing and vice versa. Whether it is punishing or rewarding depends upon the norms of the peer group, the social class, or cultural group. This is especially important in dealing with divergent behavior.

Teachers and counselors also need to be aware of the effects of another technique for implementing the unfriendly-environment technique, that of isolation from the group. One particularly damaging effect of this practice is that these sanctions are frequently exercised against talented students simply for functioning at their ability or thinking creatively, not just against those who manifest socially undesirable behavior. Whether the sanction is against desirable or undesirable behavior, counselors should be aware of the disorganizing effects of social isolation and should assist group members in becoming aware of their isolating practices.

The strategy of the friendly, loving environment is well-known in the rapidly developing field of social psychiatry. This is the essence of the concept of the "therapeutic community" used in many psychiatric treatment centers. The total environment is friendly and loving, making it safe for the patient to think, to be himself, and to find his anchors in reality. The patient meets a friendly attitude in the food service personnel, nurses, attendants, recreation workers, office personnel, and psychotherapists. This does not mean that such an environment is "soft" and unrealistic, but it does mean that human beings show their concern for the welfare of others. Even if it were unrealistic, such an environment might be necessary for enough creative growth to take place so that the individual can later cope with an unfriendly environment.

To illustrate how this principle may be used to bring about growth, the following account by a fifth-grade teacher is offered. This teacher experimented with the friendly environment to help Helen, a highly creative child with serious behavior problems and learning difficulties. First, he visited Helen's family. At first, they were alarmed, fearing that Helen had done something serious at school and was "in trouble." When they discovered only a friendly interest in the child, they warmed to this interest. Through two or three contacts the parents apparently developed a better understanding of Helen and her problems and a greater sympathy for what the teacher was trying to do to help Helen. Next, the teacher selected four girls in the class whom he thought he could depend upon to help Helen. He encouraged them to permit Helen to participate in activities with them and to help her with some of her school problems. During a thirty-day period, much of Helen's hostile and aggressive behavior towards her teacher and classmates disappeared. She dropped almost entirely her childish and immature behavior, replacing it with behavior appropriate to a fifth-grade girl. The teacher estimates that Helen learned more in the succeeding thirty-day period than she had learned during the previous eight months of the school year.

Safety and affection rank high in man's hierarchy of needs, and only in a friendly environment can we expect creative growth of a healthy kind to take place.

A coercive agent may disguise or conceal his activities in such a way that the victim may be unaware that he is being pressured. The purpose is to catch the victim "off guard" and trick him into compliant behavior. An effort is made to make the contact appear friendly and casual rather than "official." As a result of this technique, men unwittingly give the enemy information sought and accept indoctrination quite unconsciously. For example, one serviceman captured by the Communists in Korea steadfastly maintains that he never received any indoctrination, yet he repeatedly parrotted much of the ideology and even the speech pattern of the Chinese Communists. His indoctrinator was a man who posed as his physician, giving him medical care so poor as to cause suspicion as to whether or not he had any medical training whatsoever. The attempt to indoctrinate was completely unsuspected by the victim.

This strategy is morely likely to be used by the untrained or poorly trained counselor or the teacher or administrator untrained in the principles and techniques of counseling. Of course, there will always be attempts to influence others through informal contacts and social relationships, in an effort to avoid resistance. Such a strategy is fraught with dangers. It is well that the teacher or counselor recognizes that it is futile to try to trick students into changing their behavior. The change in behavior might take place, but when the student becomes aware that he had been tricked, the net effect may be far from beneficial for creative growth. Even if the student never realizes this, his capacity for dealing with his problems realistically and creatively may be impaired.

It seems rather universal that man does not like to be manipulated by other men. In fact, my own experiments (1959d) show that men respond more favorably to what they perceive as direct influence than to what they perceive as indirect influence. "Unsuspected pressure" is frequently placed in this category. A common reaction is increased resistance, and man seems to have the capacity to resist attempts to manipulate him even on an unconscious level.

The answer to the strategy of unsuspected pressure is, in my opinion, the strategy of mutual understanding. No two people are going to communicate effectively and positively about anything unless there are mutual understandings. Each must understand what he can expect of the other. For example, the teacher or counselor has certain conceptions of his role and what he is supposed to do. The student he deals with likewise has certain expectations of him. If the teacher or counselor behaves contrary to these expectations and attempts to exert influence which the student considers as not legitimate—not right and just—there will be trouble. It is the teacher or counselor's job to interpret his legitimate role to the student in an attempt to develop mutual understandings.

RESPECT FOR DIGNITY AND WORTH

The last of the coercive strategies which I shall discuss may be called the strategy of ego inflation. In this strategy, the person in control plays on the victim's vanity or need for status (to be thought important by someone), and then contrives a situation wherein the victim "loses face" if he does not comply. The purpose is to influence the victim to behave according to the desires of the coercive agent in order to protect his ego—"to be important" to someone. In the first stage, he seeks to magnify the victim's value, his intelligence, his understanding, his talents and skills, and his virtue and goodness. After the victim begins enjoying this appreciation, the agent then threatens to withdraw it unless he proves his intelligence, ability, skill or the like by complying with his wishes. In other words, the victim is given the "VIP treatment" and made to enjoy it; then the coercive agent "moves in for the kill."

Parallels in teaching and counseling are almost too obvious to require elaboration. The teacher or counselor is keenly aware of the need for establishing good rapport. He has been trained concerning its essentiality or has read that there must be rapport before good teaching or counseling can occur. Unfortunately, little training has been given in sound techniques of gaining rapport. Therefore, many must rely upon their unconsciously learned ones. Since the strategy of ego inflation is a powerful one, it is difficult for the inexperienced or untrained teacher or counselor to avoid using it. It is also true that many creative individuals come with very strong needs for support and are therefore easily suscep- tible to such a strategy. The teacher or counselor's objective should be to help the student achieve a realistic self-concept, not an inflated one.

Plainly the replacement strategy for ego inflation is respect for human dignity and worth. All really satisfying human relations and interper- sonal influence rest fundamentally on this concept. If the school coun- selor or teacher does not genuinely respect students, there is little chance that any strategy or technique is going to improve his effectiveness. If we do not respect the human dignity and worth of creative individuals, there is little we can do to help them in their struggle to function fully.

SUMMARY

In this chapter, I have sought to develop a recognition of the need for creative relationships in teaching and counseling highly creative individuals. I have attempted to develop a concept of this relationship which is especially suited to the guidance of highly creative individuals. The concept suggested is an adaptation of Moustakas' creative counseling relationship and resembles closely the creative process. It requires a will- ingness to permit one thing to lead to another and to "break out of the mold." It is contrasted with the reaction or stimulus-response kinds of relationships now described in texts on teaching and counseling. In order to elaborate upon the concept, an examination was made of the coercive strategies which men use in controlling and influencing other men. An attempt was made to describe a reversal of these strategies which would facilitate the healthy creative processes of highly creative individuals. Emphasis was placed on experiencing genuine pleasure in the creative powers of the counselee; respecting creative ways of learning; being a helpful guide; engendering genuine empathy rather than stimu- lating identification processes; exploring the positive forces in person- ality rather than exploiting personality vulnerabilities; mutual search- ing for the truth rather than giving the "big lie"; following the lead of the counselee rather than maintaining a singleness of purpose; providing a friendly environment; making a stand for mutual understanding; and respecting the dignity and worth of the individual.

Chapter 10

COUNSELORS, TEACHERS, AND ADMINISTRATORS FOR GUIDING CREATIVE TALENT

Guiding creative talent effectively is never routine for counselors, teachers, or administrators. They are never safe in following traditional rules, strict schedules, tested and practiced methods and materials, or standard ways of assessing situations. They must continue to experiment, even when everything seems to be working well. Even the usual, unconscious kinds of self-deception may be glaringly obvious to a fully-alive, highly creative youngster. Thus, it is an understatement that successful guidance of creative talent requires qualities in counselors, teachers, and administrators which are not now very common among them.

In 1941, Hughes Mearns described quite aptly the difficulties involved in guiding creative talent in the following words:

It takes a brave tolerance and an unashamed openmindedness to accept youth as it really is and as it loves to be, to move into the world with scientific detachment, that is, without prejudice or blame, and there to approve whatever is done with affectionate interest. The growth of creative power begins at that exact spot and, more important, the approving elder is at that moment established in a position of slowly increasing control.—Mearns, 1941, p. 12.

What kinds of counselors, teachers, and administrators does this take? From the conceptualizations which have been presented concerning the personalities and abilities of highly creative individuals, the processes and stages by which the creative thinking abilities develop, the problems of creative individuals, the goals for guiding them, and the relationships most likely to be successful in achieving these goals, it should be possible to formulate a few special qualifications for each of the three groups. In this chapter, I shall attempt to summarize some of my own ideas and those of others who have thought about the problem. Since members of each of the three groups of major concern bring to the problem different roles, talents, and qualifications, I shall discuss separately the roles, talents, and qualifications possessed by the counselor, teacher, and administrator.

COUNSELOR QUALIFICATIONS

General Requirements

It would be very easy to say that it requires a highly creative counselor to counsel highly creative individuals. It is frequently maintained that one must be a handicapped person in order to counsel the handicapped, that one must have been an alcoholic to counsel an alcoholic, that one must be a member of a minority group to counsel an individual from a minority group. There are, however, many types of creative counselors. I immediately think of two types which I consider poorly qualified for counseling highly creative individuals.

One type of counselor who probably would be extremely unsuccessful in counseling the highly creative individual is the one who is so absorbed in his own creativity that he gives counselees little opportunity to be creative themselves. Such a counselor upsets the creative thinking processes of his counselees completely. A counselor of this type is likely to let every impulse rush out, and he manifests little control of his responses. Such counselors may, however, have good scientific training, and may learn gradually how to control their impulses. Some, however, are likely to show little evidence of desiring to control their impulses and may themselves need psychotherapy.

The type of counselor just described would be, according to McPherson's (1960) categories, dedicated to the primary processes. The other type of creative counselor likely to be especially unproductive with highly creative individuals would fall at the opposite extreme and be dedicated to the secondary processes. That is, he is rigid, constricted, overly dedicated to method and technique, and lacking in spontaneity. He may be able to think of ways by which the counselee can solve his problems, but he is unable to establish a warm relationship. He is afraid of his unconscious and is cautious and careful to make accurate statements. His emotions are overcontrolled and he demands a high degree of order in his life. Counseling interviews must go according to his plan. He is likely to suppress childishness, be afraid of his softness and femininity, and repress all weaknesses.

It may be argued, of course, that both of the types described above are not genuinely creative. It might be said that they are "merely facile," to borrow a term from Hammer (1961). It may also be argued that both of these types need psychotherapy themselves and that they would be unproductive in counseling anyone. It would be my contention, however, that both of the above types might be effective in guiding a narrow range of counselees, but that highly creative individuals would not be among them. Both types would be ineffective in counseling such individuals.

Ideally, the counselor of highly creative individuals should have achieved a fusion of primary and secondary creativeness, to use McPherson's (1960) terminology. They are able to control their impulsiveness, but have maintained their ability to use their preconscious, to play, to fantasy, to laugh, to be spontaneous, to accept weaknesses in themselves. On the other hand, they have freed themselves of their rigidity and constriction, but have maintained their control, their contact with reality, their organization, and reasonable cautiousness and carefulness. Above all, the counselor of highly creative individuals must feel free to be himself, to be an "authentic" person without pretense or evasion.

Specific Requirements

In support of this over-all requirement, a number of specific ones are rather obvious.

The counselor of highly creative individuals must, of course, possess an openness. He must be able to listen and hear what his client says. He needs to be completely alive, taking in clues through all of his senses. His intuition must be functioning fully. He must communicate a warmth which will make the highly creative individual feel safe enough to enable him to "warm up" so that his creative processes can function. The counselor must himself understand the creative process and permit it to operate. At the same time, he must be able to maintain adequate contact with reality.

This formulation has a number of possible implications for counselor training. Some of these implications may be derived by asking, "What kind of counselor training will contribute most to the production of the kind of counselor described above?" It is quite obvious that the kind of counselor described above must not feel easily threatened. He must have achieved a creative acceptance of himself, a confidence in his own organism in perceiving his world, an awareness of those areas in his life which arouse his defenses and cut off awareness of some area of life. For most counselor "trainees" this may require psychotherapy. It is suggested, therefore, that counselors preparing to counsel highly creative individuals first undergo psychotherapy themselves.

From the requirements which have been sketched, it should also be obvious that the counselor of highly creative individuals should be trained in intuitive thinking. In examining this need in counselor training, it might be well to examine the nature of intuitive thinking. Bruner (1960, p. 13) defines it as "the intellectual technique of arriving at plausible but tentative formulations without going through the analytic steps by which such formulations would be found to be valid or invalid conclusions."

This training in "hunch-getting," or hypothesis-making, however, has been rather neglected in educational psychology and thus in the training of school counselors. Educational psychologists have traditionally applied themselves with great vigor to the study of aptitude and achievement and to the social and motivational aspects of learning and adjustment. The point has been repeatedly made that courses in counseling and guidance are typically taught with excessive emphasis upon techniques, tools, statistics, testing and measurement, and correctness of response. Much more attention needs to be given to the development of counselors who have an intuitive feel for counseling, counselors who are skillful in integrating case data, discovering causes of behavior, foreseeing possible consequences, imagining how counselees feel. The failure of counselor training to develop such intuitive skills is manifested in many of the studies (Meehl, 1954) which have demonstrated the superiority of actuarial prediction over clinical prediction.

As Bruner (1960) cautions, it is "wrong" to regard intuition as "all à la mode and no pie." The highly intuitive person may have been born with something special, but its effectiveness requires solid knowledge of the subject, a familiarity that "gives intuition something to work with."

During the training of counselors this caution is especially relevant to the problem of determining the degree to which counselors should be encouraged to guess. Usually guessing is heavily penalized in most classes and is associated with laziness and dishonesty. When guessing is used to solve a problem it should be followed up by verification and confirmation. Probably it is better for counseling students to guess, however, than to be struck dumb when they cannot immediately give the right answer. It should be plain that counselors need training in recognizing the plausibility of guesses. Very often we are forced to act on the basis of incomplete knowledge; then, calculated guessing is necessary. In fact, the secret of creative thinking lies largely in the ability and willingness to set up hypotheses or incomplete patterns and reach out in search of new relationships among ideas.

Whether or not you possess the qualifications which I have just outlined, the counselor interested in doing a good job in guiding creative talent needs to understand the creative process, the personality dynamics of creative individuals, and new developments from research in this particular field. You will find many clues in the list of references at the end of this book. Since you will not be able to read everything, I would like to suggest the following six books which I believe will be especially helpful to counselors and other student personnel workers:

Anderson, H. H. (Ed.), *Creativity and Its Cultivation.* New York: Harper & Brothers, 1959.

Hammer, E. F., *Creativity*. New York: Random House, 1961.

Kubie, L. S., *Neurotic Distortion of the Creative Process*. Lawrence, Kansas: University of Kansas Press, 1958.

Moustakas, C. E., *Psychotherapy with Children*. New York: Harper & Brothers, 1959.

Moustakas, C. E. (Ed.), *The Self: Explorations in Personal Growth*. New York: Harper & Brothers, 1956.

Osborn, A. F., *Creative Imagination*. (3rd rev.) New York: Charles Scribner's Sons, 1957.

TEACHER QUALIFICATIONS

Apparently far more thought has been given to the problem of identifying and developing creative teachers rather than counselors. This condition may have resulted from the widespread concept that creative growth must be stimulated rather than guided. There has been little or no empirical research to determine the characteristics of creative teachers or teachers who are effective in guiding creative growth. But at least there are some excellent descriptions of creative teachers.

Descriptions of Creative Teachers

Hobelman (1957) has described three creative teachers with whom she has had experience. The first of these teachers she describes as a brilliant manipulator of children as media for his own creative expression. He was very popular with pupils, parents, and administrators. He was quick to fan creative sparks which emanated accidentally from children's minds. He was sometimes less popular with fellow teachers, perhaps due in part to his spectacular results and in part to personality factors. He saw to it that things happened in his class. Being this kind of creative teacher requires unusual talents and relentless zeal for personal success. Such a teacher is dominated primarily by the stimulus-response concept, and there may be some question about the degree of depth of the creativity which he inspires. One gains the feeling that he becomes so absorbed in his own creativity that the opportunities of his pupils for the development of genuine creativity are limited. They may become "facile" or fluent without becoming flexible and original.

The second creative teacher was not always able to inspire. He encouraged creativity which came from the individual's own resources. He recognized the gifted when he taught them and tried to provide them the time, place, and materials to carry out their ideas, although different from his own.

Hobelman's third creative teacher is described as "mousy as mice" and dull to see, but dull like flint from which life is fired. He was vitally creative in his own right. He was often quite popular but this didn't matter much. Children wakened in his room whether it was kindergarten, laboratory or homeroom. They never wanted to sleep.

Barkan (1960) has also presented an interesting set of descriptions of creative teachers from kindergarten through the sixth grade. His kindergarten teachers provided an interesting contrast in personality and are described as follows:

> Miss Joslin is a person with boundless enthusiasm. Recorded music fills the air in her classroom, and regardless of the activities in process, it is never a surprise to hear her burst into song with the children or to join them in a dance. Her classroom is a kindergartener's treasure house with something fascinating in every corner. It indeed would be an understatement to say that Miss Joslin encourages her children to create and express ideas. She literally lives the process with them.—*Barkan*, 1960, p. 11.

> Miss Lee is a very orderly person. She is not too demonstrative toward her children. She arranges her work carefully and systematically, and reacts calmly and sympathetically. Miss Lee loves stories and poems, and she truly has an unlimited fund of them. Individually and in chorus her children speak and sing the poems she has taught them. They are delighted with the tingle of the language and the images evoked. . . . —Barkan, 1960, p. 40.

There are also contrasting personalities in Wessel's (1961) descriptions of four teachers he has known:

> . . . Mrs. K's uniqueness shows up here; she is a person in her own right; there is no one quite like her. She holds children to achievement of their very best. She has no use for the slipshod or the almost correct. She sets a high standard of precision, but she has in common with the others a deep sensitivity to the problems of youth today in trying to live up to their potential. Children are, at first, perhaps a little intimidated by her forthrightness, but they quickly come to think of her as a "great old girl."
>
> In contrast to Mrs. K., Mrs. M., a gifted teacher in the field of fine arts, is all gentleness, a sensitive artist in her own right. Unlike Mrs. K., she seems not to be aware of orderliness and precision; she is not in the least troubled when her studio is messy. She has sensitivity toward all children, and has used her own creative self to bring out latent creativity among

all the children in her classes. She is more concerned that the child's creative ability be developed than that the product he produces be judged by
some external standards. . . .

And now for Mr. H. . . . He recognized the positive qualities in each
of his pupils, the dull as well as the bright. When he wanted to display
class papers or projects on the bulletin boards he made sure that every
member of his classes had something on display. For him this was not a
reward, but a motivation for all pupils who could proudly claim their own
achievement. He was always innovating ways to enrich learning and to
motivate the pupils to further achievement. Young at teaching as he
was, he had a firm grasp on the content; but his own motivation for
further learning was infectious. . . . When he left last June for further
study there was an astounding outpouring of affection on the part of
his students and this surprised him. For he had come to us shy and not too
sure of himself. . . . He emerged as a person who carried the authority
not of age and experience, but the authority of commitment and true
caring.

Common Characteristics

In spite of all of the diversity described by Hobelman, Barkan,
and Wessel, there is actually a tremendous core of commonality among
the creative teachers they describe. All of them are highly sensitive, resourceful, flexible, and willing to "get off the beaten track." Perhaps
much of their secret lies in their very uniqueness or diversity. However,
perhaps most important, is their capacity to form good relationships
with their creative students. We find in their behavior characteristics
which would ordinarily alienate many students from them. These characteristics apparently become unimportant, since they have such great
capacities for creative relationships with students.

There are, in fact, a number of characteristics common to many
creative teachers which may be upsetting to their colleagues on the
school staff. For example, they are likely to tackle difficult tasks, sometimes too difficult. This means hard work—sometimes overwork and
the irritation that accompanies fatigue. Attempting tasks that are too
difficult also means that occasional failures must be expected. Highly creative teachers are likely to make mistakes—*all* of their guesses about
what will help children to learn and think won't work. They may have
some oddities, be nonconforming, and at times be childish. They may even
defy conventions of courtesy, seem uncultured and primitive, and be

unsophisticated and naive about many things. They are too absorbed in helping children develop to be concerned with being sociable or socially skilled.

There are several characteristics of highly creative teachers which may keep others from tapping their resources. Outwardly they are frequently rather bashful, and somewhat withdrawn and quiet. Their ideas have perhaps been laughed at so often, that others may have to demonstrate the genuineness of their friendliness and interest. At times creative teachers may seem haughty and self-satisfied, but this just exemplifies their independence in thinking. They may also appear discontented and fault-finding. And at times, they may feel that "the whole parade is out of step." This may be a part of their ability to sense problems and defects. If they are creative, however, they will have some constructive ideas about how the deficiencies may be alleviated or remedied.

Although it is important that highly creative teachers maintain their uniqueness, I would offer to them the same model adapted from Stein that I proposed in Chapter 8 for preventing creative children from becoming obnoxious without sacrificing their creativity.

In-Service Programs

The development of teachers who can guide successfully creative talent may be considered from the viewpoint of both in-service education and teacher education programs. First, I shall call attention briefly to some of the promising things now happening in the field of in-service education, and then I shall treat somewhat more systematically what I consider the needs of teacher preparation programs themselves.

The various professional associations to which teachers belong appear to work very hard to communicate to their membership through national and regional meetings and journals the results of research which will be helpful to teachers. Some professional associations have secured the help of research leaders in the field to aid them in preparing materials for classroom teachers. Some of them, such as the Association for Supervision and Curriculum Development, have sponsored workshops and stimulated projects in specific school systems. A number of local boards of education have also sponsored and supported such workshops, with specific projects being the outcome. Others have injected such content in their regular in-service programs for teachers.

Summer workshops already have been developed in a number of universities and seem to be stimulating considerable activity. A number of University short courses and institutes have also given attention to the dissemination of accumulated knowledge concerning creative thinking. Many experimental programs are being developed and evaluated. From these will come many curricular materials and methods which will be especially useful to teachers of creative talent.

Already the accumulation of information concerning creativity is beginning to have an effect upon education textbooks, children's books, professional development materials, and curricular materials.

In spite of the array of books now appearing on creativity in education, no book has yet appeared which makes use of the accumulation of knowledge. What has been known for the past seventy or eighty years has been largely ignored. Worthwhile contributions, however, have been made by Zirbes (1959), Wilt (1959), Barkan (1960), Peet (1960), and Miel (1961). The book edited by Miel, however, contains a chapter by Foshay on research. Some attention to research on creativity in education is to be found in such texts as: *Education for Effective Thinking* by Burton, Kimball, and Wing (1960); *The Psychology of Thought and Judgment* by Johnson (1955); *Applied Imagination* by Osborn (1957); *Children's Thinking* by Russell (1955); *The Pupil's Thinking* by Peel (1960); and *The Psychology of Thinking* by Vinacke (1951).

In many areas, curriculum specialists, writers, and research personnel are beginning to produce special materials designed to help individuals learn creatively. The materials developed by the various professional groups in mathematics, physics, chemistry, and biology have been included in experimental texts and teacher commentaries. These are producing interesting results and many of them are now rather well developed. Professional writers of popular books for children, adolescents, and adults are beginning to reflect the influence of the accumulating information and the interest in creativity in education. Examples of these are Alastair Reid's *Ounce, Dice, Trice* (1958) and *Supposing* (1960); *The Elephant's Wish* (1959), *The Birthday Present* (1959) and others by B. Munari; and *The Poetry-Drawing Book* edited by William Cole and Julia Colmore (1960).

There have also been some beginnings toward the development of programmed experiences in creative thinking. My associate, Robert Myers, has developed some workbook programs which have various stages of the creative process built into them and which apply many research findings in their construction. And in line with this Cunnington has developed some audio-taped programs. O. K. Moore's (1961) work in teaching preschool children to type, read, write, and take dictation has attracted nation-wide attention. Moore is working with New Jersey's Thomas A. Edison Research Laboratory in designing automated equipment to simplify his technique which he calls the "responsive environment." Out of this development may come teaching machines with which children can learn both creatively and by authority.

Teacher Education Programs

There is already quite an accumulation of evidence from research in industry and education that the effects of training in creative thinking transfers to other activities requiring creative thinking (Maltzman, 1960; Meadow and Parnes, 1959; Nicholson, 1959; Parnes and Meadow, 1960; Torrance, 1959b; True, 1956). Faced, then, with rather strong evidence that it is important and possible to identify and promote creative thinking, how do we do it in teacher training programs? What retooling is required?

As I see it, retooling is required in at least the following six areas:

1. Development and use of instruments and procedures to supplement present devices for selecting and guiding students.
2. Change in the objectives of courses to include the development of skills in creative thinking about course content.
3. Curricular changes whereby students learn creatively many of the things now taught by authority and gain experience in applying creatively scientific information.
4. Development of methods and materials which will foster creative growth and stimulate students to learn creatively.
5. Development of instruments for assessing achievement in courses which involve creative thinking.
6. Development of teacher-pupil relationships and principles for rewarding creative thinking (other than through testing).

1. *Instruments for Use in Selection and Guidance.* As Getzels (1960) pointed out at the annual meeting of the American Educational Research

Association in 1960, the usual criteria of tests, recommendations, and rank in class for college admission are all biased in favor of the student with "convergent" intellectual ability and social interests. From his study of the tests used as aids in the selection of students, Getzels showed that most of the items required only recognitive types of thinking. His plea is for the development of admissions procedures which would identify superior divergent students as well as superior convergent students.

To accomplish the retooling necessary to do the job, I see several kinds of instruments as being useful. These include:

1. Easily administered and scored tests of the creative thinking abilities.
2. Personality and life experience inventories which would reflect creative motivations and motivations which are obstacles to creative growth.
3. Behavior check lists which would reflect creative interests.

Developments in each of these areas have been discussed in Chapters 2, 3, and 4.

2. *Changing Objectives.* In statements of objectives by teachers of what they teach, one has to search perseveringly for much evidence of concern about developing any of the thinking abilities, much less the creative thinking abilities. I believe that it is important to establish objectives which would encourage the full mental functioning of teachers. I offer the following statement of objectives as an example of how such a set of objectives might sound:

1. Familiarization with and understanding of the scientific information and major theoretical concepts in the field of personality development and mental hygiene.
2. Acquisition of knowledge (able to recall or remember) at least two conceptualizations of stages of personality development and a generalized framework for organizing and using knowledge in this field.
3. Skill in applying the concepts and knowledge acquired in the correct solution of professional problems.
4. Skill in thinking imaginatively and intuitively about problems of personality development and mental hygiene.

5. Skill in evaluating new ideas and research being done in the field and in making and supporting decisions concerning problems of personality development and mental hygiene.

To be meaningful, such objectives must of course be supported by assignments, exercises, and evaluation procedures, which will contribute to their achievement.

3. *Curriculum Changes.* As I see it, curricular change may follow any one or combination of three different directions. Perhaps the easiest and most effective to accomplish would be to inject into present courses in education assignments, exercises, and projects which would stimulate students to leap the barriers from learning to thinking. This can be done in a variety of ways. As a term project, I require my students to develop some original idea. They are asked to state their idea, describe how it occurred to them, develop a psychological rationale for the idea, state how the idea could be tested, and think out the consequences of the idea, if found valid.

They read research articles both critically and creatively. In the reports of the articles read creatively, they are asked to include the following:

1. A brief statement of the new possibilities suggested by the statement of the problem, possible consequences stemming from its solution, and other assumptions and theoretical formulations which might have been brought to bear on the problem.

2. A listing of other possible hypotheses related to the problem, including facts which might have been used in sharpening or modifying the hypotheses.

3. A description of improvements which might have been made in the procedures for collecting and analyzing the data, including selection of samples, methods and instruments of data collection, techniques of analysis, and report of findings.

4. A description of other possible conclusions, interpretations of the findings, implications, and analogies to situations with which they are familiar.

5. An appraisal of the possibilities stemming from the findings and the extent to which the research reported represents a step forward in knowledge concerning personality development and mental hygiene.

At appropriate points, they are given a series of problems which require creative and evaluative thinking. Some of these are given during
class sessions; others are given as "take-home" problems. The following
are samples of some of the more brief problems:

1. Using our knowledge of the creative problem-solving process
and concepts of coping with stress, what characteristically "goes
wrong" with the thinking of psychopathic deviates (delinquents)?
(Develop a theory.) If your theory could be verified, how should
the treatment of delinquents be changed?
2. Make up five questions and answers about yourself which you
think you would be most likely to remember at any time in the
future and under any condition of stress. What makes you think
you would be able to remember these answers? Now, think up a
principle, rule, or generalization about the process of remembering
and forgetting on the basis of the foregoing thinking.
3. Until recently it was widely believed, even among some eminent
scholars of human behavior, that all creative geniuses are mentally
ill or "crazy." List as many guesses as you can to explain why this
concept arose and persisted so long. Now draw up a list of possible
educational practices which might prevent future generations from
being shackled by this misconception.

A second direction for curricular change would be the addition of
courses in the psychology of thinking. Such courses are already appearing occasionally in engineering, journalism, business administration, and
psychology curriculums. Thus far, the only ones that I know about in
education take the form of summer workshops. Sidney Parnes, an educational psychologist with the Creative Education Foundation at the
University of Buffalo, offers a course in creative problem-solving. This
is not offered as a part of the teacher education program, however.

A third direction would be through the reconceptualization of present psychology and education courses. Let me cite my own course
(Personality Development and Mental Hygiene) as an example of what
might be done. Going on the simple assumption that the mentally
healthy person is a fully functioning person, I conceptualized a major
portion of this course. After offering a theoretical formulation concerning the general processes by which personality develops, "goes wrong,"
or breaks down, we take a deeper look at what is really meant by full

mental functioning. We examine one by one the cognitive, memory, convergent thinking, divergent thinking, and evaluative abilities as defined by Guilford (1959) and their role in personality development and mental health. Following each one, we examine research and theory concerning the conditions which free these abilities to develop and function.

4. *Methods and Materials.* I have already mentioned my own use of self-initiated learning experiences, original projects, exercises in creative applications and decision-making, and the critical and creative reading of research articles. We need to know much more than we do about all of these and other methods.

Another promising development is in the reading field (Guilford, 1960; Lorge, 1960; Stauffer, 1960). Reading is conceptualized as a thinking process. In my own classes, I have experimented with the assignment of memory, evaluative, and creative sets in reading course assignments (Torrance and Harmon, 1960). Although students are unable to hold these sets throughout the reading of an assignment, even after three days of practice, the assignment of these sets makes a difference in the kinds of things students achieve. The "creative applications" set in three replications resulted in better performance on tasks requiring creative applications of the text material read. The "evaluative" set resulted in better decision-making and supporting of decisions and, in two out of three cases, better recognition as measured by multiple-choice items. The memory set in two out of three cases tended to result in better recall of information read as measured by completion items. These findings suggest many possibilities for accomplishing different types of objectives through the encouragement of different kinds of reading sets. Perhaps what is needed is the recognition that all reading does not need to be done with a memory set (for retention), or that all drill does not have to be carried out with a memory set. In a separate volume my colleague, Robert Myers, and I are attempting to present some of the ideas which we have developed and tested, and summarize what is known about methods and materials for guiding creative development.

5. *Measurement of Achievement.* Students tend to learn and develop along whatever lines they find rewarding. School grades and measures of achievement are important to students, and they will tend to achieve whatever is necessary to obtain these grades. They take many of their cues concerning what is important from the tests which teachers administer. Thus, if teachers change their objectives and expect pupils to

achieve them, it will be necessary for them to develop evaluation procedures which will assess the achievement of these changed objectives.

It is common knowledge that most of the examinations now used in evaluating achievement, determining grades, awarding scholarships, and determining college admission, rely most heavily upon the cognitive abilities. Memory and convergent thinking also receive considerable attention. The general practice seems to be to judge students almost entirely upon *what* they know, that is, the philosophy of the quiz program. If we are to judge them on what they can generate from what they know, new types of tests have to be devised.

Some measurement specialists insist that all educational objectives can be measured satisfactorily by objective-type machine-scored tests. But others have grave doubts concerning the possibility of assessing creative and evaluative thinking objectives in this way. The objections of several authorities have been summarized in Chapter 2.

6. *Teacher-Pupil Relationships.* As I have already pointed out, the thinking processes are automatic, swift, and spontaneous when not disturbed by other influences. The trouble is that our relationships and the structure of educational situations interfere with this process. Chapter 9 has been devoted to a discussion of this problem. The concepts presented should be as applicable to teacher-student relationships in teacher education programs as well as elsewhere.

ADMINISTRATOR QUALIFICATIONS

Many creative teachers bring to me numerous complaints concerning their administrators, especially their principals and supervisors. The following excerpt from the letter of a thirty-three-year-old, fifth-grade teacher is fairly typical:

> Your article mentioned that teachers, parents, and peers dull creativity in children. Perhaps teachers do so on the direction of their principal or supervisor. When in _____, both my principal and supervisor looked askance at my ideas. The supervisor said I was overstimulating the children. (I was nervous because of her always critical comments.) I love to learn and to see others learn. . . .
>
> Too many teachers are hindered by all the physical chores which administrators judge them on. My room was probably the messiest in the school because we were so interested in ideas there. If books were askew

in the desk and paper on the floor, we didn't notice, because we were learning. Of course, maybe I taught messiness, but I hope I fostered the love of learning and of creativity.

The principal said I shouldn't let the children decide about things, because they weren't old enough (10–11) to have good judgment. I believed in respecting their ideas, because they might come up with as good an idea as I, in a different way. I tried to stir their imagination and let them express themselves freely in such things as a story of a trip to Mars, a drawing of their house of the future, or an invention, with no limitations as to cost and feasibility. I would be so proud some day if one of my ex-students contributed great ideas to the world! . . .

From scattered research evidence, my guess is that these complaints of teachers have in them an element of legitimacy. Just as teachers prefer the high IQ pupil to the highly creative one, school administrators prefer less creative teachers to more creative ones. One study (Jex, 1959) showed that the ratings by principals and supervisors of a group of science teachers were negatively and significantly related to their scores on a test of creativity and tests of their knowledge about the subjects which they were teaching. Just as the highly creative child causes classroom problems, the highly creative teacher creates problems for the school administrator. To be creative is to be unpredictable. This always makes others uneasy. We like to be able to predict because we feel safer, more secure, and more in control of things. This creates in the administrator an uneasiness, or perhaps even hostility towards the creative teacher. Resentment may be reflected in recommendations and ratings which administrators receive from other administrators concerning candidates for new or more responsible positions.

Creative teachers do not cause problems, however, if they have "creative" supervision. Such teachers don't stop with a forty-hour week. Nevertheless, administrators, who can't tolerate an independent spirit, will find it difficult to supervise the work of creative teachers. They can avoid and solve many problems, if they recognize the characteristics of creative people. Let's look at a few of them.[1]

The creative teacher becomes completely absorbed in his work. Have you ever tried to suggest a change in the work of a creative teacher

---

[1] This material has been adapted from the author's article entitled "The Creative Teacher and the School Team: Problems and Pleasures of the Principal" in *Professional Growth for Principals*, April 1961 (Arthur C. Croft Publications) and used by permission.

just as he is finishing the job? The chances are that there was an explosion. Such an explosion is easy to explain. The work at that point had become a part of him. The best approach is to wait a while. Later, he will be more willing to make alterations.

The truly creative teacher doesn't work for status or power, but he does like to be appreciated. He works in order to live with himself. The freedom to create—to think and to do something with what he knows —brings him his greatest rewards. He may prefer to work alone at times rather than on a team. He may insist upon setting his own pace, and he may resist regimentation. The creative mind needs an incubation period of seeming inactivity to hatch ideas.

Since creativity involves divergent thinking, administrators can expect the creative teacher to express ideas which differ from some of education's time-honored practices and their own ideas. Furthermore, since the creative teacher does not care for power, he is not likely to change his thinking just to curry favor with the administrator.

The creative teacher may become restless and be difficult to hold under conventional restraints. He works best when there are difficult, challenging problems, or when the project he has is his "baby." There will be times when he will defy precedent, and he may try a new idea without asking the administrator's permission.

Probably because of the way highly creative persons are almost always treated, they develop other traits which may upset the harmony of the staff. They may at times appear haughty and self-satisfied, impolite, fault-finding, naive and childish, bashful, and withdrawn. They may lack business ability and make mistakes which are irritating. This may cause administrators to ask, "Are creative teachers worth the trouble?"

Yes, most creative teachers are worth the trouble. There are limits, but administrators can afford to tolerate a few mistakes. Otherwise, the teacher's fear of failure will prevent true creative initiative. At times the administrator can buffer his contact with others. Some people just don't understand the creative process. Creative teachers have a breadth of vision. They see relationships between seemingly remote things and bring them together in meaningful ways. If the administrator does not take the time to find out how creative teachers relate these seemingly remote things, they, too, may be unjustly critical.

To keep an harmoniously productive team, administrators need to reward the creative efforts of their teachers. This is something our society must learn how to do more effectively in almost every field of work. Today, it is difficult for the creative worker in almost any field to receive rewards in proportion to his contribution without accepting something he does not want, a position of power. Frequently such a position places him where he cannot continue making his creative contribution. This does not mean that we do not need creative administrators. We do, but creative administration may require quite different talents, skills, and motivations from creative teaching.

Research in business and industry has revealed many ways of dealing with creative workers and keeping teams harmoniously productive. The following are a few of them which may be applicable to the school administrator (principal) interested in guiding creative talent:

1. Lets teachers know that he respects creativity and creative teaching.
2. Uses some regular system for obtaining teachers' ideas.
3. Tolerates disagreement with his own ideas.
4. Encourages experimentation.
5. Avoids loading teachers with too many extra duties.
6. Makes it possible to try out new ideas without failure being "fatal."
7. Makes school atmosphere an exciting, adventurous one.
8. Avoids *overemphasis* on teamwork.
9. Holds meetings in which ideas are evaluated honestly.
10. Helps develop sound but exciting ideas from failure experiences.
11. Exposes teachers to the creative work of other teachers.
12. Makes it easy for new teachers to generate new ideas and stimulate the staff.
13. Facilitates communication between teachers in his school and teachers elsewhere working on related problems.
14. Occasionally questions established concepts and practices.
15. Carries on a continuous program of long-range planning.
16. Recognizes and tries to relieve tension when frustration becomes too severe.
17. Maintains frequent communication with individual teachers but lets them make most decisions alone.

From research in a variety of fields, we can also make some good guesses about what kind of person the creative administrator is.[2] The following are a few of my guesses:

1. He is a man of curiosity and discontent. He is always asking, "Why did this happen?" or "What would happen if we did it this way?"

2. He is a man of unlimited enthusiasm for his job. He is restless, intense, strongly motivated—completely wrapped up in what he is doing.

3. He is a man with the talent of transmitting his enthusiasm to his associates. He creates an atmosphere of excitement and urgency.

4. He is flexible. He keeps an open mind and is willing to accept and use new information. He listens to new ideas and does not flatly dismiss ideas with "don't be ridiculous" or "we tried that before."

5. He is unorthodox and boldly questions conventional ideas. He is goal-oriented, *not* method-oriented. He is willing to pay the price in physical and mental labor to achieve goals and is impatient with anything that gets in the way.

Let us take a look at some of the assets and liabilities of these characteristics.

To improve a school system, the administrator has to be discontented with things as they are. He has to start asking questions about the things that are wrong and make some guesses about causes, possible solutions, and possible consequences. If he transmits his enthusiasm to others, there will come a flood of ideas. He can become overwhelmed with ideas. There are certain dangers even in his being an idea man. The idea man tends to become simultaneously engrossed in a new idea and bored with a partly developed old one. Gradually all who work with him fear this trait in him. This includes not only board members but teachers, assistants, and parents. The administrator must strive for the balance that makes the difference between trusting and distrusting an idea man.

[2] This material is adapted from the author's article, "The Teacher as a Team Member: Team Leadership Through Creative Administration" in *Professional Growth for Administrators*, April 1961 (Arthur C. Croft Publications) and used by permission.

Although the creative administrator can set most of his associates afire with his enthusiasm, there are always some who refuse to be sparked. They will feel overworked and will try to pour cold water on his enthusiasm. If board members are among these, the administrator will have to be especially creative in getting his ideas accepted. He must learn to anticipate their dampening attitude and "create ideas to sell his ideas." He must figure out in advance the benefits and make it easy for them to say "yes." He must think of the other problems the implementation of his idea will create and figure out ways of handling them.

The creative administrator's flexibility is a great asset to him as an executive. He is not enslaved by any one best method and is able to shift his approach and develop new strategies and ways of working with people.

The creative process of the administrative leader can be a particularly lonely one. Frequently, he finds himself an isolated man, although surrounded by assistants, principals, teachers, and others who talk and argue almost incessantly. In order to create plans and programs which will satisfy the needs of all of the groups in the school system, he must at times close his ears to the special claims of each and view the picture with detachment.

The creative administrator must guard against being so carried away with his own creativity that he robs others of the chance to be creative.

The administrative leader might do well to check himself on the following behaviors which seem to be characteristic of leaders who are successful in developing a high level of productive creativity in their organizations:

1. Makes certain that principals and teachers know that he respects creative thinking.
2. Uses some regular system for obtaining the ideas of teachers, principals, and board members.
3. Develops pride in the school system.
4. Makes it possible to try out ideas without failure being "fatal."
5. Offers opportunities and resources for exploration.
6. Does not settle school problems by fiat.
7. Does not coerce conformity to his own ideas.
8. Gives others credit for ideas.
9. Finds a place for divergent talents in the system.

10. Helps teachers and principals obtain financial resources to implement or demonstrate new ideas.

11. Facilitates communication among teachers in different schools within the system working on similar problems.

12. Leads a continuous program of long-range planning.

13. Avoids screening out the truly creative in selecting teachers.

14. Sees that divergent or minority ideas receive a hearing.

15. Maintains frequent communication with individual principals but gives them freedom to make certain decisions alone.

16. Gives principals and teachers time to work out and test new ideas.

17. Finds fascination in every facet of education.

18. Browses extensively in many fields of interest, other than education.

The suggestions which I have made concerning creative administrators have been limited largely to things which the administrator must do for himself. For this reason, I should add that most of the ideas I have presented concerning educational programs for teachers apply equally to programs for the preparation of administrators.

SUMMARY

On the basis of the formulations presented in earlier chapters concerning the problems of highly creative individuals, the creative process itself, and the relationships and strategies needed in guiding creative talent, an effort was made to outline some qualifications for counselors, teachers, and administrators who can guide creative talent successfully.

In discussing the qualifications of counselors, emphasis was placed on the fusion of the primary and secondary creativeness of the counselor and the need for openness, warmth, understanding of the creative process, good contact with reality, relative freedom from threat, and tolerance for divergency. The roles of personal psychotherapy and training in intuitive thinking in counselor preparation were also discussed.

Several descriptions of creative teachers were presented and both divergent and common characteristics observed. All gave evidence of being tremendously sensitive to the needs and potentialities of students, able to maintain their own uniqueness, and above all able to maintain good relationships with students. Creative teachers often have characteristics which are upsetting to others, such as attempting tasks which are too difficult, being nonconforming, appearing uncultured or unsophisticated, and appearing bashful. Examples of in-service education programs and resources for personal development among teachers were described. Suggestions were also made concerning the retooling needed in teacher education programs to produce teachers who can guide creative talent more effectively. Ideas were presented concerning the following six areas: (1) instruments and procedures for selecting and guiding students, (2) changing course of objectives, (3) curricular changes, (4) methods and materials, (5) assessment of achievement, and (6) teacher-pupil relationships.

If creative teachers are to retain their creativity, they must be supported and guided intelligently by school administrators. Suggestions from research done in business, industry, and other sources were made to aid the administrator in guiding creative teachers and other subordinates.

Appendix

ADMINISTERING
THE MINNESOTA TESTS
OF CREATIVE THINKING

A wide variety of tasks has been developed by my colleagues and me for use in assessing creative thinking from kindergarten through graduate school. It is possible to arrange various combinations of these tasks for specific groups and purposes. Although the program continues to develop much work remains to be done on simplifying the scoring, developing more powerful and meaningful kinds of scores, and developing norms. The tasks have already demonstrated their potential usefulness. In this appendix, I shall describe each task, give information concerning administration, and present general instructions for scoring.

The tasks developed may be classified into three major categories: non-verbal tasks, verbal tasks using non-verbal stimuli, and verbal tasks using verbal stimuli. Information concerning tasks will be presented according to this organization.

NON-VERBAL TASKS

Four non-verbal tasks have thus far been used with apparent success in the Minnesota studies: Incomplete Figures, Picture Construction, Circles and Squares, and Creative Design. By having subjects write titles for their constructions and compose imaginative‚stories concerning them, any of these tasks may be extended to make them verbal tasks. Some pilot work along this line has been done already.

Incomplete Figures Task

The Incomplete Figures Task is an adaptation of the Drawing-Completion Test developed by Kate Franck and used in studies of creativity by Barron (1958) and others. We selected some of the incomplete figures from Frank's test and constructed for our purpose two forms which we called the Incomplete Figures Test. Productions resulting from their use permitted us to assess elements of originality, elaboration, and penetration.

Figure 3 shows the two forms used. On an ordinary sheet of paper an area of fifty-four square inches is divided into six squares, each containing a different stimulus figure.

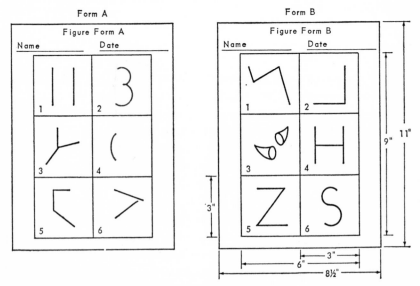

FIGURE A1. *Forms A and B of the Incomplete Figures Test.*

Subjects are given the following instructions concerning this task:

> By adding lines to the six figures below, sketch some object or design
> that no one else in the class will think of. Try to include as many different
> ideas as you can in your drawing. In other words, don't stop with your
> first idea for completing the figure; keep building onto it. Make up titles
> for each of your pictures and write one at the bottom of each block next
> to the number of the figure.

Before the subjects begin, the tester gives them four examples for the
first incomplete figure. It is emphasized that these are just examples and
should not be copied.

Subjects are allowed to work for ten minutes on each form. Some
children will not use this much time, but those who develop complex
ideas and do considerable elaboration will not have sufficient time. Since
the instructions are designed to encourage both originality and elaboration, the examiner should give the entire ten minutes before calling time.

Responses to this task are evaluated along four different dimensions:
originality, closure (penetration), complexity (elaboration), and productivity.

"Originality" has been defined in this task as uncommonness of response in a statistical sense. The scale used is based on frequency counts
of the responses of 217 pupils from kindergarten through sixth grade.
A scale value of zero has been assigned to responses given by twelve per
cent or more of the subjects. Responses given by from five to twelve
per cent are assigned a value of one; from two to five per cent, a value
of two; from one to two per cent, a value of three; and less than one
per cent, a value of four. The interscorer reliability for Form A is .82
and for Form B, .86.

"Complexity" refers to the elaboration of the basic idea by the addition of supporting ideas. Here we attempt to assess the person's capacity
to implement and build onto the basic idea. Two types of scoring have
been devised: a seven-point complexity scale and an index determined
by the number of details or ideas used in elaborating upon the idea. The
points on the complexity scale are defined by examples of typical responses for each of the figures. Interscorer reliabilities of .93 and .95
have been obtained for Forms A and B respectively.

The scoring of penetration is based theoretically on the concept of
closure. It is assumed here that an incomplete figure of any kind makes

an individual feel tense. The tendency on the part of the subject is to reduce this tension by closing the figure in the simplest way possible, i.e., by the use of a straight or circular line. If the individual closes the figure by means other than a straight or curved line, we assume that he is able to delay or resist the tendency to closure in the simplest way possible. Those who can conceive of an object in which closure of the incomplete figure is not necessary are assumed to be able to overcome the pressures toward closure completely. On the basis of these considerations, a seven-point scale of closure (penetration) was established. Interscorer reliabilities of .94 and .91 were obtained for Forms A and B respectively. It has also been found that this scale yields developmental phenomena at least through the sixth grade, older children being better able to resist pressures to premature closure or delay gratification. Finally, the number of incomplete figures attempted is the productivity score. Since most subjects attempt all figures, this score has not contributed very much to the total score or to the fluency score. In individual cases, however, it provides insights into the subject's tendencies to sacrifice productivity for elaboration or originality, mental blocking, and the like.

Picture-Construction Task

The Picture-Construction or Shape Task is another non-verbal test developed by the author. In this task, subjects are required to think of a picture in which the given shape is an integral part. The task can be administered in a group from kindergarten through graduate school. As shown in Figure A2, the materials used for this task include a

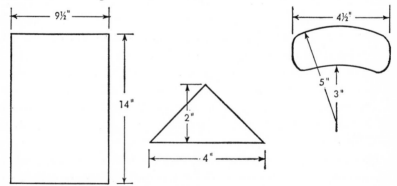

FIGURE A2. Materials for Picture Construction Task.

blank sheet of paper and a piece of glued, colored paper. Thus far, data have been collected with two shapes, a triangle and a curved jelly bean shape.

These materials are given to the subjects with the following instructions:

> You have been given a piece of paper in the form of a triangle (curved shape). Think of a picture or an object which you can draw with this form as a part. Then lift up the shape and glue it wherever you want it on this sheet of paper and add lines with pencil or crayon to make your picture. Try to think of something that no one else in this class will think of. Keep adding things onto it, putting into your picture as many interesting ideas as you can. When you have completed your picture, think up a name or title for it and write it at the bottom.

A time limit of ten minutes has been found to be satisfactory, and norms have been based on this time limit. Many children will draw their pictures immediately and will not use but two or three minutes. Some will draw pictures immediately but will continue to add to them throughout the period. Others will plan elaborate pictures which require time for implementation. Still others will sit for three or four minutes thinking of ideas before beginning work.

It is frequently difficult for the examiner to refrain from trying to stimulate further those individuals who sit and think. This may "throw off course" the thinking processes, however, and should be prevented. For example, one kindergarten boy sat for at least four minutes before doing any work. I kept wanting to urge him to draw something, to explain the task to him. I decided not to interfere with him, however, and he produced an interesting picture. In the instructions to kindergartners, it is desirable to demonstrate by drawing a picture, using the shape. I had shown his class how the triangle could be used as the roof of a bird house. I stressed the fact that they were not to copy this but to think of something else. This boy was thinking about how the inside of a bird house would look and he tried to draw this.

In the lower grades, it is necessary for the examiner to write the titles. This can be done as each child thinks of a title or after time has been called.

Responses are scored for originality, elaboration, sensitivity, communication, and activity. Factor analyses may produce results which will call for the abandonment of some of these scores.

An elaboration score may also be obtained by counting the number of different elaborating ideas or details. We are not yet able to determine the superiority of one type of scoring over another.

Sensitivity is judged by means of a five-point scale based on the following considerations. The individual may respond to the task in such a manner that he may or may not use the shape in such a way that the color, shape, and proportion is consonant with the object or picture sketched. We assume that the stimulus induces tendencies in the individual to produce associations, i.e., objects or pictures which are in harmony with the different aspects of the shape. The sketched object or picture for which the given shape is used normally has the particular color and shape of the stimulus figure. Furthermore, the stimulus figure is used in an appropriate size relationship to the sketched object or picture as a whole. We assume that the individual who is able to overcome the limitations of the stimulus figure can use limitations creatively and can resist the tendency to produce usual associations.

"Communication" refers to the degree to which the product created by the subject communicates an idea, story, or situation. The scorer is asked to judge the degree of communication achieved according to a number of specified rules.

Responses are scored for movement by means of a five-point activity scale. We assume that the person who is able to perceive his environment in a dynamically related way will be able to express movement in his responses to a greater extent than an individual who perceives his environment in a static way.

The originality of a response is evaluated by means of an originality scale based on a frequency analysis of responses by 341 children from kindergarten through sixth grade. Responses given by six or more per cent of the subjects is scored zero. A score of one is given if from three to five per cent of the subjects gave the response; two for responses having frequencies of from 1.5 per cent to three per cent; three for responses appearing from 0.5 to 1.5; and four for responses less frequent than 0.5 per cent. More simply, an originality score may also be determined by counting the number of responses not in the zero category.

The most common responses using the triangle are: roof (on house), hat (on person), umbrella, skirt (on person), tree (Christmas), kite, design, face, mountain, and rocket. The most common for the curved shape include: boat, hat (on head), hot dog (wiener), human body, cloud, dog, body of animal, car, and roof.

"Elaboration" or complexity refers to the number of different ideas used to build or construct the particular picture. The elaboration or complexity scale defines five different scale-points and gives a number of examples corresponding to these points. The more complex or better elaborated an individual's response is the higher will be his score. This scale attempts to assess an individual's ability to carry out an idea, i.e., to implement his "big idea" by adding other ideas to it. We assume that an individual who operates on a relatively high level of differentiation and integration concerning his environment is able to conceive and draw a relatively more complex idea than an individual who is operating on a relatively low level of differentiation and integration.

The interscorer reliability coefficients for the scales are: Originality, .97 and .83 respectively for triangle and curved shape; Sensitivity, .67 and .60; Elaboration, .90 and .95; Communication, .57 and .84; Activity, .87 and .88.

Circles and Squares Task

The Circles and Squares task was originally designed as a non-verbal test of ideational fluency and flexibility. The directions were then modified in such a way as to stress originality and elaboration. Although some information will be given concerning scoring and results from both sets of instructions, emphasis will be placed on developments related to the instructions designed to motivate originality and elaboration.

The materials used in the Circles and Squares Test are two printed forms. On one of them, thirty-five ($1'' \times 1''$) squares are printed, and on the other, forty-two small circles ($1''$ diameter). The rough sketch of these forms and figures is given in Figure A3.

The Circles and Squares tasks may be administered either individually or in groups. Our use of the task has been as a group administered one with a ten-minute limit.

In our first use of these tasks, the instructions were quite minimal. For example, the following constituted the directions for doing the Circles task:

> In ten minutes see how many objects you can sketch which have a circle as the main element in their design. Just use a few lines on the

circles below to identify your ideas which might start: wheel, tire, steering wheel, etc.

In addition, examples were drawn on the blackboard showing how objects could be sketched by adding lines inside or outside, or both inside and outside the circles.

In present forms using the Circles task, the instructions are as follow:

> In ten minutes see how many objects you can make from the circles below. A circle should be the main part of whatever you make. With pencil or crayon add lines to the circles to complete your picture. Your lines can be inside the circle, outside the circle, or both inside and outside the circle. Try to think of things that no one else in the class will think of. Make as many things as you can and put as many ideas as you can in each one. Add labels or titles, if the identity of the object is not clear.

As in the original instructions, examples are drawn on the blackboard. Under all conditions, if they ask, subjects are permitted to use more than one circle or square. Although this is not included in the original instructions, some use two or more circles or squares without asking. Others ask if this is permissible.

At one time during the early development of these tasks one of them was used as a practice exercise and the other as a test exercise. There is some indication that there is a slight practice effect even when no instruc-

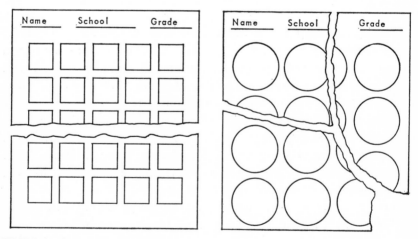

FIGURE A3. Sample Format for Circle and Squares Task.

tion accompanies the practice. There are also some indications that the Squares task is slightly more difficult than the Circles task.

In the kindergarten, first and second grades, it is necessary for the examiners to label the objects sketched. This can be done immediately after completion of the task, if several assistants are available, while the children are still seated in their desks. Or, this task can be accomplished through individual interviews. Some third graders may also need help in labeling their responses. Accurate scoring cannot be done on this task, if care is not exercised in obtaining labels.

Under the original set of instructions, responses were scored for: fluency, flexibility, and originality. Fluency was obtained by counting the number of different objects sketched. Flexibility was obtained by counting the number of different categories of objects sketched. The same categories are still used in obtaining this score. Originality was obtained by eliminating all highly common objects, such as human faces, balls, clocks, designs, and planets. Now, originality can be scored by means of scales developed in the same way as for the preceding two tasks or by the initial method used for this purpose. The following are the most common responses found in the responses of 588 subjects:

Balloons	Human faces (excluding expressive and fantasy faces)
Balls	Pans (excluding pans with some content)
Buttons	Pie
Doughnuts	Symbols (alphabet, numbers, etc.)
Earth, moon, sun	Tires
Fruits	Wheels

With the change in instructions, scores are now obtained for Elaboration. Experimental scoring schemes have included both the complexity scales of the type described for the previous two tasks or the counting of the number of ideas used in elaborating the basic ideas. The latter appears to be the more promising and is obtained by counting the total number of ideas communicated by each object and then finding the sum.

Suppose the subject sees the circle as an "apple" and labels the circle thus with no further elaboration. This would be scored "zero." The subject has, of course, been awarded a point for ideational fluency, and he may or may not receive a credit for flexibility but this response represents no elaboration. If he colors the apple red or yellow with no further elaboration, he will be given a score of one. Other possible elaborations would include: a stem, leaves, a rotten spot, a worm coming out of the apple, a pitted shape, the stem, mixed coloration such as green and red. One point would be added for each of these ideas.

Creative Design Task

Paul R. Hendrickson has designed a simple Creative Design Task which seems to be promising, but scoring procedures are being tested but have not been perfected yet. The materials consist of circles and strips of various sizes and colors, a four-page booklet, scissors, and glue. With a thirty-minute time-limit, subjects are instructed to construct pictures or designs, making use of all of the colored circles and strips. Subjects may use one, two, three, or four pages; alter the circles and strips or use them as they are; add other symbols with pencil or crayon.

VERBAL TASKS USING NON-VERBAL STIMULI

The Ask-and-Guess Test

As we departed from Guilford's models, it seemed to me that much of the essence of creative scientific thinking is captured in the processes of asking and guessing—guessing particularly about causes and consequences. The Ask-and-Guess Test is an effort to replicate this process to some extent in a test situation. First, a brief psychological rationale will be presented. The testing materials, procedures, and scoring will be described.

Curiosity. Although curiosity has long been recognized as an important human characteristic, the amount of firm scientific information concerning the nature and development of curiosity is actually rather small. Murphy (1947) defined curiosity as the "tendency to investigate any novelty perceived, tendency to seek information about anything." Murphy regards curiosity as instinctive in the broad sense that one inherits sense organs, a peripheral nervous system, and a brain. He sees curiosity as learned in the sense that the type of objects which stimulate the sense organs, peripheral nervous system, and brain, the type of pursuit of them, and the general tendency to persist in this quest, depend largely on the way the social order treats childish needs of this sort.

Murphy maintains that curiosity is at first nonspecific in direction, pointing out that puppies, monkeys, and men all are forever poking their noses into what obviously does not concern them.

Ausubel (1958) discusses the development of curiosity in terms of the number and kinds of questions asked by children. The frequency of questions increases with the spurt in language development between the second and third years of life. At this stage, questions constitute ten to fifteen per cent of all linguistic utterances. At first, questions concern the names of objects and persons in the environment. *Why* and *how* questions, according to Ausubel, are a somewhat later development. Questions are at first motivated by current rather than distant events and are concerned largely with human actions and intentions. Girls ask more questions than boys about interpersonal relations, and boys make more inquiries about causation. Ausubel also maintains that children use questions as a technique for establishing and maintaining social contact, as well as a means for obtaining information.

McKeller (1957) has examined the nature of individual differences in terms of willingness to permit their curiosity to be satisfied by an explanation. He offers as an illustration three levels of reaction to two of Coleridge's poems. Most people are uninterested in how "The Ancient Mariner" and "Kubla Khan" came to be written and how they assumed the forms they did. Others, according to McKeller, are interested but their curiosity is satisfied upon learning that Coleridge wrote "Kubla Kahn" from a dream he had after reading a passage from "Purchas's Pilgrimage." Only a few remain curious until the causal determinants of the poem have been found and analyzed. Of these graded attitudes, the last is obviously more representative of scientific curiosity.

Reik (McKeller, 1957, pp. 171–172) has labeled this phenomenon as "the courage not to understand." Apparently there are individual, cultural, and occupational differences in this willingness to let one's curiosity rest. Actually this may represent a conflict between two necessary kinds of scientific motives: curiosity versus the urge to explain.

Causes and Consequences. Although Western scientific thought has divided causal conditions from the results of these conditions, developmental psychology has apparently given far more consideration to the development of causal thinking than to thinking concerning consequences. This does not mean, however, that psychology has not been interested in man's ability to predict behavior. The ability of the clinician to predict human behavior, for example, has received considerable attention. Some attention has been given to what has been referred to as "cause-and-effect" thinking. Piaget (1954) differentiates between causal thinking and effect thinking, but in his own research has apparently been concerned primarily with the former.

Perhaps the most important studies of the development of causal thinking are those of Piaget (1954) and Werner (1957). Piaget on the basis of experiments with preschool children has identified the following six stages in the development of causative thinking:

1 and 2—making contact between internal activity and the external environment and the causality peculiar to the primary schemata.
3—magico-phenomentalistic causality.
4—elementary externalization and objectification of causality.
5—the real objectification and spatialization of causality.
6—representative causality and the residues of the causality of preceding types.

According to Piaget (1954, p. 315), causality "consists of an organization of the universe caused by the totality of relations established by action and then by representation between objects as well as between objects and subjects." Piaget points out that from the first months of life the child knows what his mother will do in the day's events: nursing, bath, etc., but that this does not imply objectified causality. These are only images which succeed each other with regularity and make possible the formation of habits.

Werner (1957) in his studies of causal thinking in children and primitive peoples, has emphasized a characteristic implied in the above observation of Piaget. Werner maintains that the traditional explanations of primitive peoples and of children are most often descriptive and narrative in form. Such explanations are not derived from principles of necessary conditions but stem from an individual history—"how it came to pass." Werner further maintains that causal thinking in the child generally has the same characteristics as a primitive thought, namely, subjectivity, concreteness, and diffuseness. According to Werner (1957, p. 321), the law of development insofar as causality is concerned is one of increasing abstraction and generalization. In other words, the highest stage of causal reasoning is attained when the explanation is in terms of universal, abstract, necessary causes.

Ausubel (1958, p. 568) agrees with Piaget and Werner that children pass through gross qualitative stages of causal thinking, and that there is a gradual change in the quality of children's causal explanations. He emphasizes the fact that there is much overlapping between age groups and that all kinds of causal explanations are found at all age levels. He states, nevertheless, that children rarely appreciate antecedent-consequent relationships before the age of eight or ten.

Testing Materials. The materials required for the Ask-and-Guess Test include a test booklet for recording the subject's responses and a picture. Several pictures were tested experimentally before the present set was chosen. Although all of the pictures tested (mother and son, father and son, male social group, committee meeting, a dog being dunked in the ocean by a ship's crew, a boy and a dog, a man training a horse) produced satisfactory results, the present set seems to be most suitable for all ages and to arouse interest at all age levels. All are Mother Goose prints [1] depicting children's behavior problems.

The first print, and the one for which the most complete data are available, is based on the story of Tom, the Piper's Son. Tom is shown running with a black and white pig in his arms and his cap blowing off. The gate of the pen has been left open; one of the remaining pigs is looking up and the others are busily eating. A figure in the background is running toward the pen with a pitch fork in hand. The dress of the human figures and the structures appear to be of medieval vintage. The second print is based on the story of "who put the cat in the well." One boy is holding a cat over the well. A girl of apparently similar age is looking on and a second boy has turned his back on the scene. In the background is a barn. Prints of Little Boy Blue and Little Bobby Shaftoe have also been used. All of these prints are colorful and have human interest appeal. The prints are used for individual administration, and colored slides for group administration.

Administration Procedures. The test may be administered either orally and individually or written and in a group. Having to write out one's ideas, however, clearly inhibits their flow, and the two types of administration do not yield equivalent results. Thus far, the proce-

---

[1] *Mother Goose Prints,* Penn Prints, New York.

dure has been administered below the fourth grade as an individual test and above this grade as a group test. In both cases, a time limit of five minutes for each of the three parts was imposed. Differences in performance under group and individual administrations in grades three through six are being investigated.

Subjects are told that this is a test of how curious they are about the world in which they live and of how good they are at guessing causes and results or consequences. In introducing the first part, the examiner states that the main way we show our curiosity and obtain information is by asking questions. They are then instructed to think of all the questions they can about what they see in the picture. They are encouraged to ask questions about any or all parts of the picture and of the event depicted but are cautioned to ask only questions which cannot be answered by looking at the picture. In asking for hypotheses concerning causes, subjects are told that they cannot always obtain the information they want by asking questions; there are times when they must make guesses and then test their guesses through further investigation or study. They are then instructed to make all of the guesses they can concerning the possible causes of the event depicted. Similarly, for the third part, subjects are instructed to give as many possible consequences (both immediate and long-range) as they can of the action depicted.

In the oral, individual administration, examiners attempt to form as friendly a relationship as possible with the child and to record his responses as accurately as possible. Obviously, it would be desirable to record responses electrically for purposes of detailed analysis of the development of the functions under study.

Scoring Procedures. Thus far, the scoring of protocols has been kept quite simple. A score for fluency is obtained simply by counting the number of relevant responses given (questions or guesses). A score for adequacy has required the establishment of a set of simple principles which has resulted in satisfactory interscorer reliability (product-moment coefficients of correlation as follows: questions = .92; causes = .95; consequences = .95). A procedure is being developed now for obtaining an originality score.

QUESTIONS

The general rule for scoring the adequacy of a question is: Could the question be answered simply by looking at the picture? If the question cannot be answered by looking at the picture, the response is scored as adequate. To obtain reliability of scoring, several arbitrary assumptions are made concerning the "givens." For "Tom, Tom, the Piper's Son," these include:

The boy's name is Tom.
The pig belongs to the farmer.
Tom is taking the pig.
The farmer is chasing Tom.
The farmer has a pitch fork in his hand.

Since the title was printed on the picture and the story is familiar to most American children, it seems that memory would be involved in most of the above, and the elimination of questions to obtain this information seems justified.

The following are typical of the questions scored as adequate:

Why is Tom stealing the pig?
Where is Tom taking the pig?
Is Tom scared?
When did this happen?
In what country did it happen?
Why did Tom steal the spotted pig instead of one of the others?
Will the farmer catch Tom?
What will he do to Tom?
Why don't the other pigs run out?
Will the boy run back and get his cap?

Examples of inadequate responses to Little Bobby Shaftoe include:

Why is the grass green?
Why is the sky blue?
Why is the house brown?

Examples of adequate responses include:

Where is the boy going?
Why are they waving to each other?
Is the sun going up or down?
Where do the steps lead? (other side of house)
Is the house near a town?
What country is this?

What year is it?

Is she his mother?

In scoring the adequacy of questions the scorer must keep in mind the level of knowledge of the child and the implications of questions for determining the action in the picture. Certain facts or relationships may be beyond the grasp of younger children, and questions about these facts and relationships which represent curiosity about the picture are scored as adequate. For example: "Why is the grass green?" and "Why is the doorknob white?" are more universal questions not particularly related to the picture; hence they would be scored as inadequate. Conversely, "Why are the sails purple?" "Why is the upstairs window half blue and half white?" "What are those pots on the chimney for?" and "Is the boat coming or going?" would be scored as adequate because they are more related to the picture and represent legitimate curiosity about the picture.

CAUSES

Responses were scored as adequate if the explanation reflected "universal, abstract, necessary causes." Sequences of events of the "this-is-the-way-it-happened" type were not scored as adequate. The causes must also refer to the action of the picture. The following are examples of responses judged to be adequate for "Tom, Tom, the Piper's Son":

Tom and/or his family were hungry or starving.

Tom was compelled to steal the pig by his parents, gang, or other party.

The pig rightfully belonged to Tom (the farmer had stolen it from Tom, the pig had wandered away, Tom had worked for it, etc.).

Tom wanted it as a pet.

Tom wanted it to sell for money.

Tom bought the pig and the man is waving good-bye.

Tom took the spotted pig because it was the biggest, was a boy pig, etc.

Tom just liked to steal.

Tom is playing a joke on the farmer.

Tom disliked the man.

The farmer wanted to kill the pig and Tom is protecting it.

Tom thought that the farmer was away and that he could get away with stealing the pig.

The farmer wants to give Tom the pitch fork.

The farmer was alerted by the squealing of the pigs or by some chance occurrence.

Examples of inadequate responses to the print of Little Bobby Shaftoe include:

The grass is green because it's summer.

The steps lead to a porch on the other side of the house.

They just had breakfast.

Adequate responses:

The boy was sailing away to college.

He was going to get help for his sick mother.

He was going to the store for some bread.

CONSEQUENCES

The rules for scoring the adequacy of consequences are essentially the same as those for scoring causes. The consequence must follow as a logical outcome of the behavior in the picture to be considered adequate.

In scoring sequential stories, each act or action in the story is scored as a separate response and is given one point. One modifying rule is that in sequential stories where the first act is not a logical consequence, the first response is not scored as adequate but succeeding responses are considered as adequate if they follow from the first.

Tom was (not) caught.

The pig got away (did not get away).

Tom was punished (scolded, spanked, put to bed without supper, compelled to work for the farmer, put in jail, etc.).

Tom was forgiven by the farmer.

The farmer gave Tom the pig.

Tom was expelled from school.

Tom escaped from prison and got caught again for stealing.

Tom kept stealing more and more.

Tom had to work for his father to pay the farmer back.

Tom was scared, amused, angry, etc.

The other pigs ran away.

The man tripped for some reason and fell.

The man became exhausted because of age and overweight.

Tom did not ever steal again (learned lesson).

The farmer is jailed for assaulting Tom.

Tom's parents attack the farmer for assaulting Tom.

Product Improvement Tasks

The Product Improvement test is another complex task with a high degree of face validity. This task almost always "makes good sense" to teachers and parents. Both groups almost always recognize that what they consider a desirable type of thinking is involved. The task is also attractive from the standpoint of administration and scoring. To most subjects, it is an interesting task. It permits them to "regress in the service of the ego" and enables them to play around with ideas which they would not dare do in a more serious task. In the individual administration, it provides an object for manipulation, making obvious certain aspects of the creative thinking process in children. The colored slides used in the group administration also stimulate interest.

This task offers interesting possibilities for scoring on a variety of dimensions: fluency, flexibility, originality, inventiveness, and the like. With each response, we ask the question, "What kind of thinking did this idea require?"

Testing Materials. Thus far, four different toys have been used: a toy nurse kit, a friction fire truck, a stuffed small toy dog, and a stuffed small toy monkey. Originally, the first three toys were used with each subject. Only one of the toys, the stuffed dog or the stuffed monkey, is included in batteries in current use.

In addition to the toy, the materials required include a test booklet for recording responses and observations, a small table and chair for the subject, a chair for the examiner, and a stop watch. In the group administration, a colored slide is used. It is also desirable to display the toy itself in the group administration, even though subjects do not have a chance to manipulate it.

The test booklet contains a general orientation to be used by the examiner in establishing rapport, the key instructions for the task, and space for observations.

The nurse kit was selected as a typically "girl's toy" and includes a variety of items suitable for playing the role of the nurse: plastic cap, candy pills, absorbent cotton, eye chart, tongue depressor, hypodermic needle, thermometer, stethoscope, spoon, and spectacles. The items are contained in a cardboard box illustrated with drawings of a nurse.

The friction fire truck was selected as a typically "boy's toy" and is of an inexpensive variety with a number of defects. It has rubber wheels, is painted red, and has an extension ladder. There is no driver in the cab, no hose, no sirens, and no safety net.

The toy dog was selected for its appropriateness for both boys and girls. The model selected is a small one covered with red and blue velvet. The tail is very short; the long, droopy ears are of black velvet; the nose is of a hard black substance; and the eyes are made of yellow and blue felt. A thin green ribbon decorates the neck. The toy monkey is about the same size as the toy dog and similarly constructed.

Early experimental work did show that boys in the first grade gave fewer responses than girls for the nurse's kit and more responses than girls for the fire truck. Beginning with the second grade, these kinds of differences fade out, and by the third grade boys gave more responses than girls for all three toys, including the nurse kit. It was partially for this reason that most of our developmental work has been done with the toy dog and monkey. Neither seems to have any "sex taint." The monkey can be used as the stimulus for an alternate task.

Administration. The task must be administered individually to children in the early school years but may be administered as a group task to older children, adolescents, and adults. Originally, no time limit was placed on the oral administration. In current work, a time limit of eight minutes is placed on both oral and written testings.

The examiner seeks to make the child feel at ease while he ascertains and records the essential identifying information. He then proceeds with the brief orientation printed on the cover of the test booklet, explaining the general nature of the task. It is suggested that at the outset the teacher or chief examiner give the entire class a general orientation and ask them to keep their answers "secret" until all have completed the task. The examiner then proceeds with the Product Improvement task or tasks. The subject is permitted to handle the toys but not specifically encouraged to do so. The examination proceeds according to the script provided in the test booklet.

The following arbitrary rules have been devised for the guidance of the examiner:

1. To the extent practical, pace the subject according to his own speed. At the end of eight minutes conclude the task promptly and go ahead to the next task. If a subject obviously runs out of responses or can give no responses, go ahead to the next item.

2. With exceptionally shy and inarticulate children who are unable to give any responses, say, "All right, let's leave this for a while and maybe you'll think of something later." After this, go ahead with the next task and at the end of the battery return, asking if they can think of something now.

3. Try to obtain maximum performance but stay within the instructions contained in the test booklet to the extent possible. Where appropriate the examiner may add, "Can you think of another way?" or "What else would improve it?" Reinforce irrelevant responses minimally and attempt to move the subject to relevant responses, if a large number of irrelevant responses are given.

4. If the subject does not grasp the idea of "changing or improving the toy so that it will be more fun to play with," one or two alternatives may be used. One of the more successful is, "If you had a magic wand and could make this toy be any way you wanted it to be, how would you make it different?" Another reasonably successful question is, "If you could tell Santa just how to make this toy so that boys and girls would have the most fun with it, how would you tell him to change it?"

5. With some children, there is a problem of reducing test anxiety, in spite of all efforts to prevent the arousal of such anxiety. With many children, we have found it helpful to say, "Come on and tell me just for fun! It doesn't count. I'd just like to know what you think about it." Thus, reassured some children will immediately respond with a rapid flow of ideas after being completely silent for some time.

6. Write down all of the responses given by the subject no matter how irrelevant or fantastic they may seem. This material is essential in assessing irrelevance and fantasy. It is also rewarding to the child, making him feel that what he is saying is being accepted. The examiner may accompany his recording of responses by such verbal

responses as "Umm," "Good thinking," and the like, if it is needed to reduce test anxiety. The general impression is, however, that children give more responses when no such evaluative remarks are made than when they are.

7. To the extent possible, record in the space at the bottom of the page of each sheet of the test booklet any unusual behavior observed, the extent of manipulation of the toy, etc. Record other observations and impressions upon completion of the battery.

For the stuffed toy dog, the instructions are as follows for the oral administration: "Try to think of the cleverest, most interesting, and most unusual ways you can for changing this toy dog so that boys and girls will have more fun playing with it. Don't worry about how much it would cost—just so it would make it more fun to play with. As fast as you think of ideas, tell them to me and I'll write them down for you."

The instructions for the group administration are as follows: "List below the cleverest, most interesting, and most unusual uses you can think of for changing the toy dog you will be shown so that children will have more fun playing with it. Don't worry about how much it will cost— just so it would be more fun to play with."

Scoring Procedures. The ideational fluency score is obtained simply by counting all of the separate responses given by the subjects, regardless of the quality. The flexibility score for each task is obtained by counting the number of approaches used in improving the product. Guides for scoring flexibility are included in the section which follows. The inventivlevel score was devised by adapting the criteria used by the U. S. Patent Office in assessing inventivlevel. Redefined, these criteria are as follows: stride forward, newness, challenging and thought provoking, rarity, constructiveness, and surprisingness. The scoring guide will be presented in a later section. The originality score was developed from a tabulation of the frequency of responses given.

FLEXIBILITY

Twenty or more general principles may be used in thinking of new ideas for improving almost any product, process, organization, or plan. The flexibility score is the number of different principles or approaches used in responding to the task. Their application is illustrated in the following categories for the toy dog:

Toy Dog

1. *Adaptation*—Change it to a cat, mouse, etc. Uses other than as a toy dog.

2. *Addition*—Leash, ribbon on ear, squeaker for nose, hat, hat with flowers, toes, collar and license, "wee-wee" thing to go to bathroom, motor, dog sweater, carrying a bone, decoration.

3. *Change Color*—All red, all black, brown all over, more like real dog, like a particular kind of dog, pink dog, yellow nose, different colored eyes, red ribbon instead of green ribbon, etc.

4. *Change Shape*—Hold ears up, make rear stick up, change shape of nose more like real dog, fatter neck, floppy ears, tongue inside mouth, etc.

5. *Combination*—Put with dog house, puppies, mommy, master, mate, bag for dog and house, car for master and dog, cat to chase, road to go on, stake for hitching dog, a bowl, remote control.

6. *Division*—(Thus far, we have no responses using this approach).

7. *Magnification*—Bigger: dog, head, tongue, hind legs; longer: tail, legs, tongue; wider: ears; so big you could sit on it.

8. *Minification*—Smaller: mouth, etc.; shorter: ears, etc.; baby dog.

9. *Motion*—Legs so that they bend or move; eyes move, open, close; jump around; sniff; wag tail; wind up toy; touch button and runs by himself; wheels on feet; ears that move; mouth that opens and closes; grins, shows teeth.

10. *Multiplication*—Litter of dogs, pairs, etc.

11. *Position*—Sit up, stand up, lie down, stand on head, stand up straighter.

12. *Quality of Material*—Make it out of rubber, ears should be strings, real dog fur, flexible material, etc.

13. *Rearrangement*—Eyes on same level, detachable parts, etc.

14. *Reversal*—Put head where tail is, etc.

15. *Sensory Appeal* (ear)—Marbles in ear so it makes a noise, barks, makes a noise when you push it; squeeze ears and he barks; tape

recorder inside to sing a song; tiny computer to translate human speech into dog language, etc.

16. *Sensory Appeal* (eye)—Nose that glows, eyes that glow, eyes that light up, etc.

17. *Sensory Appeal* (nose)—Make it smell sweet; put catnip on it to make it a toy for cats, etc.

18. *Sensory Appeal* (touch)—Holes in nose; a cold nose; nose made of sponge that stays moist, etc.

19. *Substitution*—Collar in place of ribbon, chain in place of ribbon, ears like bean bags, etc.

20. *Subtraction*—Take seal (tag) off, take bow (ribbon) off, etc.

INVENTIVLEVEL

The "inventivlevel" concept was adapted from U. S. Patent Office usage, suggestions made by McPherson at the 1955 Utah Conference on the Identification of Creative Scientific Talent (1956), Rossman (1931), and others. The first scoring guide proved to be too bulky and cumbersome to be used effectively. The guide presented here is a revision of the original one and is much briefer and easier to use. Interscorer reliabilities have been consistently in the .90's and upper .80's.

The following criteria (with examples from this task and the unusual uses of the toy dog task) have been found useful for our purposes:

Stride Forward Does the idea present a new and original plan? How useful is the idea? Does this usefulness extend in a practical, realistic direction? Examples: *Improvements*—Give him a beard and/or mustache; have him do acrobatics. *Unusual Uses* —Make him into a barrette or brooch; make him into an ear muff.

Newness Is the idea unusual, remarkable? Is it of recent origin? Does it show innovation, new effects? Examples: *Improvements*—Give him a doggy smell, make him inflatable. *Unusual Uses*—Make an autograph dog, a garbage disposal, a kitchen timer, a pendulum weight, fire starter, etc. from him.

Challenging and Thought Provoking

Does the idea lead to new and additional ideas? Does it, or can it generate new ideas? Examples: *Improvements*—Have him growl with a record inside; have leg scratch ear; make paws shake hands, etc. *Unusual Uses*—Puzzle (make it in very small pieces); camera (twist tail for shutter release); character in a good book; communication device.

Rarity

Is the idea different from those generally given? Is it produced by only a few individuals? Examples: *Improvements*—Make his eyes/nose light up, sparkle, glow in dark; squirt water from mouth; smelly nose; holes in nose; make him able to lick face. *Unusual Uses*—Toilet paper dispenser, lint remover (give it an electrostatic charge); squeeze bottle (made out of plastic).

Constructiveness

Does the idea tell how to bring about the change or how to apply the principle or how to solve the problem? Examples: *Improvements*—Have him stand by pushing button, or pulling his tail. *Unusual Uses*—Make a sleep inducer by adding a tape recorder inside it; give it an electric brain so he can be a computer, can answer questions, etc.

Surprisingness

Does the idea produce astonishment, wonder, or surprise? Does the idea introduce reasons to produce feelings of astonishment or surprise? (The suggested idea must not be a part of any toy dog insofar as you [the scorer] know). Examples: *Improvements*—Make him wet or warm to touch; make him have doggy smell. *Unusual Uses*—Back scratcher, decoy, burglar alarm, nose as a horn.

A point value of one is given for each category one through six. Each response is given a value. The total score for inventivlevel is the sum of the point values of all responses.

ORIGINALITY

In order to develop information to construct some measure of originality or unusualness of response, tabulations were made of the responses of 146 elementary school children from grades one through six and 448 high school students. Frequencies and percentages were computed, and on the basis of these data weighted values were assigned to each response for the elementary level, the high school level, and the elementary and high school combined. Experience has not yet shown what is the best way of determining originality scores. One procedure would be to assign a value to each response on the basis of the tables. If it is desirable to show developmental trends, the weighted value for grades one through twelve should be used for all subjects. A simpler procedure which might possibly provide a more meaningful score would be to award one point each for each response having a value of four or for each response having a value of three or four. Not enough scoring has been done thus far to determine the relative advantages of the several possible procedures.

The following is a list of the most common responses. It is suggested that a score of zero be assigned to each of these responses, and that a score of one be assigned to all other appropriate responses showing evidence of creative intellectual energy:

Bark, speak
Bells on it
Bigger
Change Color
Clothing on it, cap, shoes, glasses
Collar, add
Ears flap
Eyes roll (when tongue is pulled,
    etc.)

Fuzzy or hairy
Hat on head
Leash, add
Legs move
Mouth move
Squeak when squeezed
Tail longer
Tail wags
Walk, able to

Unusual Uses (Toy Dog/Monkey)

Basically, the Unusual Uses task involving the toy dog or the toy monkey requires the subject to redefine the object after spending eight minutes thinking of ways to improve it as "something to play with." The redefinition abilities are now considered as required in creative thinking by Guilford and his associates (Guilford and Merrifield,

1960). These abilities belong in Guilford's convergent-production category and originally were not included among the abilities believed to be involved in creative thinking.

The materials are the same as used in the Product Improvement Task and in general this task should not be used except in conjunction with the Product Improvement Task.

The task can be administered orally and individually or written and in a group. In the individual administration, the following instructions are given: "Think of the cleverest, most interesting, and most unusual uses you can for this toy dog (monkey) other than as a plaything. These uses can be for the toy as it is or as it can be changed. For example, you could use it as a pin cushion as it is. Or, you could make it larger and stronger and use it to sit on. Think of as many uses as you can and tell them to me." In the group administration, the instructions are as follows: "List below the cleverest, most interesting, and most unusual uses you can think of for this dog other than as a plaything. Think of uses as it is or as it could be changed. For example, it could be used as a pin cushion as it is. If you make it larger and stronger, you could use it to sit on."

The time limit is five minutes for both individual and group testing. Responses are scored for fluency, flexibility, inventivlevel, and originality. The scoring concepts are essentially the same as those employed in evaluating responses to the Product Improvement Task. The flexibility categories, however, were derived in the same way as those for Circles.

VERBAL TASKS USING VERBAL STIMULI

Unusual Uses (Tin Cans, Books)

The Unusual Uses tasks using verbal stimuli are direct modifications of Guilford's Brick Uses Test. After preliminary tryouts, we decided to substitute tin cans and books for bricks. It was believed that children would be able to handle tin cans and books more easily, since both are more available to children than bricks. The writer was familiar with the potentialities of tin cans as a stimulus to invention through the experiences of prisoners of war in World War II and in survival training.

It was recognized at the outset that both tin cans and books create in many individuals rigid sets which are difficult for them to overcome. It is easy to define a tin can as "a container" and then to think of all the different things which can be put into tin cans, making it difficult to think of other types of response. Similarly, book is readily defined as "something to read," making redefinition somewhat difficult. This type of rigidity seems to increase with age and with mental illness. About 87 per cent of the responses given by a group of schizophrenic fall in the "container" category, compared to 34 per cent for a group of college freshmen and juniors and 17 per cent for fourth, fifth, and sixth grade children.

Thus far, the task has been administered only as a group test. The time limit established is five minutes. In early administrations, subjects were simply instructed "to think of as many uses as you can for tin cans or books," as the case might be. The instructions were then changed to read as follows: "Now try to think of some unusual uses of tin cans (books). List below the cleverest, most interesting, and most unusual uses you can think of for tin cans (books). The tin cans (books) may be of any size and you can change them in any way they can be changed."

Responses are scored for fluency, flexibility, and originality. The fluency score is obtained by counting the number of different relevant responses. Flexibility is measured by the number of different categories used. The scoring guide for categorizing responses is included herewith. Thus far, originality has been measured by counting the number of uncommon responses. More specifically, the following categories and/or responses have been eliminated from the tin can task:

1. Container (unless the container use is really surprising, heretofore unheard of, etc.)
2. Dipper or water glass.
3. Destruction or waste.
4. Growing plants.
5. Noise maker.
6. Recreation (unless something really surprising or unusual). Such recreational uses as "kick the can" and "stilts" are eliminated.

The following categories for books are rated as commonplace and eliminated in the scoring for Originality:

1. Buy
2. Destruction
3. Gift
4. Information
5. Pleasure
6. Record

Impossibilities Task

The Impossibilities task is used by Guilford and his associates (1951) as a measure of fluency involving complex restrictions and large potential. In a course in personality development and mental hygiene, this author has experimented with a number of modifications of the basic task, making the restrictions more specific. For example, one task required students to think of all the impossibilities concerning changing adult personality through psychotherapy. Another required them to state impossibilities concerning the control of children's behavior; another, the control of adolescent behavior.

The task is given as a part of a battery and imposes a five-minute time limit. The instructions state simply: "List as many impossibilities as you can think of."

Although we are not certain that we are justified in doing so, we have scored responses for fluency, flexibility, and originality. As in the other tasks, fluency is determined by counting the number of relevant responses, i.e., things usually regarded as impossible to accomplish. Flexibility is determined by the number of different categories of impossibilities listed in a scoring guide. In obtaining the Originality score, the following types of responses are eliminated as not being original:

1. Things which are actually possible and have been or are being done.
2. Irrelevant responses.
3. Commonplace impossibilities, frequently talked about impossibilities in folklore, mythology, etc. These include:
    a. Men and animals flying without mechanical aids.
    b. A cow jumping over the moon.
    c. Making one's self invisible.
    d. Animals and birds talking.

Consequences

The Consequences task was chosen by Guilford and his associates (1951) to yield measures both of Ideational Fluency and Penetration. Low quality responses were counted in obtaining a measure of fluency with simple restrictions and large potential. Remote consequences were used in obtaining a measure of Remote Associations or Penetration.

For our modifications of the task, we chose three improbable situations for each form from a list of impossibilities obtained from the testing of our staff with the Impossibilities task. Those used in Form A were:

1. What would happen, if man could become invisible at will?
2. What would happen, if a hole could be bored through the earth?
3. What would happen, if the language of birds and animals could be understood by man?

The following constituted Form B:

1. What would happen, if the days were twice as long as they are?
2. What would happen, if a man could live forever on the earth?
3. What would happen, if men could fly without mechanical aids?

The administration of the Consequences task has been as a group test with a time limit of five minutes for the three problems combined. Responses are scored for fluency, flexibility, and originality along the same pattern as the Impossibilities task.

Just Suppose

The Just Suppose test is an adaptation of the Consequences type of test designed to elicit a higher degree of spontaneity and to be more effective with children. As in the Consequences task, the subject is confronted with an improbable situation and asked to predict the possible outcomes from the introduction of a new or unknown variable. In this adaptation, the verbal statement of the improbable situation is accomplished by a black and white drawing of the situation. The drawing faces the verbal description and there are blanks under the verbal statement for responses. The accompanying illustration of the soap bubble situation is taken from Form A.

Two forms have been developed, each consisting of six sets of these improbable situations and illustrations. The improbable situations in Form A are:

1. Just suppose—When it was raining all the rain drops stood still in the air and wouldn't move—and they were solid.

2. Just suppose—I could walk on air or could fly without being in an airplane.

3. Just suppose—I went through the wringer of the washing machine and came out flat.

4. Just suppose—A great fog were to fall all over the earth and all we could see would be feet.

5. Just suppose—Someone got caught in a big soap bubble and couldn't get out.

6. Just suppose—While you were looking at a movie about something that took place a long time ago you walked right into it.

Form B contains the following situation:

1. Just suppose—Sunshine was solid.

2. Just suppose—Our shadows were to become real.

3. Just suppose—Clouds had strings attached to them which hung down to earth.

4. Just suppose—You could stretch your body any way you wanted.

5. Just suppose—We should all turn black.

6. Just suppose—The picture you drew became real.

The following instructions are given in administering this task:

On the pages which follow are six improbable situations or conditions—at least they don't exist now. This will give you a chance to use your imagination about all of the other exciting things which might happen IF these improbable conditions might come to pass.

In your imagination JUST SUPPOSE that each of the situations described were to happen. THEN think of all of the other things that would happen because of it. What would be the consequences? Make as many guesses as you can.

Write your guesses as rapidly as you can in the blank spaces on the page opposite the picture. You will be given five minutes for each of the improbable situations. As soon as time is called, turn the page and proceed immediately to the next situation. Do not worry too much about spelling, grammar, and the like, but try to write so that your ideas can be read.

Five minutes are allowed for each task. Responses are scored for fluency, flexibility, and originality in much the same way as the Consequences task.

FIGURE A4. *Sample Item from Just Suppose Test.*

Situations

The Situations tasks were modeled after Guilford's (1951) test designed to assess the ability to see what needs to be done, one of the measures of the factor labeled "sensitivity to problems."

These tasks are included in a booklet along with other verbal tasks and have been included in Forms A and G.

Subjects are told that they will be given three common problems and that they will be asked to think of as many solutions to these problems as possible. The problems are stated as follows:

1. How would you handle a friend who likes to kid others but cannot stand to be kidded by them?

2. You have been made responsible for spending the money for your club. One of the members of the club is out to make the group think that you are dishonest. What would you do?

3. If all schools were abolished, what would you do to try to become educated?

A time limit of five minutes for the three problems has been followed. Responses are scored for fluency, flexibility, and originality using scoring guides developed in the same manner as outlined for Impossibilities.

Common Problems

The Common Problems task is an adaptation of Guilford's (1951) test designed to assess the ability to see defects, needs, and deficiencies and found to be one of the tests of the factor termed "sensitivity to problems."

Subjects are instructed that they will be given two common situations and that they will be asked to think of as many problems as they can that might arise in connection with these situations. In Form A, the situations are:

1. Taking a bath.
2. Doing homework.

The ones in Form B are:

1. Making a sandwich.
2. Getting to school in the morning.

A time limit of five minutes is imposed for the two situations in each form.

Responses are scored for Fluency, Flexibility, and Originality, as in the other tasks in this section, according to a scoring guide.

Improvements

The Improvement tasks were adapted from Guilford's (1952) Apparatus Test which was designed to assess ability to see any kind of defects, an aspect of sensitivity to problems. In the Apparatus Test, subjects are asked to suggest two improvements on each of several appliances. In our task, subjects are asked to think of as many improvements as they can for three common objects in five minutes.

Subjects are told that they will be given a list of three common objects and that their task is to suggest as many ways as they can to improve each object. They are cautioned not to worry about whether or not it is possible to make this change. They are also asked to refrain from suggesting something that has already been done to make the object better. (This instruction is commonly violated, however.)

In Form A, the objects are: bicycles, shoes, and clothes. In Form B, the products are: coats, telephones, and skates.

A time limit of five minutes is imposed on the task. The general scoring plan for this task is the same as for the Situations and Common Problems tasks, with scoring based on guides.

Mother Hubbard Problem

The Mother Hubbard Problem was conceived as an adaptation of the Situations Task for oral administration in the primary grades. It has proved useful in older groups as a group administered task, however. The administration of this task has stimulated a number of ideas concerning factors which inhibit the development of ideas. For example, we observed early that many children were inhibited in thinking about ideas for getting Mother Hubbard out of her predicament because they were so obsessed with the idea that she should have prevented the predicament. As evidence has accumulated from other sources, this observation has emerged as a part of the emphasis in American education on prevention and on success rather than on the development of skills for coping with inevitable frustrations and predicaments.

Instructions for the task are included in a booklet containing a battery of tasks. The instructions included in the booklet are as follows: "Now we are going to try something a little different. You probably know the Mother Goose story which goes something like this:

> Old Mother Hubbard went to the cupboard
> To get her poor doggie a bone
> But when she got there
> The cupboard was bare. . . .

Now I want you to think of all the things Mother Hubbard could have done when she found that there were no bones in the cupboard."

The task has been administered in grades one through four as an individual task and to adults as a group task. Under both conditions, a time limit of five minutes has been imposed.

Thus far, major attention has been given to scoring for fluency and quality. As in other tasks, the Fluency score is obtained by counting the number of relevant responses. In the earlier grades, it has also been found useful to obtain Irrelevant and Fantasy responses. Quality responses are defined as those which show sensitivity to problems and some degree of penetration in imagining the consequences of the predicament. Eliminated in the Mother Hubbard problem are responses clearly dependent upon memory, as "the little dog had none," and such obvious responses as "Mother Hubbard went to the store to buy a bone." Scoring guides have been developed and good interscorer reliability has been attained.

Cow Jumping Problem

The Cow Jumping Problem is a companion task for the Mother Hubbard Problem and has been administered to the same groups, under the same conditions, and scored according to similar procedures. The task is to think of all of the possible things which might have happened when the cow jumped over the moon. A time limit of five minutes is used. As with other verbal tasks, it is administered individually and orally to children in the kindergarten and primary grades.

Such responses as the following are scored as "poor quality": cow came down, cow landed on something hard, cow was killed, plate sang, dish ran away with spoon, cat played fiddle, little dog laughed to see such sport, cow fell down, cow broke whole self, cow hurt herself, etc.

Imaginative Stories

The Imaginative Stories task has been designed as a test of creative writing ability. The instructions for this task are as follows:

> In the next twenty minutes, we would like for you to write the most interesting and exciting story you can think of about one of the topics listed below. Try to write legibly but do not worry too much about your writing, spelling, and the like. Instead, try to put into your story as many good ideas as you can. Choose any one of the following topics or make up a similar one of your own:

The following titles are suggested in Form A:

1. The dog that doesn't bark.
2. The man who cries.
3. The woman who can but won't talk.
4. The cat that doesn't scratch.
5. Miss Jones stopped teaching.
6. The doctor who became a carpenter.
7. The rooster that doesn't crow.
8. The horse that won't run.
9. The duck that doesn't quack.
10. The lion that doesn't roar.

The following titles were suggested in Form B:

1. The teacher who doesn't talk.
2. The hen that crows.
3. The dog that won't fight.
4. The flying monkey.
5. The boy who wants to be a nurse.
6. The girl who wants to be an engineer.
7. The cat that likes to swim.
8. The woman who swears like a sailor.
9. The man who wears lipstick.
10. The cow that brays like a donkey.

All titles involve animals or persons with divergent characteristics.

A detailed scoring guide for this task has been prepared by Yamamoto (1961). Yamamoto devised a set of six rating scales, each involving five elements. The five scales and their constituent elements are as follows:

1.—Organization
   Balance
   Arrangement
   Consistency
   Conciseness
   Clarity

2.—Sensitivity
   Stimulus Perception
   Association
   Relevancy of Idea
   Specificity
   Empathy

3.—Originality
   Choice of Topic
   Idea
   Organization
   Style of Writing
   Sense of humor

4.—Psychological Insight
   Causal Explanation
   Perspective
   Meaningfulness
   Ego-involvement
   Understanding

5.—Richness
   Expression
   Ideas
   Emotion
   Curiosity
   Fluency

An average interscorer reliability of .78 was obtained among three independent judges, using the scoring guide for the above criteria.

Since the instructions for writing the imaginative stories were designed to encourage originality and interestingness, I attempted to develop detailed scoring instructions for originality and interest. In determining the Originality score the following nine points or characteristics were judged and one point is given for the presence of each.

Picturesqueness   Suggests a picture is colorful, is strikingly graphic, or is objectively descriptive.

Vividness   Story told with liveliness and intenseness; description is so interesting, or even exciting, that the reader may be stirred emotionally; is vigorous, fresh, alive, spirited.

Flavor   Possesses a noticeable, characteristic element, or taste, or appeals to the sense of taste or smell.

Personal Element   Author involves himself in the account or expresses his personal feelings or opinions about the events described.

Original Solution or Ending (Surprising)	A "punch-line"; need not be funny though it may; must be unexpected, unusual, surprising.
Original Setting or Plot	The setting, plot, theme, or moral is unusual or original.
Humor	Has quality of portraying the comical, the funny, the amusing; may make the reader laugh or smile; brings together some incongruities which arise naturally from situation or character, frequently so as to illustrate some fundamental absurdity in human behavior or character.
Invented Words, Names, etc.	Parts of two or more words are combined to express some concept, when animals and persons are given amusing names or names appropriate to their character, or the like.
Other Unusual Twists in Style or Content	A category for giving credit for a high type of originality not reflected in the eight foregoing categories.

In deriving a set of criteria for use in assessing Interest, we have been guided largely by the work of Flesch and his associates (Flesch and Lass, 1955). The following nine indicators are considered and one point is awarded for the presence of each:

Conversational Tone	Story told just as though author were carrying on a conversation with the reader, lack of conscious formality.
Naturalness	Free of artificial and stilted language, form, etc.; "written just as it was thought."
Use of Quotations	Direct words of speaker are given whether or not quotation marks are used.
Variety in Kind of Sentences	May vary according to use (declarative, interrogative, exclamatory, etc.) or according to form (simple, compound, complex, and compound-complex).
Variety in Length of Sentence and in Structure	Mixture of short and long sentences; variation in structure of sentences, such as predicate before subject, dependent clause before independent clause, and the like.

Personal Touch	Same as in Originality.
Humor	Same as in Originality.
Questions and Answers	Questions and answers in the direct words of speakers, or questions and answers between the writer and the reader.
Feelings of Characters	Feelings of characters of story given either through their own words or through the eyes of the writer.

The average interscorer reliability among three judges was .86 for Originality and .83 for Interest.

It has been suggested that the scoring criteria developed provide teachers with concepts which are useful in talking with children about their writing.

Other Tasks Under Development

Several other tasks have been developed for assessing the creative thinking abilities and evaluating creative growth. In most cases, we have not yet had enough experience with them for inclusion here. Some of these tasks will be described briefly and manuals will be issued at a later date after sufficient experience has been accumulated.

Picture Titles. In the Picture Construction and Incomplete Figures tasks, subjects have been asked to make up interesting titles for their pictures. Procedures are being developed for scoring these for originality and synthesis. It is also planned to have subjects write stories about their pictures.

Make-Up Problems. Following the design of Getzels and Jackson (1958), simple sets of data have been prepared with the instructions to make up as many problems as possible which could be solved with the data supplied. One is a mathematics problem and the other a social studies problem.

Filling-in-Gaps. The Filling-in-Gaps Task is designed to provide a measure of sensitivity to problems. It consists of a set of the first and last frames of a series of cartoons. The subjects problem is to formulate hypotheses concerning possible intervening events which would follow from the first and result in the last. Preliminary tryouts have been promising but other developmental work awaits completion.

Creative Activities Check Lists.   Several check lists and inventories of activities, life experiences, and the like have been developed. One is a list of activities which children do on their own in various fields. Another is an inventory of reading interests and habits, and still another is a set of life experience inventories composed of items hypothesized as being related to creative growth.

The following is a sample of one of the briefer check lists which have been developed. It will be noted that it includes activities related to language arts, science, social studies, art, and other fields. There are more detailed check lists that have been constructed for special purposes. A detailed inventory in the science field is the *Things Done* inventory available from: Science Service, 1719 N. Street, N.W., Washington 6, D.C.

THINGS DONE ON YOUR OWN

Name_____ Grade_____ School_____ Date_____

DIRECTIONS: Below is a list of activities boys and girls sometimes do on their own. Indicate which ones you have done during this school term by checking the blank at the left. Include only the things you have done on your own, not the things you have been assigned or made to do.

( )   1. Wrote a poem
( )   2. Wrote a story
( )   3. Wrote a play
( )   4. Kept a collection of my writings
( )   5. Wrote a song or jingle
( )   6. Produced a puppet show
( )   7. Kept a diary for at least a month
( )   8. Played word games with other boys and girls
( )   9. Used *Roget's Thesaurus* or some other book in addition to a dictionary
( )   10. Recorded on a tape recorder an oral reading, dialogue, story, discussion, or the like
( )   11. Found errors in fact or grammar in newspaper or other printed matter
( )   12. Acted in a play or skit
( )   13. Directed or organized a play or skit
( )   14. Made up and sang a song
( )   15. Made up a musical composition for some instrument
( )   16. Made up a new game and taught it to someone else

( )   17. Pantomimed some story
( )   18. Acted out a story with others
( )   19. Wrote a letter to a member of family or a friend away from home
( )   20. Made up an original dance
( )   21. Played charades
( )   22. Visited a zoo
( )   23. Explored a cave
( )   24. Read a science magazine
( )   25. Read a science book
( )   26. Mixed colors
( )   27. Made a fire cracker
( )   28. Printed photographs
( )   29. Grew crystals
( )   30. Made a leaf collection
( )   31. Made a wildflower collection
( )   32. Made an electric motor
( )   33. Made a musical instrument
( )   34. Planned an experiment
( )   35. Dissected an animal
( )   36. Grafted a plant or rooted one from a cutting
( )   37. Distilled water
( )   38. Used a magnifying glass
( )   39. Made ink
( )   40. Made leaf prints
( )   41. Started a fire with a lens
( )   42. Used a magnet
( )   43. Raised rats, mice, rabbits, or guinea pigs
( )   44. Collected insects
( )   45. Collected rocks
( )   46. Kept a daily record of weather
( )   47. Been a bird watcher
( )   48. Kept a science notebook
( )   49. Kept a science scrapbook
( )   50. Attended a science fair or display
( )   51. Used a chemistry set
( )   52. Produced static electricity
( )   53. Constructed a model airplane
( )   54. Designed a model airplane
( )   55. Counted annual rings in a log
( )   56. Made a stamp collection
( )   57. Made a collection of post marks
( )   58. Organized or helped to organize a club
( )   59. Served as officer in a club organized by boys and/or girls
( )   60. Figured out a way of improving a game we play at school or home
( )   61. Figured out a way of improving the way we do something at home

( )   62. Figured out a way of improving the way we do something at school
( )   63. Figured out a way of improving the way we do something in a club, Scouts, etc.
( )   64. Solved a problem about getting along with my parents
( )   65. Solved a problem about getting along with other boys and girls
( )   66. Helped act out some historical event
( )   67. Found out about the history of my city or community
( )   68. Found out about the way some government agency (post office, court, etc.) operates
( )   69. Wrote a letter to someone in another country
( )   70. Wrote a letter to someone in another state
( )   71. Made a map of my community
( )   72. Made my own decision about the use of money
( )   73. Asked questions about the way some business operates
( )   74. Made a poster for some club, school, or other event
( )   75. Organized or helped organize paper drive, rummage sale, etc.
( )   76. Sketched landscape with pencil and/or charcoal
( )   77. Designed stage settings for play or skit
( )   78. Developed a design for jewelry
( )   79. Developed a design for cloth
( )   80. Illustrated a story of my own or one in a book
( )   81. Took color photographs
( )   82. Took black and white photographs
( )   83. Made an illustrated map of a local community
( )   84. Made plaster molds with which clay objects can be cast
( )   85. Drew cartoons
( )   86. Designed greeting card for some holiday or special event
( )   87. Made linoleum cuts
( )   88. Made block prints in color
( )   89. Made a watercolor painting of a familiar scene
( )   90. Made an oilcolor painting of some type
( )   91. Made animal figures in the paper sculpture technique or paper mache
( )   92. Made a toy for a child
( )   93. Built a scale model of a park, playground, farm, etc.
( )   94. Made a wood carving
( )   95. Made a soap carving
( )   96. Made basket for ornamental purposes
( )   97. Drew up plans for an invention, apparatus, etc.
( )   98. Constructed a model of an invention, apparatus, etc.
( )   99. Made up recipe for some kind of food dish (meat, salad, dessert, etc.)
( )   100. Made up recipe for some kind of drink mixture

BIBLIOGRAPHY

Abramson, J. *Essai d'Etalonnage de Deux Tests d'Imagination et d'Observation,* *Journal de Psychologie,* 1927, pp. 370–379.

Allen, A. B. *Imagination and Reality in Colour.* London: Frederick Warne & Co., Inc., 1939.

Anderson, H. H. (Ed.) *Creativity and Its Cultivation.* New York: Harper & Brothers, 1959.

Anderson, H. H. "Developing Creativity in the Child" Paper presented for the 1960 White House Conference on Children and Youth. Mimeographed. East Lansing, Michigan: Michigan State University.

Anderson, J. E. "The Nature of Abilities," in E. P. Torrance (Ed.) *Education and Talent.* Minneapolis, Minnesota: University of Minnesota Press, 1960, pp. 9–31.

Andrews, E. G. "The Development of Imagination in the Pre-School Child," *University of Iowa Studies in Character,* 1930, *3 (4).*

Applegate, Mauree. *Helping Children Write.* Scranton, Pa.: International Textbook Co., 1949.

Asch, S. E., *Studies of Independence and Submission to Group Pressure. I. A Minority of One Against a Unanimous Majority.* Swarthmore, Pa.: Swarthmore College, 1955.

Ashby, W. R. and M. Bassett. "The Effect of Leucotomy on Creative Ability," *Journal of Mental Science,* 1949, *95,* 418–430.

Ausubel, D. P. *Theory and Problems of Child Development.* New York: Grune & Stratton, Inc., 1958.

Barkan, M. *Through Art to Creativity.* Boston, Mass.: Allyn and Bacon, Inc., 1960.

Barlow, F. *Mental Prodigies.* New York: Philosophical Library, Inc., 1952.

Barron, F. "Some Relationships between Originality and Style of Personality," *American Psychologist,* 1954, *9,* 326.

——. "Originality in Relation to Personality and Intellect," *Journal of Personality,* 1957, *25,* 730–742.

——. "The Psychology of Imagination," *Scientific American,* 1958, *199,* 151–166.

Bartlett, F. *Thinking*. New York: Basic Books, Inc., 1959.

Barzun, J. *The House of Intellect*. New York: Harper & Brothers, 1959.

Benham, E. "The Creative Activity," *British Journal of Psychology*, 1929, 20, 59–65.

Berg, Esta. "A Simple Objective Technique for Measuring Flexibility in Thinking," *Journal of General Psychology*, 1948, 39, 15–22.

Biber, Barbara. "Premature Structuring as a Deterrent to Creativity," *American Journal of Orthopsychiatry*, 1959, 29, 280–290.

Binet, A. *Les Idées Modernes sur les Enfants*. Paris: E. Flamarion, 1909.

Blakely, R. J. "Is Individuality Maladjustment?" *NEA. Current Issues in Higher Education*, 1957, pp. 12–24.

Bloom, B. S. "Studies of Creative versus Non-Creative Individuals: University of Chicago," in C. W. Taylor (Ed.) *The 1955 University of Utah Research Conference on the Identification of Creative Scientific Talent*. Salt Lake City: University of Utah Press, 1956, pp. 183–184.

Bond, J. A. "Analysis of Observed Traits of Teachers Rated Superior in Demonstrating Creativeness in Teaching," *Journal of Educational Research*, 1959, 53, 7–12.

Boraas, J. *Teaching to Think*. New York: The Macmillan Co., 1922.

Broadley, Margaret E. *Square Pegs in Square Holes*. Garden City, N.Y.: Doubleday & Company, Inc., 1943.

Brown, Sister Patrick Ann. "A Study of Highly Creative and Highly Intelligent Children on School Adjustment." Unpublished Master's Paper. Milwaukee, Wisc.: Marquette University, 1960.

Bruner, J. S. "Learning and Thinking," *Harvard Educational Review*, 1959, 29, 184–192.

————. *The Process of Education*. Cambridge, Mass.: Harvard University Press, 1960.

Buck, J. N. "The H-T-P Technique, a Qualitative and Quantitative Scoring Manual," Monograph Supplement, *Journal of Clinical Psychology*, 1948, 5, 1–120.

Buhl, H. R. *Understanding the Creative Engineer*. New York: American Society of Mechanical Engineers, 1961.

Burchard, E. M. L. "The Use of Projective Techniques in the Analysis of Creativity," *Journal of Projective Techniques*, 1952, 16, 412–427.

Burkhart, R. "Four Creativity Personality Factors in Art and Teacher Education." (Mimeographed) Mt. Pleasant, Mich.: Central Michigan University, 1961.

Burton, W. H., R. B. Kimball and R. L. Wing. *Education for Effective Thinking*. New York: Appleton-Century-Crofts, Inc., 1960.

Carlson, Ruth Kearney. "Emergence of Creative Personality," *Childhood Education*, 1960, 36, 402–404.

Cattell, R. B. and J. E. Drevdahl. "A Comparison of the Personality Profile (16 P.F.) of Eminent Researchers with that of Eminent Teachers and Administrators, and that of General Population," *British Journal of Psychology*, 1955, 46, 248–261.

Chassell, J. M. "Tests for Originality," *Journal of Educational Psychology*, 1916, 7, 317–328.

Chisholm, B. *Can People Learn to Learn?* New York: Harper & Brothers, 1958.

Christensen, P. R., J. P. Guilford, and R. C. Wilson. "Relations of Creative Responses to Working Time and Instructions," *Journal of Experimental Psychology*, 1957, 53, 82–88.

Cole, Natalie Robinson. *The Arts in the Classroom.* New York: the John Day Company, Inc., 1940.

Cole, W. and Julia Colmore (Ed.) *The Poetry-Drawing Book.* New York: Simon & Schuster, Inc., 1960.

Coleman, J. S. *Social Climates in High Schools.* Washington, D.C.: Government Printing Office, 1961.

Colvin, S. S. "Invention versus Form in English Composition: An Indicative Study," *Pedagogical Seminary*, 1902, 9, 393–421.

————, and I. F. Meyer. "Imaginative Elements in the Written Work of School Children," *Pedagogical Seminary*, 1906, 13, 84–93.

Compton, A. H. "Case Histories of Creativity: Creativity in Science," in *The Nature of Creative Thinking*. New York: Industrial Relations Institute, Inc., 1953.

Conant, J. B. *The Identification and Education of the Academically Talented Student in the American Secondary School.* Washington, D.C.: Academically Talented Pupil Project, National Education Association, 1958.

————. *The American High School Today.* New York: McGraw-Hill Book Co., Inc., 1959.

Dearborn, G. V. "A Study of Imagination," *American Journal of Psychology*, 1898, 5(9), 183.

DeHaan, R. F. and R. J. Havighurst. *Education for Gifted Children.* Chicago: University of Chicago Press, 1957.

Deutsch & Shea, Inc. *Company Climate and Creativity.* New York: Industrial Relations News, 1959.

Doig, D. "Creative Music: I. Music Composed for A Given Test," *Journal of Educational Research*, 1941, 35, 263–275.

————. "Creative Music: II. Music Composed on a Given Subject," *Journal of Educational Research*, 1942, 35, 344–355.

————. "Creative Music: III. Music Composed to Illustrate Given Musical Problems," *Journal of Educational Research*, 1942, 36, 241–253.

Drevdahl, J. E. "Exploratory Study of Creativity in Terms of Its Relationships to Various Personality and Intellectual Factors," *Dissertation Abstracts*, 1954, 14, 1256.

————. "Factors of Importance for Creativity," *Journal of Clinical Psychology*, 1956, *12*, 21–26.

Drews, Elizabeth M. "Freedom to Grow," *NEA Journal*, September 1960, *49(6)*, 20–22.

————. "New Light on Gifted Adolescents," in E. P. Torrance (Ed.) *New Educational Ideas: Third Minnesota Conference on Gifted Children*. Minneapolis, Minnesota: Center for Continuation Study, University of Minnesota, 1961. (a)

————. "A Critical Evaluation of Approaches to the Identification of Gifted Students," in A. Traxler (Ed.) *Measurement and Evaluation in Today's Schools*. Washington, D.C.: American Council on Education, 1961, pp. 47–51. (b)

Edgerton, H. A. "Two Tests for Early Identification of Scientific Ability," *Educational and Psychological Measurement*, 1959, *19*, 299–304.

Educational Policies Commission of the NEA and American Association of School Administrators, *Contemporary Issues in Elementary Education*. Washington, D.C.: National Education Association, 1960.

Eyring, H. "Scientific Creativity," in H. H. Anderson (Ed.) *Creativity and Its Cultivation*. New York: Harper & Brothers, 1959, pp. 1–11.

Feder, D. D. "Perspectives and Challenges." Presidential address presented to American Personnel and Guidance Association Convention. Denver, Colorado, March 28, 1961.

Fiedler, F. E. "The Concept of an Ideal Therapeutic Relationship," *Journal of Consulting Psychology*, 1950, *14*, 239–245.

————. "A Comparison of Therapeutic Relationships in Psychoanalytic, Non-directive and Adlerian Therapy," *Journal of Consulting Psychology*, 1950, *14*, 436–445.

Fisichelli, V. R. and L. Welch. "The Ability of College Art Majors to Recombine Ideas in Creative Thinking," *Journal of Applied Psychology*, 1947, *31*, 278–282.

Flanagan, J. C. "Definition and Measurement of Ingenuity," in C. W. Taylor (Ed.) *The Second University of Utah Research Conference on the Identification of Creative Scientific Talent*. Salt Lake City: University of Utah Press, 1958, pp. 109–118.

————. "The Relation of a New Ingenuity Measure to Other Variables," in C. W. Taylor (Ed.) *The Third (1959) University of Utah Research Conference on the Identification of Creative Scientific Talent*. Salt Lake City: University of Utah Press, 1959, pp. 104–123.

Flesch, R. and A. H. Lass. *The Way to Write*. New York: McGraw-Hill Book Co., Inc., 1955.

Fletcher, F. M. "Manpower for Tomorrow . . . A Challenge," *Personnel and Guidance Journal*, 1958, *37*, 32–39.

Fredericksen, N. *Development of the Test "Formulating Hypothesis": A Progress Report.* Princeton, N.J.: Educational Testing Service, 1959.

French, J. R. P., Jr. and B. Raven, "The Bases of Social Power," in D. Cartwright (Ed.) *Studies in Social Power.* Research Center for Group Dynamics, Ann Arbor, Mich.: University of Michigan, 1958.

Freuchen, P. *Ice Floes and Flaming Water.* New York: Julian Messner, Inc., 1954.

Fritz, R. L. "An Evaluation of Scholastic Achievement of Students Attending Half-Day Sessions in the Seventh Grade." Unpublished research paper. Minneapolis, Minnesota: University of Minnesota, August 1958.

Gallagher, J. J. *Analysis of Research on the Education of Gifted Children,* Springfield, Illinois: Office of Superintendent of Public Instruction, 1960.

Gesell, A. L. *The Child from Five to Ten.* New York: Harper & Brothers, 1946.

Getzels, J. W. "Non-IQ Intellectual and Other Factors in College Admission," in *The Coming Crisis in the Selection of Students for College Entrance.* Washington, D.C.: American Educational Research Association, 1960.

————, and P. W. Jackson. "The Meaning of 'Giftedness'—An Examination of an Expanding Concept," *Phi Delta Kappan,* 1958, 40, 75–77.

———— — ————. "The Highly Intelligent and the Highly Creative Adolescent: A Summary of Some Research Findings," in C. W. Taylor (Ed.) *The Third (1959) University of Utah Research Conference on the Identification of Creative Scientific Talent.* Salt Lake City: University of Utah Press 1959, pp. 46–57.

———— — ————. "Occupational Choice and Cognitive Functioning: Career Aspirations of Highly Intelligent and Highly Creative Adolescents," *Journal of Abnormal and Social Psychology,* 1960, 61, 119–123. (a)

———— — ————. "The Social Context of Giftedness: A Multi-Dimensional Approach to Definition and Methods," in E. P. Torrance (Ed.) *Creativity: Second Minnesota Conference on Gifted Children.* Minneapolis, Minnesota: Center for Continuation Center, University of Minnesota, 1960. (b)

———— — ————. "Family Environment and Cognitive Style: A Study of the Sources of Highly Intelligent and Highly Creative Adolescents," *American Sociological Review,* 1961, 26, 351–359.

Glueck, S. and Glueck, Eleanor. *Unraveling Juvenile Delinquency.* New York: The Commonwealth Fund, 1950.

Goertzel, Mildred G. and V. H. Goertzel. "Intellectual and Emotional Climate in Families Producing Eminence," *Gifted Child Quarterly,* 1960, 4, 59–60.

Griffin, D. F. "Movement Response and Creativity," *Journal of Consulting Psychology,* 1958, 22, 134–136.

Griffiths, Ruth. *A Study of Imagination in Early Childhood.* London: Kegan Paul Trench, Traubner & Co., 1945.

Grippen, V. B. "A Study of Creative Artistic Imagination in Children by the Constant Contact Procedure," *Psychological Monograph*, 1933, *45(1)*, 63–81.

Guilford, J. P. "Creativity," *American Psychologist*, 1950, *5*, 444–454.

———. "Structure of Intellect," *Psychological Bulletin*, 1956, *53*, 267–293.

———. "The Relation of Intellectual Factors to Creative Thinking in Science," in C. W. Taylor (Ed.) *The 1955 University of Utah Research Conference on the Identification of Creative Scientific Talent*. Salt Lake City: University of Utah Press, 1956, pp. 69–95.

———. *A Revised Structure of Intellect*, (Rep. Psychol. Lab., No. 19). Los Angeles: University of Southern Calif., 1957, pp. 69–95.

———. "Basic Traits in Intellectual Performances," in C. W. Taylor (Ed.) *The Second (1957) University of Utah Research Conference on Identification of Creative Scientific Talent*. Salt Lake City: University of Utah Press, 1958, pp. 66–81.

———. *Personality*. New York: McGraw-Hill Book Co., Inc., 1959. (a)

———. "Three Faces of Intellect," *American Psychologist*, 1959, *14*, 469–479. (b)

———. "Factors and Psychological Theory," *American Psychologist*, 1959, 434. (c)

———. "Intellectual Resources and their Values as Seen by Scientists," in C. W. Taylor (Ed.) *The Third (1959) University of Utah Research Conference on the Identification of Creative Scientific Talent*. Salt Lake City: University of Utah Press, 1959, pp. 128–149. (d)

———. "Frontiers in Thinking Teachers Should Know About," *Reading Teacher*, 1960, *13*, 176–182.

———. "Creative-Thinking Abilities of Ninth-Grade Students." Paper presented at annual meeting of American Educational Research Association, Chicago, February 24, 1961.

——— and P. R. Christensen. *A Factor-Analytic Theory of Verbal Fluency*. (Rep. Psychol. Lab., No. 17). Los Angeles: University of Southern Calif., 1956.

———, ———, J. W. Frick, and P. R. Merrifield. *The Relations of Creative-Thinking Aptitudes to Non-Aptitude Personality Traits*. (Rep. Psychol. Lab., No. 20). Los Angeles: University of Southern Calif., 1957.

———, J. W. Frick, and P. R. Christensen. *A Factor-Analytic Study of Flexibility in Thinking*. (Rep. Psychol. Lab., No. 18). Los Angeles: University of Southern Calif., 1957.

———, B. Fruchter, and H. P. Kelley. "Development and Application of Tests of Intellectual and Special Aptitudes," *Review of Educational Research*, 1959, *29*, 26–41.

———— and P. R. Merrifield. *The Structure of Intellect Model: Its Uses and Implications. (Rep. Psychol. Lab., No. 24)*. Los Angeles: University of Southern Calif., 1960.

————, R. C. Wilson, P. R. Christensen, and D. J. Lewis. *A Factor-Analytic Study of Creative Thinking. I. Hypotheses and Description of Tests.* Los Angeles: University of Southern Calif., 1951.

————, R. C. Wilson, and P. R. Christensen. *A Factor-Analytic Study of Creative Thinking. II. Administration of Tests and Analysis of Results. (Rep. Psychol. Lab., No. 8)*. Los Angeles: University of Southern Calif., 1952.

Hammer, E. F. *Creativity.* New York: Random House, 1961.

Harding, Rosamond E. M. *An Anatomy of Inspiration.* Cambridge: W. Heffer and Sons, Ltd., 1948.

Hargreaves, H. L. "The Faculty of Imagination," *British Journal of Psychological Monographs, Supplement,* 1927, 3(10).

Harms, E. "The Psychology of Formal Creativeness: I. Six Fundamental Types of Formal Expression," *Journal of Genetic Psychology,* 1946, 69, 97–120.

————. "A Test for Types of Formal Creativity." Paper read during the 47th annual meeting of American Psychological Association, Sept. 1939. *Psychological Bulletin,* 1939, 36, 526–527.

Harris, D. "The Development and Validation of a Test of Creativity in Engineering," *Journal of Applied Psychology,* 1960, 44, 254–257.

Hart, H. H. "The Integrative Function of Creativity," *Psychiatric Quarterly,* 1950, 24, 1–16.

Hebeisen, Ardyth A. "The Performance of a Group of Schizophrenic Patients on a Test of Creative Thinking," in E. P. Torrance (Ed.) *Creativity: Third Minnesota Conference on Gifted Children.* Minneapolis, Minnesota: Center for Continuation Study, University of Minnesota, 1960, pp. 125–129.

Hobelman, Lucile. "Three Creative Teachers," *Clearing House,* 1957, 32, 161–162.

Hoffman, B. "The Tyranny of Multiple-Choice Tests." *Harper & Brothers,* March 1961, 222, 37–44.

Holland, J. L. "Some Limitations of Teacher Ratings as Predictors of Creativity," *Journal of Educational Psychology,* 1959, 50, 219–222.

————. "Creative and Academic Performance among Talented Adolescents." Paper presented at annual meeting of American Educational Research Association, Chicago, February 24, 1961.

———— and L. Kent. "The Concentration of Scholarship Funds and Its Implications for Education," *College and University,* Summer 1960, 35(4), 471–483.

Holm, Joy Alice. "Guidance through Art Education." Master of Science Research Project. Chicago: Illinois Institute of Technology, 1957.

Hutchinson, E. D. *How to Think Creatively*. Nashville, Tenn.: Abingdon Press, 1949.

Jackson, P. W., J. W. Getzels, and G. A. Xydis. "Psychological Health and Cognitive Functioning in Adolescence: A Multivariate Analysis," *Child Development*, 1960, *31*, 285–298.

Jex, F. "Negative Validities for Two Different Ingenuity Tests," in C. W. Taylor (Ed.) *The Third (1959) University of Utah Research Conference on the Identification of Creative Scientific Talent*. Salt Lake City: University of Utah Press, 1959, pp. 124–127.

Johnson, D. M. *The Psychology of Thought and Judgment*. New York: Harper & Brothers, 1955.

Kelley, E. C. "The Significance of Being Unique," in S. I. Hayakawa (Ed.) *Our Language and Our World*. New York: Harper & Brothers, 1959, pp. 152–171.

Kettner, N. W., J. P. Guilford, and P. R. Christensen. "A Factor-Analytic Study Across the Domains of Reasoning, Creativity and Evaluation," *Psychological Monographs*, 1959, *73*, No. 479.

Kirkpatrick, E. A. "Individual Tests of School Children," *Psychological Review*, 1900, *5(7)*, 274.

Kubie, L. S. *Neurotic Distortion of the Creative Process*. Lawrence, Kansas: University of Kansas Press, 1958.

Kupferberg, Tuli, and Silvia Topp. *Children as Authors*. New York: Birth Press, 1959.

LaBrant, Lou. "The Dynamics of Education," *Saturday Review*, 1959, *42(37)*, 28.

Lally, Ann and Lou LaBrant. *The Gifted Child*. Boston: D. C. Heath & Company, 1951.

Lehman, H. C. *Age and Achievement*. Princeton, N.J.: Princeton University Press, 1953.

———. "Reply to Dennis' Critique of *Age and Achievement*," *J. Gerontology*, 1956, *11*, 333–337.

Levinger, Leah. "The Teacher's Role in Creativity: Discussion," *American Journal of Orthopsychiatry*, 1959, *29*, 291–297.

Ligon, E. M. *The Growth and Development of Christian Personality*. Schenectady, N.Y.: The Union College Character Research Project, 1957.

Lorge, I. "The Teacher's Task in the Development of Thinking," *Reading Teacher*, 1960, *13*, 170–175.

Lowenfeld, V. and K. R. Beittel. "Interdisciplinary Criteria of Creativity in the Arts and Sciences: A Progress Report," *Research in Art Education (9th Yearbook NAEA)*. Washington, D.C.: National Art Education, 1959, pp. 35–44.

McCardle, H. J. "An Investigation of the Relationships Between Pupil Achievement in First-Year Algebra and Some Teacher Characteristics." Doctoral Dissertation. Minneapolis, Minnesota: University of Minnesota, 1959.

McCarty, Stella Agnes. *Children's Drawings: A Study of Interest and Abilities.* Baltimore: The Williams and Wilkins Co., 1924.

McClelland, D. C. "The Calculated Risk: An Aspect of Scientific Performance," in C. W. Taylor (Ed.) *The 1955 University of Utah Research Conference on the Identification of Creative Scientific Talent.* Salt Lake City: University of Utah Press, 1956, pp. 96–110.

McCloy, W. "Creative Imagination in Children and Adults," *Psychological Monographs,* 1939, *51, No. 5,* 88–102.

———. "Passive Creative Imagination," *Psychological Monographs,* 1939, *51, No. 5,* 103–107.

——— and N. C. Meier. "Re-creative Imagination," *Psychological Monographs,* 1939, *51, No. 5,* 108–116.

McDowell, M. S. and S. R. Howe. "Creative Use of Play Materials by Pre-School Children," *Childhood Education,* 1941, *17,* 321–326.

McGuire, C., E. Hindsman, F. J. King and E. Jennings. "Dimensions of Talented Behavior," *Educational and Psychological Measurement,* 1961, *21,* 3–38.

McKeller, P. *Imagination and Thinking.* New York: Basic Books, Inc., 1957.

MacKinnon, D. W. "What Do We Mean by Talent and How Do We Test for It?" *The Search for Talent.* New York: College Entrance Examination Board, 1960, pp. 20–29.

McMillan, Margaret. *Education Through the Imagination.* New York: Appleton-Century-Crofts, Inc., 1924.

McNeil, E. B. "The Paradox of Education for the Gifted," *Improving College and University Teaching,* 1960, *8(3),* 111–115.

McPherson, J. H. "A Proposal for Establishing Ultimate Criteria for Measuring Creative Output," in C. W. Taylor (Ed.), *The 1955 University of Utah Research Conference on the Identification of Creative Scientific Talent.* Salt Lake City: University of Utah Press, 1956, pp. 62–68.

———. "What is Creativity? Its Nature and Implications for Management," in *Creativity: Key to Continuing Progress.* New York: American Management Association, 1960.

Maltzman, I. "On the Training of Originality," *Psychological Review,* 1960, *67,* 229–242.

Markey, F. V. *Imaginative Behavior in Pre-School Children.* New York: Bureau of Publications, Teachers College, Columbia University, 1935.

Maslow, A. H. *Motivation and Personality.* New York: Harper & Brothers, 1954.

———. "Self-Actualizing People: A Study of Psychological Health," in C. W. Moustakas (Ed.) *The Self.* New York: Harper & Brothers, 1956.

————. "Toward a Humanistic Psychology," in S. I. Hayakawa (Ed.) *Our Language and Our World*. New York: Harper & Brothers, 1959, pp. 180–201.

Mearns, H. *The Creative Adult*. Garden City, N.Y.: Doubleday & Company, Inc., 1941.

————. *Creative Power*. New York: Dover Publications, Inc., 1958.

Mednick, S. A. "Development of Admission Criteria for Colleges and Universities That Will Not Eliminate Such Applicants as the Bright Nonconformist, the Underchallenged and the Individual with Highly Specialized Ability," in *Current Issues in Higher Education*. Washington, D.C.: Association for Higher Education, National Education Association, 1961, pp. 87–88.

Meehl, P. E. *Clinical versus Statistical Prediction*. Minneapolis, Minnesota: University of Minnesota Press, 1954.

Meier, N. C. "An Instrument for the Study of Creative Artistic Intelligence," *Psychological Monographs*, 1936, 48, 164–172.

————. "Reconstructive Imagination," *Psychological Monographs*, 1939, 51, 117–126.

Meyer, Priscilla. "A Study of Production of Creative Ideas," *American Psychologist*, 1953, 8, 404.

Miel, Alice (Ed.). *Creativity in Teaching: Invitations and Instances*. San Francisco, Calif.: Wadsworth Publishing Co., Inc., 1961.

Miles, Catherine Cox. "Crucial Factors in the Life History of Talent," in E. P. Torrance (Ed.) *Talent and Education*. Minneapolis, Minnesota: University of Minnesota Press, 1960, pp. 51–65.

Miller, I. E. *The Psychology of Thinking*. New York: The Macmillan Co., 1909.

Moore, O. K. "Orthographic Symbols and the Pre-School Child—A New Approach," in E. P. Torrance (Ed.) *New Educational Ideas: Third Minnesota Conference on Gifted Children*. Minneapolis, Minnesota: Center for Continuation Study, University of Minnesota, 1961, pp. 51–101.

Morgan, E. S. "What Every Yale Freshman Should Know," *Saturday Review*, 1960, 43(4), 13–14.

Mork, G. M. A. "Science Lesson on Rockets and Satellites," Lawerence, Kansas: *University of Kansas Bulletin of Education*, 1959, 13, 86–91.

Mosing, L. W. "Development of a Multi-Media Creativity Test," *Dissertation Abstracts*, 1959, 19, 2137.

Moustakas, C. R. *Psychotherapy with Children*. New York: Harper & Brothers, 1959.

Munari, B. *Who is There? Open the Door!* Cleveland: The World Publishing Co., 1957.

————. *The Elephant's Wish*. Cleveland: The World Publishing Co., 1959.

————. *The Birthday Present.* Cleveland: The World Publishing Co., 1959.

Murphy, G. *Human Potentialities.* New York: Basic Books, Inc., 1958.

Murray, H. A. "A Mythology for Grownups." *Saturday Review,* 1960, *43(4),* 10–12.

————."Vicissitudes of Creativity," in H. H. Anderson (Ed.), *Creativity and Its Cultivation.* New York: Harper & Brothers, 1959.

Nicholsen, P. J., III. "An Experimental Investigation of the Effects of Training Upon Creativity," Doctoral Dissertation. Houston, Texas: University of Houston, 1959.

Ornstein, J. "New Recruits for Science," *Parents' Magazine,* February 1961, *36(2),* 42ff.

Osborn, A. F. *Your Creative Power.* New York: Charles Scribner's Sons, 1948.

————. *Creative Imagination* (3rd Ed.). New York: Charles Scribner's Sons, 1957.

Owen, W. A., C. F. Schumaker, and J. B. Clark. "The Measurement of Creativity in Machine Design," *Journal of Applied Psychology,* 1957, *41,* 297–302.

Palm, H. J. "An Analysis of Test-Score Differences Between Highly Creative and High Miller Analogies Members of the Summer Guidance Institute," *Research Memo* BER-59-13. Minneapolis, Minnesota: Bureau of Educational Research, University of Minnesota, 1959.

Parnes, S. J. and A. Meadow. "Effects of 'Brainstorming' Instructions on Creative Problem-Solving by Trained and Untrained Subjects," *Journal of Educational Psychology,* 1959, *50,* 171–176.

———— — ————. "Evaluation of Persistence of Effects Produced by a Creative Problem-Solving Course," *Psychological Reports,* 1960, *7,* 357–361.

Patrick, Catherine. *What is Creative Thinking?* New York: Philosophical Library, Inc., 1955.

Peel, E. A. *The Pupil's Thinking.* London: Oldbourne Book Co., 1960.

Peet, Harriet E. *The Creative Individual: A Study of New Perspectives in American Education.* New York: The Ronald Press Company, 1960.

Pepinsky, Pauline N. *Originality in Group Productivity. I. Productive Independence in Three Natural Situations.* Columbus, Ohio: Research Foundation, Ohio State University, 1959.

————. "Study of Productive Nonconformity," *Gifted Child Quarterly,* Winter 1960, *4,* 81–85.

Piaget, J. *The Psychology of Intelligence.* London: Routledge and Kegan Paul, Ltd., 1951.

————. *The Construction of Reality in the Child.* New York: Basic Books, Inc., 1954.

Piers, Ellen V., Jacqueline M. Daniels, and J. F. Quackenbush. "The Identification of Creativity in Adolescents," *Journal of Educational Psychology,* 1960, *51,* 346–351.

Reid, A. *Ounce, Dice, Trice.* Boston: Little, Brown & Co., 1958.

———. *Supposing.* Boston: Little, Brown & Co., 1960.

Ribot, T. *Essay on the Creative Imagination.* London: Kegan Paul, Trench, Trubner & Co., 1906.

Riesman, D. " 'Tootle': A Modern Cautionary Tale," in Margaret Mead and Martha Wolfenstein (Eds.) *Childhood in Contemporary Cultures.* Chicago: University of Chicago Press, 1955, pp. 236–242.

Roe, Anne. *The Making of a Scientist.* New York: Dodd, Mead & Co., 1952.

———. "Personal Problems and Science," in C. W. Taylor (Ed.) *The Third (1959) University of Utah Research Conference on the Identification of Creative Scientific Talent.* Salt Lake City: University of Utah Press, 1959, pp. 202–212.

———. "Crucial Life Experiences in the Development of Scientists," in E. Paul Torrance (Ed.) *Talent and Education.* Minneapolis, Minnesota: University of Minnesota Press, 1960, pp. 66–77.

Rogers, C. R. "Toward a Theory of Creativity," *ETC: A Review of General Semantics,* 1954, *11,* 249–260.

Rosen, J. G. "The Barron-Welsch Art Scale as a Predictor of Originality and Level of Ability Among Artists," *Journal of Applied Psychology,* 1955, *39,* 366–367.

Rossman, J. *The Psychology of the Inventor.* Washington, D.C.: Inventors Publishing Co., 1931.

———. "A Study of the Childhood, Education, and Age of 710 Inventors," *Journal of Patent Office Society,* 1935, *17,* 411–421.

Runner Associates. *Runner Studies of Attitude Patterns* (11th Revision). Golden, Colo.: Runner Associates, 1954.

Runner, K. "Some Common Patterns," *Adult Leadership,* 1954, *3(6),* 15–17.

Russell, D. H. *Children's Thinking.* Boston: Ginn & Company, 1956.

Schafer, R. "Regression in the Service of the Ego," in G. Lindzey (Ed.) *Assessment of Human Motives.* New York: Rinehart & Company, 1958, pp. 119–148.

Schimek, J. G. "Creative Originality: Its Evaluation by the Use of Free-Expression Tests." Doctoral Dissertation. Berkeley, Calif.: University of California, 1954.

Shands, H. C. *Thinking and Psychotherapy.* Cambridge, Mass.: Harvard University Press, 1960.

Sharp, Stella Emily. "Individual Psychology," *American Journal of Psychology,* 1899, *5(10),* 371–373.

Simpson, R. M. "Creative Imagination," *American Journal of Psychology,* 1922, 33, 234–243.

Smillie, D. "Tests and Definitions of Intelligence." Dittoed. Merrill-Palmer School, Detroit, 1959.

Spearman, C. *Creative Mind.* London: Cambridge University Press, 1930.

Spencer, L. "Implementation—The Effective Use of Identification Techniques," in J. B. Conant (Ed.) *The Identification and Education of the Academically Talented Student in the American Secondary School.* Washington, D.C.: National Education Association, 1958, pp. 35–45.

Sprecher, T. B. "A Study of Engineers' Criteria for Creativity," *Journal of Applied Psychology,* 1959, 43, 141–148.

Springbett, B. M. "An Approach to the Measurement of Creative Thinking," *Canadian Journal of Psychology,* 1957, 11, 9–20.

Stauffer, R. G. "Productive Reading-Thinking at the First Grade Level, *Reading Teacher,* 1960, 13, 183–187.

Stein, M. I. "A Transactional Approach to Creativity," in C. W. Taylor (Ed.) *The 1955 University of Utah Research Conference on the Identification of Creative Scientific Talent.* Salt Lake City: University of Utah Press, 1956, pp. 171–181.

———— and Shirley J. Heinze. *Creativity and the Individual.* Glencoe, Ill.: Free Press of Glencoe, Inc., 1960.

Stephenson, W. *Testing School Children.* London: Longmans, Green & Co., 1949.

Stern, G. G. *Preliminary Manual: Activities Index and College Characteristics Index.* Syracuse, N. Y.: Psychological Research Center, Syracuse University, 1958.

Strang, Ruth. "Developing Creative Powers of Gifted Children," in *Creativity of Gifted and Talented Children.* New York: Bureau of Publications, Teachers College, Columbia University, 1959.

Strawbridge, D. and N. Kahn. *Fighter Pilot Performance in Korea.* Chicago: Institute for Air Weapons Research, University of Chicago, 1955.

Sullivan, H. S. *The Interpersonal Theory of Psychiatry.* New York: W. W. Norton & Company, Inc., 1953.

Taton, R. *Reason and Chance in Scientific Discovery.* London: Hutchinson Scientific and Technical Publications, 1957.

Taylor, C. W. (Ed.) *The 1955 University of Utah Research Conference on the Identification of Creative Scientific Talent.* Salt Lake City: University of Utah Press, 1956.

————. *The 1957 University of Utah Research Conference on the Identification of Creative Scientific Talent.* Salt Lake City: University of Utah Press, 1958.

————. *The Third (1959) University of Utah Research Conference on the Identification of Creative Scientific Talent.* Salt Lake City: University of Utah Press, 1959.

————. "The Creative Individual: A New Portrait in Giftedness," *Educational Leadership*, 1960, *18(1)*, 7–12. (a)

————. "Identifying the Creative Individual," in E. P. Torrance (Ed.), *Creativity: Second Minnesota Conference on Gifted Children*. Minneapolis: Center for Continuation Study, University of Minn., 1960. (b)

Taylor, I. A. "The Nature of the Creative Process," in P. Smith (Ed.), *Creativity*. New York: Hastings House, Publishers, Inc., 1959, pp. 51–82.

Terman, L. W., *et al*. *Mental and Physical Traits of a Thousand Gifted Children*, (*Genetic Studies of Genius*, Vol. I). Stanford, Calif.: Stanford University Press, 1925.

———— and Melita H. Oden. *The Gifted Child Grows Up*. (*Genetic Studies of Genius*, Vol. IV). Stanford, Calif.: Stanford University Press, 1947.

Thurstone, L. L. "Creative Talent," in L. L. Thurstone (Ed.) *Applications of Psychology*, New York: Harper & Brothers, 1952.

————. "A Psychologist Discusses the Mechanism of Thinking," in *The Nature of Creative Thinking*. New York: Industrial Relations Institute, Inc., 1953.

Torrance, E. P. "Highly Intelligent and Highly Creative Children in a Laboratory School" (Explorations in Creative Thinking in the Early School Years, No. 6), *Research Memo* BER-59-7. Minneapolis, Minnesota: Bureau of Educational Research, University of Minnesota, 1959. (a)

————. "Personality Studies of Highly Creative Children" (Explorations in Creative Thinking in the Early School Years, No. 9), *Research Memo* BER-59-12. Minneapolis, Minnesota: Bureau of Educational Research, University of Minnesota, 1959. (b)

————. "Sex Role Identification and Creative Thinking," *Research Memo* BER-59-10. Minneapolis, Minnesota: Bureau of Educational Research, University of Minnesota, 1959. (c)

————. "An Experimental Evaluation of 'No Pressure' Influence," *Journal of Applied Psychology*, 1959, *43*, 109–113. (d)

————. *Talent and Education*. Minneapolis, Minnesota: University of Minnesota Press, 1960. (a)

————. *Creativity: Second Minnesota Conference on Gifted Children*. Minneapolis, Minnesota: Center for Continuation Study, University of Minnesota, 1960. (b)

————. "Eight Partial Replications of the Getzels-Jackson Study," *Research Memo* BER-60-18. Minneapolis, Minnesota: Bureau of Educational Research, University of Minnesota, 1960. (c)

————. "Social Studies Objectives of Minnesota Elementary and Secondary School Teachers," *Research Memo* BER-60-4. Minneapolis, Minnesota: Bureau of Educational Research, University of Minnesota, 1960. (d)

———— and Kevser Arsan. "Experimental Studies of Homogeneous and Hetero-geneous Groups for Creative Scientific Tasks." Paper presented at meet-ings of Association of Educators of Gifted Children, Statler-Hilton Hotel, Detroit, April 8, 1961.

———— and J. A. Harmon. "Effects of Memory, Evaluative and Creative Sets on Test Performance," *Research Memo* BER-60-17. Minneapolis, Minne-sota: Bureau of Educational Research, University of Minnesota, 1960.

————, C. H. Rush, H. B. Kohn, and J. M. Doughty. "Fighter-Interceptor Pilot Combat Effectiveness: A Summary Report." Lackland Air Force Base, Texas: Air Force Personnel and Training Research Center, No-vember 1957.

———— and staff. *Rewarding Creative Thinking*. Minneapolis, Minnesota: Bureau of Educational Research, University of Minnesota, 1961.

————, K. Yamamoto, D. Schenetzki, Necla Palamutlu and B. Luther. *Assess-ing the Creative Thinking Abilities of Children*. Minneapolis, Minnesota: Bureau of Educational Research, University of Minnesota, 1960.

———— and R. C. Ziller. *Risk and Life Experience: Development of a Scale for Measuring Risk-Taking Tendencies*. Lackland Air Force Base, Texas: Air Force Personnel and Training Research Center, February 1957.

True, G. H. "Creativity as a Function of Idea Fluency, Practicability, and Specific Training." Doctoral Dissertation. Iowa City, Iowa: Iowa State University, 1956.

Tumin, M. "Obstacles to Creativity," *ETC*, 1953, *11*, 261–271.

Vernon, M. D. "The Development of Imaginative Construction in Children," *British Journal of Psychology*, 1948, *39*, 102–111.

Vernon, P. E. *Intelligence and Attainment Tests*. London: University of London Press, 1960.

Vinacke, E. *The Psychology of Thinking*. New York: McGraw-Hill Book Co., Inc., 1951.

Walker, D. E. "Consistent Characteristics in the Behavior of Creative Mathe-maticians and Chemists," *American Psychologist*, 1952, *7*, 371.

Wallace, H. "Tests of Creative Thinking and Sales Performance in a Large Department Store," in E. P. Torrance (Ed.) *Creativity: Second Minne-sota Conference on Gifted Children*. Minneapolis: Center for Continua-tion Study, University of Minnesota, 1960.

Wallas, G. *The Art of Thought*. New York: Harcourt Brace & World, Inc., 1926.

Weideman, Ruth A. "An Experiment with Grade Children in Making Creative Songs with Varied Stimuli." M. A. research paper. Minneapolis, Minne-sota: University of Minnesota, 1961.

Weisberg, P. S. and Kayla J. Springer. *Environmental Factors Influencing Creative Function in Gifted Children*. Cincinnati: Department of Psychiatry, Cincinnati General Hospital, 1961 (Mimeographed).

Welch, L. "Recombination of Ideas in Creative Thinking," *Journal of Applied Psychology*, 1946, *30*, 638–643.

Werner, H. *Comparative Psychology of Mental Development*. New York: International Universities Press, 1957.

Wessel, H. M. "Four Teachers I Have Known," *Saturday Review*, June 17, 1961, *44(24)*, 58–59ff.

Whyte, W. H., Jr. *The Organization Man*. New York: Simon and Schuster, Inc., 1956.

Wilson, R. C. "Adaptation of the School to the Needs of the Creative Child," in E. Paul Torrance (Ed.) *Creativity: Proceedings of the Second Minnesota Conference on Gifted Children*. Minneapolis, Minnesota: Center for Continuation Study, University of Minnesota, 1960.

————, J. P. Guilford, and P. R. Christensen. "The Measurement of Individual Differences in Originality," *Psychological Bulletin*, 1953, *50*, 362–370.

————, J. P. Christensen, and D. J. Lewis. "A Factor Analytic Study of Creative Thinking Abilities," *Psychometrika*, 1954, *19*, 297–311.

Wilt, Miriam E. *Creativity in the Elementary School*. New York: Appleton-Century-Crofts, Inc., 1959.

Wolfle, D. "Diversity of Talent," *American Psychologist*, 1960, *15*, 535–545.

Wrenn, C. G. *The Counselor in a Changing World*. Washington, D.C.: Commission on Guidance in American Schools, 1961.

Yamamoto, K. *Manual for Evaluating Imaginative Stories*. Minneapolis, Minnesota: Bureau of Educational Research, University of Minnesota, 1960. (a)

————. *Further Analysis of Ask-and-Guess Test Results*. (*Research Memorandum* BER-60-11) Minneapolis, Minnesota: Bureau of Educational Research, University of Minnesota, 1960. (b)

Ziller, R. C. "Vocational Choice and Utility for Risk," *Journal of Counseling Psychology*, 1957, *4*, 61–64.

Zirbes, Laura. *Spurs of Creative Teaching*. New York: G. P. Putnam's Sons, 1959.

SUBJECT INDEX

Utah University Conference on the Identification of Creative Scientific Talent, 39–42, 75, 235

V

Validity of creativity measures, problems on, 39–42

Validity studies, Minnesota Tests of Creativity, criteria:
achievement of basic skills, 54–64
creative behavior in a group, 50–51
industrial arts, 50
sales productivity, 48–49

Validity studies, Minnesota Tests of Creativity, criteria (*Cont.*):
sociometric nominations, 51–54

Values and purpose, creativity and developing, 150–151

Verbal skills of creative children, 109–110

Vocational choice and risk-taking, 74–76

Vocational success and creativity, 5–6

W

Wechsler-Bellevue Intelligence Test, 18, 19

"Will do" and "can do," discrepancy between, 72–76

AUTHOR INDEX